# COTTIER IN CONTEXT
## DANIEL COTTIER, WILLIAM LEIPER AND DOWANHILL CHURCH, GLASGOW

by
Juliet Kinchin, Hilary Macartney and
David Robertson

With Contributions by
Max Donnelly, Alan Ferdinand,
Kerr Jamieson and
Ranald MacInnes

Edited by
Hilary Macartney and
David Robertson

ISBN: 978-1-84917-052-9

## Historic Scotland Technical Advice Notes

| | |
|---|---|
| 1 | Preparation and Use of Lime Mortars (revised 2003) |
| 2 | Conservation of Plasterwork (revised 2002) |
| 4 | Thatch & Thatching Techniques (1996) |
| 5 | The Hebridean Blackhouse (1996) |
| 6 | Earth Structures and Construction in Scotland (1996) |
| 7 | Access to the Built Heritage (1996) |
| 8 | Historic Scotland Guide to International Conservation Charters (1997) |
| 9 | Stonecleaning of Granite Buildings (1997) |
| 10 | Biological Growths on Sandstone Buildings (1997) |
| 11 | Fire Protection Measures in Scottish Historic Buildings (1997) |
| 12 | Quarries of Scotland (1997) |
| 13 | The Archaeology of Scottish Thatch (1998) |
| 14 | The Installation of Sprinkler Systems in Historic Buildings (1998) |
| 15 | External Lime Coatings on Traditional Buildings (2001) |
| 16 | Burrowing Animals and Archaeology (1999) |
| 17 | Bracken and Archaeology (1999) |
| 18 | The Treatment of Graffiti on Historic Surfaces (1999) |
| 19 | Scottish Aggregates for Building Conservation (1999) |
| 20 | Corrosion in Masonry Clad Early 20th Century Steel Framed Buildings (2000) |
| 21 | Scottish Slate Quarries (2000) |
| 22 | Fire Risk Management in Heritage Buildings (2001) |
| 23 | Non-Destructive Investigation of Standing Structures (2001) |
| 24 | The Environmental Control of Dry Rot (2002) |
| 25 | Maintenance and Repair of Cleaned Stone Buildings (2003) |
| 26 | Care and Conservation of 17th Century Plasterwork in Scotland (2004) |
| 27 | Development and Archaeology in Historic Towns and Cities (2004) |
| 28 | Fire Safety Management in Heritage Buildings (2005) |
| 29 | Corrugated Iron and other Ferrous Cladding (2004) |
| 30 | Scottish Turf Construction (2006) |
| 31 | Stone Masonry Material and Skills (2007) |

## Guides for Practitioners

Stonecleaning – A Guide for Practitioners (1994)
Timber Decay in Buildings – The Conservation Approach to Treatment (1999)

| | |
|---|---|
| 1 | Rural Buildings of the Lothians: Conservation and Conversion (1999) |
| 2 | Conservation of Historic Graveyards (2001) |
| 3 | Conservation of Timber Sash and Case Windows (2002) |
| 4 | Measured Survey and Building Recording (2003) |
| 5 | Scottish Iron Structures (2006) |
| 6 | Conversion of Traditional Buildings parts 1 and 2 (2007) |
| 7 | Fire Safety Management in Traditional Buildings Parts 1 & 2 (2010)(this replaces TAN'S 11, 14, 22, 28) |

## Case Study

| | |
|---|---|
| 1 | Conservation of Phoebe Anna Traquair Murals at Mansfield Traquair Centre Edinburgh (2007) |
| 2 | The Investigation, Repair and Conservation of the Doulton Fountain, Glasgow Green Technical Reference Series: Saracen Foundry |

## Technical Reference Series

| | |
|---|---|
| 1 | Saracen Foundry |

Available from:

Historic Scotland Conservation Group
Longmore House
Salisbury Place
EDINBURGH
EH9 1SH
Tel       0131 668 8638
Fax       0131 668 8669
email     hs.cgpublications@scotland.gsi.gov.uk

# CONTENTS

# PLATES, FIGURES AND ILLUSTRATIONS

## LIST OF FIGURES

## LIST OF ILLUSTRATIONS (APPENDIX I)

# ACKNOWLEDGEMENTS

Many people have been involved in the preparation of this book. In addition to the individuals and organisations mentioned in the Introduction, the authors are grateful to the following people in particular, who have contributed valuable ideas, information and practical help and advice during the course of preparation: Carrick McDonald for the Index, Gavin Stamp, Sam Small, Gordon Urquhart, Robert Wilmot, Bill Church, Rev Robert Currie, Robert Gibbs, Michael Burgoyne, Ann Laird, Tom Donald, Roy Mohan Shearer, Rev Stuart Smith, Irene O'Brien, David Weston, Ezra Shales, Jennifer Melville, James Mackenzie, Matthew Hynes, John Hume, Meredith Cohen, Paul Stirton, Ingval Maxwell, Tobit Curteis, Linda Cannon, Rab MacInnes, Anne Clough, the staff at Groves Raines Architects and members of the staff at Historic Scotland Conservation Group in particular Vanesa Gonzalez.

# COTTIER'S IN CONTEXT FOREWORD

Charles Rennie Mackintosh, one of Scotland's best known architects, is widely recognised as one of the most influential designers of his generation. However, a less known figure emerged in Glasgow decades earlier who was to have a profound effect not only on Scottish and international contemporaries, but also on the generations that followed.

Scottish-born Daniel Cottier worked closely with contemporaries such as William Leiper, predominantly as a stained glass artist, decorator and furniture designer during the second half of the 19th Century. While his designs contributed to some of the most stunning building interiors in Scotland, he spent much of his career abroad and became a major influence in international circles, also as an art dealer and promoter of younger artists and designers.

At the time of printing, works are well underway to conserve Dowanhill Church, Glasgow, the only one of three major Scottish churches famously decorated by Cottier to survive from this period. This publication, the first of two volumes, explores the life, work and influence of Daniel Cottier and his contemporary William Leiper, setting the hugely significant surviving interior of Dowanhill Church into a broader context. Volume two of this series will be published on completion of the Dowanhill Church project and will document the conservation works carried out to this important interior decorative scheme.

Daniel Cottier was one of 19th Century Scotland's leading lights; a designer of enormous talent and influence internationally, he has ironically been much overlooked in his native country. I hope that this book will go some way to redressing this undeserved obscurity.

David Mitchell
Director of Conservation
Historic Scotland
March 2011

**Plate I**

Dowanhill Church from Hyndland Street, tinted postcard. Courtesy of Gordon R Urquhart.

# INTRODUCTION

Cottier's is a well-known Glasgow landmark. It opened in April 1992 as a restaurant and bar in Glasgow's West End occupying two floors of an old church hall. The buildings had been designed as part of Dowanhill United Presbyterian Church (fig 1), 1865, by William Leiper (1839-1916) (fig 2) and in the 1990s their re-use as a bar and restaurant was still considered a radical solution for an ecclesiastical building. By the time the bar and restaurant opened the great hammerbeam roof of the main church which stands alongside had also been repaired and the Church had begun its new life as a theatre.

**Fig 1** Interior before 1906, Dowanhill Church, photograph from W Dickie, 1926, *History of Dowanhill Church 1823-1923.* Courtesy of Four Acres Charitable Trust.

**Fig 2** *William Leiper,* Colin Hunter ARA, oil on canvas, 1869. Courtesy of Aberdeen Art Gallery & Museum Collection.

Eight years before the opening of Cottier's, the congregation of Dowanhill Church had been forced to vacate the church and the hall, which were both in a terrible condition (fig 3). Individual timber trusses had started to slip out of position as the deadly incursion of dry rot, which had afflicted the buildings for years, took a deeper hold. More in hope than expectation the property had been gifted to Four Acres Charitable Trust for one pound, a trust that had been formed locally with the task of renewal in its sights, but with little or no resources at its disposal.

After a period of gestation the project eventually came to life. By the time the first meal was served in the new restaurant the Trust had experienced the thrill of uncovering one of the most important decorative schemes to survive in a city where exotic schemes of Victorian church decoration were once commonplace.

The scheme of decoration by Daniel Cottier (1838-91) (fig 4) was the inspiration for the treatment of the hall conversion. 'Cottier's' was therefore a natural choice of name for the new establishment. The Trust retained ownership of Cottier's which, under the guidance of a local restauranteur engaged by the trustees, went from strength to strength.

Not only that, but the Church itself took on a new lease of life as a temporary theatre while further funds were being sought for its full conservation. The Cottier Theatre, despite the cold, draughty ambience, ran continuously until 2005 when a significant grant from the Heritage Lottery Fund was awarded, with the promise of more support from long-term funders, Historic Scotland and Glasgow City Council.

Cottier's is a local project that has acquired a national and, some would say, an international dimension. Interest in the life and personality of Daniel Cottier has been growing steadily in the last twenty-five years in his native city of Glasgow and beyond. Prior to this, the artist's name and career had been largely forgotten outside the USA.

In 1870's New York, less than a decade after the American Civil War, Daniel Cottier had established his pioneering art gallery and emporium where the very latest in European taste and fashion was brought to East Coast America (fig 5). As one art journalist wrote in 1874, 'the great majority of people bent on being up with the times must be catered for […] and the place for them is at Cottier's'.[1] Cottier became a major influence in international circles as a stained glass artist, decorator, furniture designer, as well as an art dealer and promoter of younger artists and designers.

**Fig 3** Condition of Dowanhill Church and Hall 1984-89.

**A** Condition of Dowanhill Church Hall 1987. Courtesy of Four Acres Charitable Trust, photograph Michael Burgoyne.

**B** Decayed Hammer Beam, Dowanhill Church, 1989. Courtesy of Four Acres Charitable Trust.

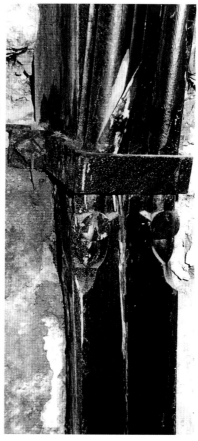

**C** Decayed Wall Post, Dowanhill Church 1984. Courtesy of Four Acres Charitable Trust.

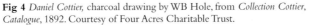

**Fig 4** *Daniel Cottier,* charcoal drawing by WB Hole, from *Collection Cottier, Catalogue,* 1892. Courtesy of Four Acres Charitable Trust.

**Fig 5** Cottier's Premises in New York. Courtesy of Ezra Shales.

By the 1980s, however, important schemes of decoration by Cottier and his company were still being lost in Scotland. In 1984, when Dowanhill Church ceased to be used as a church, the painted decoration scheme had only just been rediscovered and looked unlikely to survive.

Three major churches in Glasgow were decorated in the 1860s by Daniel Cottier at the start of his career. The first, Townhead United Presbyterian Church (fig 6), 1863, by Campbell, Douglas and Stevenson was demolished in 1989. The second, Dowanhill United Presbyterian Church, 1865, by William Leiper survives and is the subject of this study, while the third, Queen's Park

United Presbyterian Church (fig 7), 1867, by Alexander 'Greek' Thomson was destroyed by an incendiary bomb towards the end of the Second World War.

Cottier's role in the decoration of these buildings and his relationship with these three leading architects was to establish his reputation as an innovative colourist. We are fortunate in the case of Dowanhill Church that he received the commission for the stained glass as well. The scheme of glass has survived largely intact. It has now been fully conserved and justifies a separate conservation case study in a forthcoming publication.

As the only church decorated by Cottier to survive from this period, Dowanhill's significance is all the greater. It was the only one where the artist was free to produce a comprehensive work embracing stained and painted glass, structural wall painting and painted furniture, including a remarkable pulpit canopy, minister's seat and a pair of collection stands.

The extent to which Cottier was responsible for the design of the scheme of decoration and glass at Dowanhill and the extent to which this should be attributed to the architect William Leiper cannot be known. What is clear is that this was a youthful collaboration between two men still in their twenties when the building was completed. Conservation of the decorative work is now a major task

**Fig 6** Townhead Church, Glasgow, with wall decoration by D Cottier (inset). Courtesy of RCAHMS. Licensor www.rcahms.gov.uk

**Fig 7** Interior, Queens Park Church. Glasgow. Courtesy of Glasgow Life / Libraries / Glasgow City Archives.

due to the spiral of decline that took place in the 1970s and 1980s. The elements of the scheme were recorded in the 1990s but there are large areas that are covered by later paint surfaces. Only when conservation work is complete will we be able to witness the full impact of the original scheme, including the proportions of the decorative elements and the balance of the colour harmonies.

## The Social and Artistic Context

This publication represents an essential stage within the larger project to conserve and interpret the church, and has involved extensive research into the building and its archives. It commences with a review by Juliet Kinchin of the context from which the building emerged and the significance of the building for art history. This review, originally written in 2003 and updated for this publication, provides a succinct picture of Daniel Cottier's life and artistic influence, as well as of the role of the architect William Leiper and the people of nineteenth-century Glasgow who built Downhill Church. Further chapters document the history of Downhill Church and its decoration and expand contextual themes identified in the review. The publication also contains, in an appendix, an article by Ranald MacInnes. Originally written in 1993, it was intended as a guide to the building, but was never published.

The personality and career of Daniel Cottier and the existence of the 'First Glasgow School' form a vital, but largely hidden, part of Glasgow's outstanding Victorian heritage.[2] A proper perspective on decorators and designers of the 1860s and '70s has yet to emerge. They have so far been largely overshadowed by the subsequent generation of talented designers whose work at the end of the century came to be identified as the Glasgow Style. A recently uncovered scheme of church decoration by Charles Rennie Mackintosh in Dysart, Fife (fig 8), that has been dated to 1901, can be understood more fully in the context of the work of the artist decorators that came to prominence in the 1860s with the arrival of the young Daniel Cottier.

5

**Fig 8** Decoration in Dysart Church, Fife, CR Macintosh. Courtesy of Dysart Parish Church, photograph Alan Ferdinand.

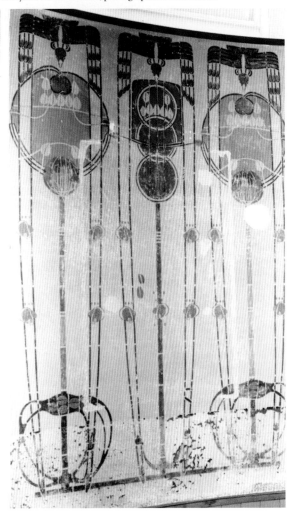

The force and impact of Cottier's first 'Glasgow School' is less hidden in countries further afield where Cottier and his circle were active, in the USA in New York and Boston, and also in Australia where his partner John Lamb Lyon brought the Cottier influence to bear on the Art Movement in both Sydney and Melbourne through the firm of Lyon, Cottier and Company. Books and articles are now available, such as Andrew Montana's *The Art Movement in Australia* (2000), confirming that art historians in that country consider Glasgow to have been one of the leading world centres for decorative finishes in the second half of the nineteenth century.[3]

At that time Glasgow was full of churches with elaborate decorated interiors (fig 9). The city was in the forefront of church and domestic decoration by the 1860s and held this position at an international level for decades to come. This same city built the fastest, most beautiful ocean-going liners that travelled the world and were decorated by many of its leading firms and individual designers. Daniel Cottier was both the father of the stained glass movement in the city and the foremost decorator of his day.

By their nature decorative schemes are vulnerable to modification, wholesale replacement, and loss through deterioration or demolition. Today very few buildings in the city survive with their original decorative schemes preserved intact. This makes it very difficult to appreciate what the interiors of these buildings were really like and the few photographs that record them cannot convey their most important aspect which was colour. Indeed the colour harmonies were a key to the artistic vision of the period.

**Artistic Theories**

Juliet Kinchin draws attention to a major influence on the development of colour theory and colour harmony in Scotland in the nineteenth century. This was David Ramsay Hay of Edinburgh, who throughout the 1830s, '40s and '50s published a body of influential work on colour and on proportion in architecture. The effectiveness of a scheme of harmonious colour decoration was conceived by Hay, and others such as George Field in England and Michel-Eugène Chevreul in France, in terms of primary, secondary and tertiary colours, where proportion both in the mixing of the colours themselves and in their combinations within the decorative scheme was the key to success.

The theory that certain ratios, and the proportions they give rise to, can be found both in nature and perceived aesthetically, has existed from Antiquity. It was prominent in the Middle Ages and the Renaissance, and remained a respectable position in the Victorian period, although undermined to a greater or lesser extent by the emergence of new aesthetic theories in the eighteenth century. For Hay, rules of proportion and ratio were as important to beauty in architecture and in the use of colour as was self evidently the case in music, where ratio determines harmonic consonance. This was not to argue that great art could be achieved through the mere application of rules. According to Hay, 'the generality of mankind may be capable of perceiving this latter kind of beauty, and of feeling its effect upon the mind, but men of genius, only, can impart it to works of art, whether addressed to the eye or the ear.'[4] Such a one was 'the genius Daniel Cottier' who set out at all times to give the impression of being 'odd and remarkable'.[5]

We know that Daniel Cottier delivered a paper to the Glasgow Architectural Society in 1866 entitled 'Colour the Handmaid of Architecture', and in much of the decorative treatment at Dowanhill, it is clear that colours are combined and contrasted in geometric motifs that echo and express the Gothic architectural forms found throughout the building.[6]

In a more self-effacing way the architect William Leiper was also setting out to be the architect of genius who studied old sources and laws to arrive at new forms of aesthetic value. There are no original drawings of Dowanhill Church but careful study of measurements

**Fig 9** Interior, Anderson Church, Glasgow, J Salmon, 1864-5. Courtesy of Glasgow Life / Libraries / Glasgow City Archives.

in the building points to numeric relationships in proportion that closely reflect the theories of Hay and of Eugène-Emmanuel Viollet-le-Duc in France. This part of the study sets out to demonstrate that careful measurement and analysis of the building itself can reveal much about the aesthetic preoccupations of the architect and his milieu. This in turn supports the view developed here that Dowanhill Church was the expression of an integrated aesthetic, not just a borrowing of styles.

### Documenting the History of the Building, its Painted Decoration, and the Role of the Congregation

This present volume is concerned with the detailed documentary research that has taken place on the history of the building and its painted decoration.

Research into the surviving documentation providing information about the building of the church, its decoration, the congregation that attended it and the ministers who served in it, has been carried out by Hilary Macartney. Many of the church records survive and these offer a detailed insight into the social concerns

and values of a nineteenth-century congregation and the ways in which society at that time sought to regulate itself and embark upon ambitious work providing a legacy for future generations.

This documentary research includes minute books, pamphlets, newsletters and periodicals generated by the congregation over the years, as well as some oral history. It is specific to Dowanhill Church which also has the benefit of an important published history written by the Reverend William Dickie in 1926. There is therefore a great deal that we know about the building and its phases of historical development.

Work undertaken since Four Acres Charitable Trust acquired ownership of the building has revealed more of the decoration and has added greatly to our understanding of the original and subsequent decorative schemes. Much of the photographic evidence gathered in this process is presented here and is supported by detailed research undertaken by Alan Ferdinand over many years. The revelation of the decoration forms part of the continuing programme of scientific investigation which will include extensive material testing and analysis during the main conservation phase that is yet to come.

Research on the history of the church has been supplemented by a project to bring together an archive of records and photocopies of material covering Dowanhill Church, William Leiper, Daniel Cottier and other key members of their circle, and many of the works they carried out. An important part of this work is the development of a comprehensive catalogue raisonné of Cottier's known work, something that will be a continuing work in progress. Max Donnelly kindly provided a copy of his original catalogue raisonné researched for his Sotheby's Institute dissertation, *Cottier & Company (1864-1915) Establishing a Context for the Second Glasgow School* prepared in 1998, and this has been supplemented where additional information has since come to light. Due to the diversity of Cottier's career, new items are continually surfacing and there is no claim that the record compiled for this study is a complete one, even in respect of known works. The catalogue raisonné presented in this publication concentrates on Scotland, Northumberland, USA and Australia since there is little published research on Cottier's output in most of England, apart from occasional references to domestic glass and furniture that come to light through auction houses and property sales.

## Conservation Principles

Conservation principles have been evolving throughout the last twenty-five years since Dowanhill Church effectively reached the nadir of its deterioration in 1984 and started a journey to recovery, care and enhancement. Today those who speculate that there could be a 'science' of aesthetics are very much on the fringe. They may yet emerge to have their day again, but meanwhile there are plenty who promote a science of conservation.

The debate about the conservation principles that should be applied to a work of restoration is no less a part of a nineteenth-century tradition than the debate about aesthetic theories. Men like John Ruskin and Viollet-le-Duc approached the repair and restoration of ancient buildings from differing philosophical standpoints that remain relevant to this case study.

The application of conservation principles has been an overarching concern of Four Acres Charitable Trust. By 1987 the Trust had started to understand the scale of the task in hand and the need to record everything and define a sequence of work that would enable this to happen while establishing new and viable uses within the building.

By 1989 the Trust was involved in a dialogue with Historic Scotland initiated by its architect Ian Begg and the director of Historic Scotland's Stenhouse Conservation Centre, Rab Snowden. Difficult decisions had to be made about what could be saved of the plaster matrix supporting the decorative scheme some of which had been lost prior

to the Trust taking ownership and some of which was evidently dangerous. Exceptional measures were taken at that time by the Trust's conservation surveyor, Alan Ferdinand, to salvage important fragments of decoration that would be lost if the severely damaged roof structure was to be retained. By 1991, once the roof structure had been saved and the water ingress and pervasive dry rot remedied, a long debate commenced about the decorative scheme, what should be revealed, what should be preserved and what, if anything, should be replicated.

The original scheme by Cottier was covered over by subsequent schemes, two of which were based on, but modified the original, and a third more recent of little perceived artistic merit. These schemes all have significance and have been researched on that basis. The original scheme however has significance of an entirely different order and it has since been generally agreed that it should be revealed as far as possible.

The conservation of Daniel Cottier's decorative scheme is now in hand and a second volume of this publication is planned which will give a detailed account of the technical work to conserve and recover the full impact of the interior.

## Dowanhill Church – Four Acres Charitable Trust

Many important changes have taken place since the building was acquired in 1984 from the then congregation of Dowanhill Church and these are continuing today. 'Cottier's', once a name applied to Daniel Cottier's fine art emporium in New York, has acquired new meaning in the city of his youth.

It was due to the minister, the Reverend Robert Currie, in his untiring efforts to preserve the building in the late 1970s and early 1980s, that the importance of Cottier and the surviving scheme was brought into focus. He negotiated with Michael Donnelly of the People's Palace in Glasgow for the preservation of the glass and decorated furniture. Michael Donnelly also uncovered areas of accessible decoration and spoke to a meeting of people interested in forming a trust to save the building about the role of Cottier, based on his publication *Glasgow's Stained Glass: A Preliminary Study* (1981). This study, written before the Trust was formed, gave an impetus to the plans for restoration.

The original idea for a community-owned resource for artistic and conservation activity was conceived by David Cruickshank (fig 10). He initiated the Trust and had a powerful vision for the building that still resonates today. It was David Cruickshank who approached the late Roy Jenkins, MP for Hillhead, to become the Honorary President. The interest taken by Roy Jenkins and his wife Jennifer led among other things to grants being awarded by the Monument Trust and Pilgrim Trust, which enabled the transfer of ownership and coverage of start-up costs. They took an interest in the decorative scheme and visited

**Fig 10** David Cruickshank in front of Dowanhill Church, *The Scotsman*, 1984. Courtesy of The Scotsman.

THE SCOTSMAN Wednesday, December 12, 1984
11

# Arts workshops scheme for former church

Mr David Cruikshank, trust chairman, outside Dowanhill Church
— a £1 bargain for the community.

Dowanhill Church in the west end of Glasgow, which was discarded by the Church of Scotland because of crippling building maintenance costs, is being converted into a theatre, arts workshops and a community complex.

The church has been sold for £1 to the Four Acres Charitable Trust, a voluntary organisation which aims to find alternative uses for the many empty, yet historically valuable buildings which have become derelict, vandalised and in danger of being demolished.

With continued support from local authorities and other groups concerned with buildings conservation, the trust hopes to have the first phase of its project completed and open to the public within a year.

Although the first step is simply to make the building wind and watertight the operation will cost almost £300,000, and will be a major achieve-

ment for the trust, considering the state of the building and the lack of financial support.

It will add yet another former church building to a list of those which have already found new roles ranging from bars and restaurants to warehouses and additional factory space.

However, the Four Acres directors are determined that their operation will be based on helping the local community and encouraging the development of small, arts-orientated businesses.

Plans have been drawn up to transform the building into a "major performance venue" with its own stage and gallery, and to restore the important and valuable interior design of Daniel Cottier. The area will also be used to stage exhibitions large and small, with display facilities where the side pews formerly stood.

Also included will be a heri-

## By DAVID CAMERON

tage museum and tourist information centre, which will cover not only the activities in the building itself, but throughout the West of Scotland.

The trust wants to make facilities available for local artists and small businesses. Workshops will eventually be built into the large outer rooms for this purpose.

The trust has already secured Manpower Services Commission project which is employing 16 people, both full and part-time.

Only one problem stands in the way of the overall success of Dowanhill. Although money has been pledged "on principle", there is still a shortfall of more than £30,000.

Unless the trust can come up with a successful financial package the cash already pledged may not be forthcoming. "If this was to happen then we could be faced with having to apply for demolition within a year," said Mr David

Cruickshank, the trust's chairman.

However, everyone at Dowanhill appears to be confident that things will go well and, that over the next five years, the building will become one of the most important focal points in the area.

The trust's activities have delighted the Rev Ian Fisher, whose committee at Glasgow Presbytery is pressing for the closure of many Glasgow churches.

Mr Fisher said he and many others believed it was inevitable that a large number of Glasgow's churches would have to be sold.

"I am delighted with what the trust are trying to do and I wish them well with their project. I am not sure that all churches could be used for this community type of project, but as we have seen recently there are commercial ventures which appear to be quite successful. I hope that there will be more of these in the future."

the building in the late 1980s and early 1990s when further new areas were being uncovered by the Trust's conservation specialist Alan Ferdinand. Roy Jenkins believed that there were parallels to be made between a city like Glasgow and one such as Boston, perhaps without the fuller knowledge we now have of Cottier's influence on the USA eastern seaboard. Dame Jennifer became the Honorary President on Roy Jenkins' death in 2003.

Many individuals have been involved in this project over the years. From the start Michael Burns, Lesley Andrews, Margaret Singleton, Alan Ferdinand and the late Roderick McKerracher helped to shape the character of the organisation while local councillors Patricia Chalmers, Christopher Mason and the late Robert Logan provided essential support and encouragement through the early stages. The Trust is grateful to everyone who has given of their time and enthusiasm to the project over the years, and Pamela Blair and Marion McIntosh deserve particular mention in this regard.

From 1987 the Trust has flourished under the watchful eye of its chairman, the author and historian Dr Oliver Thomson, and a core of trustees and office bearers, Stuart Patrick, Stephen Phillips, Donal O'Herlihy and Carrick McDonald.

A building such as Dowanhill Church needs a knowledgeable architect to manage its careful conservation. The church has been fortunate at times of greatest need to have had conservation architects of the stature of Ian Begg, until 1995, and Nicholas Groves Raines who took over on Ian Begg's retirement.

Particular mention should be made of Billy McAneney, who has run Cottier's bar and restaurant since 1992 in his role as a consultant to the Trust's wholly-owned trading subsidiary FACT TWO Ltd (fig 11). This essential role has provided the revenue to the Trust without which nothing could be done. Many individuals will have come to know the building intimately through working in this facility and in the adjacent Cottier Theatre which became established in the main church within three years of the pioneering performance of Test Department's *The Soul Machine* in 1991 (fig 12).

This performance inaugurated Dowanhill Church as Glasgow's latest 'found space' which, largely through the efforts of Sandy Maxwell, went on to win the Spirit of Mayfest award in 1995. Thereafter the Cottier Theatre ran an intense programme for a further ten years as an active if primitive performance space. This would not

**Fig 11** Cottier's Restaurant and Bar. Courtesy Four Acres Charitable Trust, photographs Alistair Devine.

**Fig 12** *The Soul Machine*, Test Department theatre poster, 1991. Courtesy Angus Farquhar.

have been possible without the support of volunteers such as Jim Mackie, willing to give of their time to work in a theatre environment. The theatre remained open while the tower and steeple were being restored without this interrupting the continuity of performance in the nave. However, following the award in 2004 of a substantial grant from the Heritage Lottery Fund, theatre use was suspended in 2005 to enable the full programme of conservation and refurbishment to get under way.

This full scheme falls into several phases. At the time of writing the completed work includes the roof repairs and stonework by Hunter and Clark Ltd, the stained glass restoration by Cannon MacInnes and the restoration of the magnificent organ by Harrison and Harrison of Durham with James Mackenzie as the Trust's organ consultant. The organ was built by Father Willis and originally installed in 1876. It will return to the building when the internal structural work and fine conservation finishes are completed. Crucially the Trust succeeded after many years of preparation and negotiation in

commissioning a new undercroft below the nave. When it is fitted out, the theatre audiences, performers and visitors to the building will have the ancillary facilities they need without any impact on the restored interior. At the time of writing the conservation of the Cottier decoration and the fit-out of the theatre undercroft remain the main funding challenges.

It is ultimately the support of the Trust's funding partners Historic Scotland, the Heritage Lottery Fund, Glasgow City Council, the Architectural Heritage Fund and the Charity Bank that has ensured that Dowanhill Church, so nearly lost, has regained its life for at least another 100 years. It is hoped that this publication about the international significance of the building will inspire and extend public interest in the heritage site and its role in Glasgow's future.

*David Robertson*
*Project Director*

[1] Cook 1874, 500-1.
[2] Donnelly, Max 1998.
[3] Montana 2000, esp 127-158; see also Ellsmore 1983, 34-43.
[4] Hay 1846, 21-22.
[5] Gould 1969, 2.
[6] McFadzean 1979, 199.

# 1 COTTIER'S IN CONTEXT:
# THE SIGNIFICANCE OF DOWANHILL CHURCH
## Juliet Kinchin

**Plate II**

*A* Pulpit Canopy, Dowanhill Church. original decoration by D Cottier, 1865. Courtesy of Historic Scotland.

*B* Cabinet by Cottier & Co decorated with figures of Amor, Mars, Fama and Fortuna, Greek masks, and urns, 1870-80. © National Museums of Scotland. Licensor www.scran.ac.uk

*C* *Gratitude,* First Presbyterian Church, New York, Cottier & Co, stained glass, 1887. Courtesy of Ezra Shales.

*D* *Titian,* Lyon, Cottier & Co, stained glass, 1884. Collection: Powerhouse Museum, Sydney. Photo: Sotha Bourn.

*It is to be hoped that in future generations no Philistine will arise to propose any departure from Cottier's design which remains, and should remain a charming work of art and a monument to his genius.* Rev Dickie, 1926.[1]

## Harbinger of International Aestheticism

Set close to the heart of Glasgow's West End, this former United Presbyterian Church, built 1865-7, encapsulates the architectural confidence, adventurous patronage and artistic experimentation that came together in 1860's Glasgow. The commission effectively launched the careers of both the young architect William Leiper (1839-1916), and Daniel Cottier (1838-91), designer of the painted interior decoration and stained glass. Although a youthful work, it is one of the few surviving and publicly accessible projects to demonstrate the stirrings of a new and distinctive design language that was to resonate in artistic centres around the world. Just as Scots had played an important role in the influential neo-classical style of the mid to late eighteenth-century, so Cottier, Leiper and a group of their close associates from Glasgow (including JJ Stevenson, J Moyr Smith, Bruce Talbert, JM Brydon) were central to the development of the international Aesthetic Movement in the 1870s and '80s. From Alexander 'Greek' Thomson, William Morris and Rhoda and Agnes Garrett, to Vincent Van Gogh, Tiffany and the Vanderbilts the two men's range of friends and associates ran the whole gamut of 'artistic' and literary society – not only in Glasgow, Aberdeen and Edinburgh, but also further afield in London, New York, Montreal, Sydney, Melbourne, Adelaide, Paris, and the Hague.

Little did they know it, but in their patronage of Cottier in particular, the Dowanhill congregation were one step ahead of the fashionable elites in both East Coast America, Canada and Australia. Within a few years of completing work at New York, Sydney and Melbourne, backed up by a European network of agents and contacts, Cottier was to have a huge impact on progressive tastes in the fine as well as decorative arts. In all these centres, apart from carrying out prestigious decorative schemes, he introduced the art-buying public to contemporary paintings of the Barbizon and Hague Schools, and supported young indigenous talent through employing artists like Matthew Maris and Albert Pinkham Ryder on decorative projects as well as exhibiting their latest work. By 1874 a leading New York magazine could write, 'The great majority of people who are bent on being in the fashion and up to the times must be cared for, and the place for them is Cottier's.'[2]

Wherever he went, Cottier attracted a following and connected with the most interesting artists, architects, designers, critics and collectors around. His various enterprises provided a magnet for a younger generation of talent, and a stepping-stone to other practices. In particular, Scottish designers seeking openings in London or abroad received a ready welcome. The long-term side effects of working with noxious pigments and processes combined with the notoriously dank weather in the west of Scotland made emigration appealing. Both Andrew Wells and Charles Gow spent a convalescent spell working for Lyon and Cottier in Australia before returning to establish partnerships in Glasgow.

In all his activities Cottier traded on the sophisticated colour sense that he had demonstrated at Dowanhill and which was rooted in technical skills acquired during his Glasgow apprenticeship as a stained-glass artist and house-painter with Cairney & Son. He and Leiper shared an admiration for the great Alexander Thomson, and for their contemporaries in the practice of Campbell Douglas and Stevenson, an admiration which infused their Dowanhill collaboration, as did their direct experience of the progressive tendencies in London during the years around 1858-62; Leiper worked briefly with the architects JL Pearson and William White and moved in the fringes of the set around William Burges and EW Godwin, while Cottier attended FD Maurice's Working Men's College in Red Lion Square. Through his mentor there, the artist Ford Madox Brown, Cottier was exposed to Pre-Raphaelite art and, significantly, witnessed the inception of Morris, Marshall, Faulkner & Co in 1861.

## The Glasgow Legacy

Arguably Dowanhill Church is the most significant survivor of a number of projects in the 1860s that made a contribution to the development of the local skill base and stimulated the kind of adventurous patronage that paved the way for the emergence of Glasgow as an international centre for progressive design around 1900. It provided a model for a new kind of 'art' architecture involving a non-hierarchical collaboration between architect and decorative artist that embraced every aspect of the building, from the railings outside through to the collection plates within the interior. The aesthetic innovations evident at Dowanhill were rapidly translated into domestic commissions, and many of the decorators and stained glass artists (such as Andrew Wells, Charles Gow, Hugh McCulloch) who went on to employ or work with Charles Rennie Mackintosh and his associates had emerged from the Cottier stable. As in the interior of Dowanhill Church, self-consciously 'artistic' paint effects integrated with vibrant stained glass were to become hallmarks of the Glasgow Style. At the core of the Glasgow contribution to international tendencies around 1900 was the concept of the room as a work of art, and a poetic, Symbolist sensitivity that distinguished the Scottish work from products of the English Arts and Crafts Movement. The spirituality, emotional intensity and subtle colouration of painters like Corot, Matthew Maris and Albert Pinkham Ryder, whom Cottier directly promoted, enriched the visual vocabulary of designers like George Walton, the Macdonald sisters and George Logan. Unlike Cottier, Leiper remained based in Scotland, apart from a brief interlude at the Académie Julian in Paris where he studied painting alongside Scottish friends like Arthur Melville, and continued his involvement with the Dowanhill Church, advising on subsequent additions and repairs in conjunction with Cottier's assistant, Andrew Wells, another figure who deserves to be better known. He also designed a further church for an affiliated congregation in Whiteinch (Victoria Park UP Church, now demolished), and developed the Early French Gothic style of Dowanhill in another UP Church at Camphill Queen's Park on the south side of the city. Although his practice came to focus on domestic work outside Glasgow, he made several other notable contributions to the cityscape, most importantly the Templeton's carpet factory by Glasgow Green in 1889 which translated the flat geometrical and coloured patterns of the earlier Dowanhill interior into a remarkable façade, this time a tour-de-force of Venetian rather than Early French Gothic (selected for the cover of the *Blue Guide to Victorian Architecture in Britain* (1987) as an iconic example of the period). Less obvious, but also significant, was Leiper's continued involvement in the world of fine and decorative arts, as an artist of note, a designer of art-lovers' houses and ship interiors, and a promoter of contemporary French and Scottish painting. He played a key role, for instance, in the commissioning and installing murals from the Glasgow Boys to adorn the Banqueting Hall of the Municipal Chambers in 1899-1902, and with John Honeyman was the first architect admitted to the ranks of the RSA, as an Associate in 1892 and a full Academician in 1896. Writing in his groundbreaking study of *The English House* in 1904, the German critic Herman Muthesius recognised Leiper as one of the leading architects in Scotland. The stylishly comfortable and modern houses he created in West-coast towns like Helensburgh and Kilmacolm (several of them decorated by Cottier & Co), were studied by the next generation of Glasgow architects, Mackintosh among them, not only for their assured blend of French and increasingly Scottish and vernacular sources, but also for their interior detailing.

**A Unique Survival**

Cottier has featured in a series of major exhibitions in America, Canada and Australia but in his native Glasgow has yet to be recognised as more than the name of a lively bar. HH Richardson's Trinity Church in Boston, which he decorated in 1878 in collaboration with John La Farge and Louis Comfort Tiffany, is promoted as a major landmark and tourist attraction within that city, whereas Cottier's three church interiors from the late 1860s in Glasgow have fared less well. As recently as 1997 the remarkable Townhead Parish Church (architect JJ Stevenson 1865-6) was demolished, and Cottier's decoration along with it. His masterful contribution to the Queen's Park UP Church (1867-9), one of Alexander Greek Thomson's most original and celebrated works, had already been destroyed during an air raid in May 1942. It was the Cottier decoration of this church that led Ford Madox Brown to describe his protégé as a colourist with 'a range of performance beyond that of any modern artist [...] I put this Thomson-Cottier church above everything I have seen in modern Europe'.[3] Cottier's work on Dowanhill, which overlapped with both of these vanished schemes, is a unique survival in every sense.

Glasgow's Victorian architecture has been subject to serious scrutiny over the last few decades, most recently in connection with the work of Alexander 'Greek' Thomson, but there is no such reliable background of research on nineteenth-century design and the decorative arts in Scotland. Despite a number of important exhibition catalogues, articles and theses, the significance of Daniel Cottier in particular has been obscured by the formidable diversity and geographical spread of his activities. As one contemporary put it, 'The late Daniel Cottier was a man of original cast of mind, a man of large outlook, and many-sided in his interests and outlook [...] "he thought in Continents".' Leiper too displayed a range of talents, not only as an architect but as a painter and photographer. The ongoing project to research, conserve and interpret Dowanhill Church is providing a major opportunity to raise general awareness of the Glasgow contribution to progressive design and architecture in a local, national and international context. Oral histories and research into business, church and estate records are also vividly illuminating the intersection of spiritual, working and domestic lives in the demographically varied community around Dowanhill.

[1] Dickie 1926, 118.
[2] Cook 1874, 500-1.
[3] Brown 1893.
[4] Wells 1902, 14.

# 2 SOCIAL CONTEXT
## Juliet Kinchin

**Plate III**

*A Villa, Gothic Style,* Boucher & Cousland, architects, ca. 1858. Courtesy of RCAHMS. Licensor www.rcahms.gov.uk

*B* The Reverend William Dickie, photograph from W Dickie, 1926, *History of Dowanhill Church 1823-1923.* Courtesy of Four Acres Charitable Trust.

*C* Advertisement for John Templeton & Son carpet manufacturers illustrating William Leiper's famous design of 1889 which was based on the Venetian Doge's Palace. © Glasgow Life (Museums).

## High Victorian Glasgow

With few planning, environmental or fiscal constraints, Glasgow in the mid-nineteenth century was experiencing change at an unprecedented level. 'We may safely assert, that there is no town in the United Kingdom where commercial progress has produced such rapid and extraordinary changes', wrote George Measom in 1859.[1] The intense mental energy and level of restless activity in the city was reflected in its architecture. Glasgow's spectacular growth in the decades leading up to the City of Glasgow Bank crash of 1878 entailed a huge amount of building work, along with the creation of physical infrastructure and transportation networks to facilitate the expansion of its industrial capitalism. Apart from the thriving textile industry, the shipyards for which Glasgow was to become famed were being established along the Clyde, and by the mid 1850s the city had become an extremely competitive and sophisticated retail environment. Glasgow's industries and trade were tied into the imperial marketplace through a communications network of steamship and railway routes centred on the city.

During his visit to Glasgow in 1857, the American novelist Nathaniel Hawthorne was alternately amazed and appalled by the spectacle of the city. His account vividly captures the shocking dislocations, both social and visual, that modernisation engendered:

> [...] we walked out and saw something of the newer portion of Glasgow; and, really, I am inclined to think it the stateliest of cities. The Exchange and the other public buildings and the shops, especially in Buchanan Street, are very magnificent; the latter, especially, excelling those of London [...] Later in the forenoon we again walked out and went along Argyle Street, and through the Trongate and the Saltmarket [...] High Street and still more the Saltmarket, now swarm with the lower orders, to a degree which I never witnessed elsewhere; so that it is difficult to make one's way among the sallow and unclean crowd.[2]

On the one hand, the stylistic assurance, originality and theatrical panache of work by an architect like Alexander Thomson was in tune with the buoyancy of Glasgow's economy, its internationalism and competitiveness. On the other, the exercise of design skills was a means of re-imposing meaning and coherence on the fluid conditions of urban life. For Thomson, the task of the architect was to counter and transcend the degenerative aspect of the city through the architectural expression of 'divine harmonies' and 'imperishable thought'. Churches were the most spiritual and publicly accessible of building types through which an architect could work. This was the context out of which the Dowanhill Church developed.

Glasgow's citizens were proud of their city's distinct economic and cultural apparatus which functioned independently from national and upper-class power structures. Inspired above all by Alexander Thomson, Glasgow was becoming a hotbed of architectural and interior innovations that could not be dismissed as the mere aping of metropolitan developments in Edinburgh or London. Design skills were at a premium, applied to both the building and enhancing of the city, and in support of a diverse range of industries. It was a time when the institutional infrastructure of the arts was being established and consolidated. Glasgow was home to one of the twelve Government Schools of Design established in 1840-2. In 1856 the Municipal Corporation acquired the buildings and collection of the coach-builder Archibald McLellan. The paintings formed the nucleus of the civic collection and the building also for a time accommodated the School of Art and Design. The establishment of the Glasgow Architectural Association in 1858, with which Leiper, Cottier, Walter Macfarlane and Alexander Thomson were involved, set the climate for interdisciplinary debate within the city's architectural, building and decorating professions, as did the Glasgow Philosophical Society. Starting in 1861 the Glasgow Institute of Fine Arts, a private exhibiting society, offered an annual exhibition of works for sale, showing the work of amateurs and professionals, Continental and Scottish artists alongside each other from the outset. In the summer of 1867, eight amateur 'gentlemen' artists, including the architect William Young (who also belonged to the circle around Leiper and Cottier) set up the Glasgow Art Club. Another related development was the growing taste for foreign pictures among collectors in Glasgow and the first appearance of dedicated art and antique dealers, among them Cottier.

The trajectory of Cottier's and Leiper's careers before and after Dowanhill exemplified the social and geographic mobility of the age, also the increasing status accorded to the arts, and the expanding market for their design skills. Born into relatively humble circumstances in 1838 Cottier initially worked as a shoe salesman before serving an apprenticeship with the stained glass firm Cairney's.[3] By the end of his career he was catering to super-rich clients like the Vanderbilts in New York or Van Horne in Montreal. Leiper came from a more professional background, his father being a schoolteacher, but he too rose to a position of considerable wealth and respectability as a Royal Academician and Justice of the Peace. Although born and trained in Glasgow, they both had experience of working in London as well as other Scottish cities by the time they came to work on Dowanhill. They travelled regularly and extensively on the Continent, Cottier also dotting between North America, Australia, and at one point North Africa. The ease of travel and efficiency of communication by letter and telegraph facilitated the conduct of business at a distance, while the phenomenal growth in printed literature – books, adverts, trade catalogues, magazines and architectural journals – also speeded up the transmission of ideas and images.

## Partick and the Dowanhill Estate

Viewed in the context of the speculative development of the area and of the local population's domestic and working lives, the history of Dowanhill Church can be seen as reflecting in microcosm wider socio-economic tendencies within the area of Glasgow as a whole.

On the edge of the city's westward development in the 1860s (although not incorporated within the city boundaries until 1912), the character of the area around the Dowanhill Church was more socially and economically diverse than that of other West End estates like Hillhead, Hyndland and Kirklee. At one end of the spectrum were the homes belonging to members of the city's industrial and mercantile elite on its upper slopes, while at the other were the industrial yards and factories being established down by the Clyde. There was more direct access to activity on the waterfront at that time, and a ferry crossing that linked Old Partick to the larger parish of Govan. Along the upper reaches of the Dowanhill area, the establishment of Great Western Road in 1836 by an Act of Parliament had stimulated a rash of impressive middle-class developments around it. In the decade or so leading up to the construction of the Dowanhill Church a series of terraces were completed along the Great Western Road – Grosvenor Terrace (1855), Kew Terrace (1849) and Kirklee Terrace (1845-64). The most monumental addition to this stretch, Alexander 'Greek' Thomson's Great Western Terrace, was soon to follow in 1869. Another remarkable development was Crown Circus, laid out by James Thomson in 1858.

In his *Rambles round Glasgow* published in the 1850s, Hugh Macdonald described the semi-rural character of the area:

> Partick altogether has a pleasant half-rural aspect, while the reputed salubrity of its air and its vicinity to the city have rendered it a favourite place of resort on holidays and on the long summer evenings [...] Numerous handsome villas and cottages have also been erected in its environs, principally by thriving business men from Glasgow, which lend it a peculiar air of prosperity and cheerfulness.[4]

In particular, the Dowanhill estate was rapidly being turned into a middle-class enclave in the leafy heights above the old settlement of Partick. It had been purchased in 1853 by the entrepreneur TL Paterson who had already tried his hand at brewing, textile manufacture, shipping, and speculation in railway and banking shares. As one of the Glasgow commissioners for the 1851 Great Exhibition in London he was becoming a figure of local prominence. By the mid 1860s some twenty-five villas had been developed within a layout plan prepared by James Smith, one of the first being that feued to Alexander Kay in 1853. As a director of the cotton-manufacturers Findlay & Co who owned the Deanston,

Catrine and Ballindalloch mills, Kay was one of the wealthiest and most influential members of the East Partick congregation who was to bankroll a significant part of the new church. Among those merchants and professionals who moved to the terrace houses being constructed in the late 1860s, at the same time as the Dowanhill Church, was Robert Stronnach, manager of the ill-fated City of Glasgow Bank and the first banker ever to be gaoled for fraud. Other prominent figures who had moved to the Dowanhill Estate during the first wave of its development were William Todd of Todd and MacGregor, the Partick shipbuilders, WF Donaldson of the Donaldson Brothers shipping line, and Robert Wylie of the furnishing and undertaking firm Wylie & Lochhead.[5] The 'surprising display of house plenishing' in the latter firm's stylish Buchanan Street showrooms was described in 1859 as 'unmistakeable proof of the luxurious habits and refined taste that have grown up among the middle classes in the west of Scotland'.[6] The firm also had commercial operations in the immediate locality of Dowanhill, with extensive stables on Byres Road in the 1860s for their hearses, delivery vans, and horse-drawn buses that ran from Partick. In 1861 they opened a 'scientifically organised' and steam-driven wallpaper factory at Whiteinch that within two decades was producing over a thousand miles of wallpaper every fortnight, some to designs in the new Aesthetic style pioneered by Cottier and Leiper. Like the adjacent Barclay Curle shipyard, Wylie & Lochhead invested in housing for their workers down by the Clyde. Another prominent firm of upholsterers and cabinetmakers in the vicinity was John Laird & Son, established 1846.

In feuing a site to the congregation of East Partick UP Church the developer TL Paterson was able to add a note of architectural distinction to the area, emphasising its middle-class respectability, and providing a focus for the next spurt of residential building. Then as now, the addition of Leiper's elegant spire in this suburban context provided a beacon to the area from multiple viewpoints. The Church Managers had considered a number of sites on the estate, two of which came with a financial incentive of £100, which they perhaps used as a bargaining tool to beat Paterson down to a price of 7/6d per square yard.[7] The level of detail in the feuing contract which specified, for example, the use of ashlar, and submission of the selected design for approval, reveal Paterson's proactive involvement in determining the architectural character of his estate. At around this time, however, Paterson was beginning to encounter major financial difficulties. The inherent riskiness of property speculation was compounded by family problems, and losses in other areas of his entrepreneurial activity. The development of Dowanhill continued in fits and starts as the financing and partners became available, but having just about managed to keep his creditors at bay, Paterson became a casualty of the failure of the City of Glasgow Bank in 1878 which led to a massive depreciation in property prices and the removal of his remaining credit. In 1884 the receivers finally moved in, and he had to leave Newhall, the house at 8 Sydenham Road which he had built and lived in since 1859.[8]

## The Congregation

As well as providing a key to the rapidly changing socio-economic and demographic character of the area, the building of Dowanhill Church and the subsequent history of the parish illuminate the fierce theological debates of the period, and the factional tussles within the United Presbyterian Church.

East Partick Church (fig 13) was established in 1823 as one of around 300 Secession congregations in Scotland which dissented from the established Church of Scotland. Their first place of worship was a classical 'preaching box' located towards the bottom of Byres Road. Geographically, it lay within the traditional parish

boundaries of Govan, and until 1848 there was a ferry allowance to assist those who came to the Church from the south side of the river. In 1847, the Secession Church and the Relief Church were united to form the United Presbyterian Church, and East Partick became one of over 500 UP congregations in Scotland which opposed the established Church of Scotland on the principle of Voluntarism. After the Free Church, which seceded from the Church of Scotland in 1843, the UP Church formed the main dissenting group outside the established Church. Church-building entered a distinctive and acutely competitive phase in Scotland's major cities, and in November 1864 the congregation of East Partick Church decided to build a new church, with school-room, vestry and Session house, relinquishing their existing place of worship to the 'Mission Congregation' that had been growing apace. A triangular plot had been identified in the 'important and rapidly increasing districts to the north' at the angle between Crown Street (now Hyndland

**Fig 13** The East Partick United Presbyterian Church.

*A* East Partick UP Church, photograph from W Dickie, 1926, *History of Dowanhill Church 1823-1923.* Courtesy Four Acres Charitable Trust.

*B* The Reverend Thomas Lawrie, photograph from W Dickie, 1926, *History of Dowanhill Church 1823-1923.* Courtesy Four Acres Charitable Trust.

*C* The Reverend William Dickie, photograph from W Dickie, 1926, *History of Dowanhill Church 1823-1923.* Courtesy Four Acres Charitable Trust.

Street) and Hyndland Road.[9] In relocating to this lofty position and specifying a Gothic spire, the congregation was deliberately aligning itself with the more prosperous middle-class development of the Dowanhill estate, rather than with the 'poor and neglected classes' of the district near the river where industrial activity was focused. 'The site chosen is a very central and desirable one' wrote the Preses George Thomson in an open letter to the congregation; 'Some might have wished it further east, others further west, and others further south, but the aim has been to place the Church where it would best accommodate the existing Congregation, as well as with a view to its future prosperity.'[10] The costs of the new-build were to be strictly controlled, with an upper limit of £5500, and a decision was made to sell the existing church to the Mission congregation for the reduced sum of £1150. Socially, the move paralleled that of the UP congregation in Cambridge Street who had relocated in 1863 to the new Gothic Lansdowne Church built in the wealthiest part of Great Western Road.[11] The upward social mobility of these congregations reflected a more general tendency among the United Presbyterians who had begun to attract a considerable number of wealthy industrialists throughout Scotland. As the historians Andrew Drummond and James Bulloch commented:

> Individualists to a man, they reflected within the Church the pattern of a pushing, competitive, bourgeois society, those of the poor in their membership were survivors from an earlier stage of development [...] On the whole it is not unfair to say that they were a one-class Church, rooted in that grade of society which was industrious, hard-working, sober and thrifty [...] their laymen, who made the decisions in these matters, repeatedly decided to move out of areas which had become socially uncongenial to them, to sell the building [...] and rebuild with foresight in districts to which their moneyed members had removed.[12]

This tendency was perhaps reflected in the somewhat mercantile character of the way in which UP churches such as Dowanhill were run. The rent of pews, for example, was priced on a sliding scale, providing a vital part of the Church's income.

## United Presbyterians and Church Architecture

In an urban context, progressive modern design was a tool through which to establish the presence of new denominations, and in Glasgow it was the United Presbyterians who seemed to be the most adventurous and imaginative in their patronage. Before Dowanhill, the way had been prepared by Alexander Thomson in his brilliantly idiosyncratic designs for the churches in Caledonia Road (1857), and St Vincent Street (1859) with their brightly polychromatic interiors. To this was added John Honeyman's Lansdowne UP church on Great Western Road of 1862-3, the first piece of home-produced, academic Gothic on a considerable scale.

While it is clear from the design of the Dowanhill Church that both Leiper and Cottier were fully aware of the most progressive developments in both English and French ecclesiastical architecture, the use of a Gothic style, polychromatic decoration and glowing stained glass assumed a very particular inflection in Glasgow. Issues of decoration and style were not merely a matter of taste or fashionable historicism. In England, AW Pugin's innovations, for example, had been tied to the rise of Anglo-Catholicism and the English Tractarian Movement of the 1840s and '50s. Likewise the Gothic Revival pioneered by Viollet-le-Duc in France was connected with the reorganisation of the French Catholic church and the huge budget for new liturgical furnishings made available under the Second Empire to replace the losses of the French Revolution.

The theological and liturgical context of Scotland's High Victorian churches was different. The first ecclesiological societies were not founded until 1886 and 1893, in Aberdeen and Glasgow respectively. However, interest in ecclesiology was evident in the new building programmes of the Roman Catholic and Scottish Episcopal churches during the first half of the nineteenth century, following the repeal of penal laws limiting their worship. Within the Presbyterian churches, concern to improve both places and forms of worship led to the formation of the Church Service Society in 1865. An influential figure in its foundation was George Washington Sprott, who was concerned to counter the impact of the English Tractarian Movement. Nevertheless, in his pamphlet of 1863, he declared, 'There is nothing in our system inconsistent with the noblest style of architecture – nothing to prevent our utilising all the parts of a Gothic Cathedral', though he felt that 'the earliest from of the Christian Church, the Basilica, suits best our worship'.[13] The Presbyterian view of Gothic, then, was often ambivalent at best. Glasgow architects frequently engaged in lively debate on the merits of the different styles of architecture. At a meeting of the Glasgow Architectural Society in 1859, for example, John Honeyman defended the Gothic style, followed by Alexander 'Greek' Thomson and Thomas Gildard who defended the classical and Grecian styles.[14] Thomson, an elder of the United Presbyterian Church, mounted famous attacks on the Gothic style in his addresses to the Architectural Society in 1864 and 1866: 'To Protestants of any sort, and still more particularly Presbyterian dissenters', he asked, 'what has the philosophic Christianity of the Reformation to do with the sensuous ritual of the Middle Ages?'.[15] For many Presbyterians, Gothic was also self-evidently 'Popish', and irrelevant to the design of a modern Scottish church. Despite these debates and reservations, however, the *Ecclesiastical Cyclopaedia* of

1862 noted that 'Gothic architecture, somewhat naked and confused indeed, is prevailing again in Scotland'; if not ideal, in the author's view it was certainly an improvement on 'the old barn form' of eighteenth-century churches; the most important guideline was that 'whatever is dedicated to God should be the best of its kind'.[16] In the case of Dowanhill Church, it is also possible that Gothic style, colour and decoration were more in tune with the personal tastes of the wealthier members of the congregation, and however egalitarian the teaching of the Church, there appears to have been a desire to distinguish the new building visually from what was to become its lower-class counterpart, the Mission Church. Moreover a Gothic spire could make an assertive, significant dint on the skyline. The East Partick congregation might specify Gothic for their new church, but the architect was still left with the problem of how to adapt the style to the requirements of Presbyterian worship without producing a 'naked and confused' looking design.

## The Competition and Building of the Church

A brief was issued to six selected architectural practices in December 1864, with a closing date of 24 January 1865, expressly stipulating the need to stick to the limited budget. The Church was to accommodate a potential congregation of about one thousand persons, on the basis of pews based at 32-inch (8.13 cm) intervals, and 21 inches (5.33 cm) of sitting room for each person. A Gothic style of architecture was specified, 'substantial but without superfluous decoration, having a spire or tower, with provision made for bell'. Although the plots in the immediate vicinity had still to be feued and developed, in keeping with requirements of the feuing contract for the site, detailed consideration was given to the relationship of the building to the emerging streetscape; those walls on the east, south and west sides were to be constructed of sturdy 'hewn courses', presenting an impression of aesthetic order and finesse to passers-by, although the architect could get away with square dressed rubble work all other walls. The winning architect's commission was set at five per cent.

William Leiper spent a busy Christmas preparing two sets of designs.[17] He had returned from London to Glasgow in 1863 and after a brief spell as an assistant with Campbell Douglas and Stevenson, entered his first partnership as a fully-fledged architect with RG Melvin, one of their earliest jobs being the completion of the Stirling Library in Miller Street following the death of James Smith. (He was filling the place vacated by John Moyr Smith who left to pursue his career in first Manchester, then

London, but was to remain an important contributor to what we might call the 'first' Glasgow Style.) The Dowanhill competition was small enough that he could prepare the drawings single-handedly while still having time for routine work, yet substantial enough for a public demonstration of his artistic prowess that might attract critical attention and potential clients. Writing in 1876, EW Godwin advised struggling young architects that the competitions in which they were most likely to succeed were those 'for public buildings where the cost ranges from 5,000l. to 20,000l. The drawings for such works you can prepare single-handed, and yet have time for pot-boilers. The cost out of pocket will be a trifling one'.[18]

Leiper was familiar with the site and had local knowledge of this rapidly developing area, not least through the work of Boucher and Cousland who designed seven villas on the estate in the late 1850s when Leiper was serving a five-year apprenticeship with the firm (fig 14). His familiarity with the site enabled him to collect information beyond any which he could glean from illustrations in the architectural press. Still more importantly, his father was one of the most respected elders of the East Partick UP Church (he had been the Session Clerk, 1855-9), which gave Leiper a head start in being able to gauge the prevailing sentiment of the locality and the agendas of influential Church members. Working within the constraints of the triangular site Leiper produced a taut composition dominated by an elegant 195-foot (59.28-m) spire. The main body of the church was spanned by a hammer-beam roof with pierced spandrels, and was to contain galleries on three sides supported by cast-iron columns. Externally it was divided into six bays by massive buttresses, while the pastoral role of the church was expressed in the more domesticated character of the outbuildings extending along the northern side of the plot.

On 4 February 1865 the judges (including the architect John Burnet as advisor and members of the Church's Building Committee) placed the two designs by 'Veritas' – subsequently revealed as the young William Leiper – in first and second place. They happened to be the cheapest of the four submissions, but the aesthetic merits of the committee's choice were validated by the international commissioners of the Paris Exposition Universelle in 1867 who selected and praised the Leiper designs. The Church Minutes record that the architect was asked to get on with the job as quickly as possible, which he appears to have done. A Foundation Stone was laid on 7 August, and by 11 November 1866 the church was open for worship.

**Fig 14**

*A Villa – Gothic Style*, Boucher & Cousland, architects, ca.1858. Courtesy of RCAHMS. Licensor www.rcahms.gov.uk

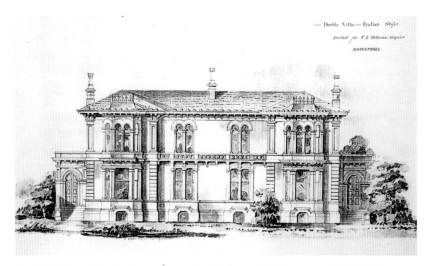

*B Villa, Italianate Style,* Boucher & Cousland, architects, ca.1858. Courtesy of RCAHMS. Licensor www.rcahms.gov.uk

## Interior Decoration and Stained Glass

Leiper had entrusted the hand-painted and stencilled decoration of the interior and several items of furniture to his friend Daniel Cottier (fig 15). On a bill of extras Cottier was paid £397 10s for this work. The original estimates made no mention of decoration and included only the cost of plain glass in the windows, while allowing for the possibility of stained glass as an extra should funding become available. For some members of this congregation any kind of stained glass was presumably considered an extravagance, plus there must have been a degree of resistance to the introduction of sensual colour and imagery with idolatrous overtones into a Presbyterian place of worship. This issue had generated fierce debate in relation to the commissioning of stained glass for Glasgow Cathedral, although there is no evidence that Thomson's highly coloured interiors for the St Vincent Street and Caledonia Road UP churches were criticised. In February 1866, presumably when he was just at the point of embarking on the decoration of Dowanhill Church, Cottier delivered a paper to the Glasgow Architectural Society entitled 'Colour, the handmaid of architecture'. Unfortunately we have no record of how he presented his ideas, but presumably he emphasised the importance of a comprehensive approach to both stained glass and painted decoration in introducing colour to any architectural scheme. It was perhaps this presentation that inspired Alexander Kay to write to George Thomson and the Building Committee, in a letter dated 19 February 1866, arguing

**Fig 15** Interior, Dowanhill Church after 1906. Courtesy of Four Acres Charitable Trust.

that the addition of stained glass was in accordance with the style of the building and would considerably enhance both the beauty and comfort of the Church; having already contributed £500 to the Building Fund Kay offered a further £300 to defray the extra expense of the coloured glass. This sum is thought to have been sufficient to enable Cottier to carry out the stained glass in the main body of the Church (fig 16) and to fill the rose window above the pulpit, with six heads of Old Testament characters (fig 17) and inscriptions around the circumference (Moses – 'Blessed are the Meek'; Jeremiah – 'Blessed are they that Mourn'; Oded – 'Blessed are the Peacemakers'; David – 'Blessed are the poor in Spirit'; Abraham – 'Blessed are the Merciful'; Jonathan

**Fig 16** Geometric Glass, Dowanhill Church, D Cottier, stained glass, 1866-7. Courtesy of Four Acres Charitable Trust.

**Fig 17** *A* Rose Window, Dowanhill Church, D Cottier, stained glass, 1866-7. Courtesy of Tom Donald.

*B Moses.* Courtesy of Tom Donald.

*C Jeremiah.* Courtesy of Tom Donald.

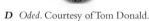

*D Oded.* Courtesy of Tom Donald.

*E Peter.* Courtesy of Tom Donald.

*F Abraham.* Courtesy of Tom Donald.

*G Jonathan.* Courtesy of Tom Donald.

– 'Blessed are in heart the Pure').[19] There seems to have been a deliberate attempt to balance representations of men and women in the iconographic scheme of the Church (see for example the David and Miriam window (fig 18), and the male and female carved heads to either side of the windows outside). Although confined to the tops of the windows under the galleries rather than the lofty rose window, women were represented in a further set of biblical heads, six from the Old Testament and two from the New: Deborah, Ruth, Abigail, Esther, Dorcas,

Lydia, Mary and Mary Magdalene (fig 19). It is tempting to also see a reference here to the women in Kay's immediate family, as he was married with seven daughters. Certainly the features have a distinctly contemporary and Pre-Raphaelite feel about them. Kay must have been pleased with the whole project as he promptly commissioned Leiper and Cottier to build and decorate a substantial house in Biggar named Cornhill to which he retired in 1873. (The house is currently run as a hotel.) This is a clear instance of how aesthetic innovations in ecclesiastical

Fig 18 Windows, South Gallery, Dowanhill Church, D Cottier, stained glass, 1866-7.

*A Vine Leaves and Grapes.*
Courtesy of Tom Donald.

*B David.* Courtesy of David Robertson.

*C Miriam.* Courtesy of David Robertson.

design and decoration were translated into a domestic context, and the importance attached by Glasgow's mercantile and industrial elite to the consistency of image projected through their personal and public lives.

Returning to the stained glass at Dowanhill, Kay's generosity was complemented by the gift of 'the Elders, Managers and Trustees' of a window depicting David and Miriam that cost about £40. (This was originally located at the back of the South Gallery which is now filled by the organ.) The inscription 'Cottier 67' appears at the foot of the Miriam figure confirming that the glass was only added after the opening of the Church.[20] Interestingly the inscriptions on the windows mentioned the first Minister of the new church, the Rev Lawrie, and the name of the architect, but not that of any of the donors, Alexander Kay having stipulated that no reference be made to his donation.

**Fig 19** Female Heads, Lower Lancet Windows, Dowanhill Church, D Cottier, stained glass, 1866-9. Courtesy of Tom Donald.

*A Lydia*

*B Dorcas*

*C Esther*

*D Abigail*

*E Mary Magdalene*

*F Deborah*

*G Ruth*

*H Mary*

## Cottier's Departure for London

In the final stages of completing the stained glass for Dowanhill, Cottier moved his main base of operations to London. In both personal and professional terms his spell in Glasgow had been intense, exhilarating and formative. During the time spent on the Church he had fallen in love, got married in June 1866, and fathered three children, all born in Glasgow between April 1867 and March 1869. He had also just completed work on the stunning interior of Thomson's Queen's Park UP Church. Despite the evident joy and fulfilment of these Glasgow years, however, 1869 was a difficult time for the rapidly growing family. For a time Cottier was dangerously ill with the rheumatic fever, initially contracted in Aberdeen, that was to plague him for the rest of his life. Then in December his eldest baby son died. Infant mortality was high. The Dowanhill Building Committee was supportive and paid him £20 up front for the stained glass, the implication being they feared Cottier himself would not survive the winter.[21] Combined with the known hazards of working with noxious pigments, the dank polluted atmosphere of Glasgow must have been the worst possible environment for Cottier. Despite the availability of stimulating work it was presumably a combination of health considerations and the desire for a new start after their bereavement that prompted the Cottiers to move south. Cottier already had contacts in London and a clutch of his old Glasgow friends associated with the architectural firm of Campbell Douglas Sellars had recently moved there, including JJ Stevenson. He soon entered a partnership with three of them, Bruce Talbert, JM Brydon and William Wallace. The Leiper-Cottier association had never been formalised – both maintained their stylistic and professional independence – but they continued to collaborate up until Cottier's death in 1891, both directly, and indirectly through Cottier's assistants, notably Andrew Wells.

## Overall Costs

Despite the Committee's best efforts to limit expenditure, the final estimates crept up to £6877 6s 8d, and the actual building costs ended up as £8651 19s 3d. Together with the 'Preliminary Expenses' – including the fees of all the professionals involved, the cost of the bell, and the painting and carving – the total cost of the Church was £11,107 12s, which left the congregation with the considerable outstanding debt of £6200 17s that took until 1881 to clear. The expense of joining a church with this kind of debt was not to be undertaken lightly, and although the congregation continued to expand, some residents moving to the area were not inclined to transfer their allegiance and membership. Some slippage in the costs seems to have been inevitable in church building of this time, but at least the project had not gone as hopelessly over budget as some, and the congregation certainly got value for their money from two young designers before they became famous.

## Fracture, Reunification, Closure

The Preses or chair of the Board of Managers of the Church, George Thomson, had been a driving force behind the building of the new church, but in 1875 he deserted the Dowanhill congregation to join the Mission congregation in Whiteinch, when the latter became fully independent from its parent church. There are hints of a clash of personalities revealed in the records, but he may also have felt that the Church was being distracted from its crucial Missionary work both at home in Glasgow and abroad. Further haemorrhaging of the UP Church in the decades that followed was allayed by a union with the Free Church in 1900, and culminated in re-unification with the Church of Scotland in 1929. The repair and redecoration of the church in 1937 gave the Church a temporary boost, but in Glasgow as elsewhere congregations continued to dwindle in the post-war period, leading ultimately to closure and deconsecration in 1983.

---

[1] Measom 1859, 252.

[2] Hawthorne 1871, vol 2, 243-4.

[3] 'The Late Daniel Cottier' 1891, 323.

[4] Macdonald 1856, 280.

[5] 1858, Inchview House, Partick; 1861, 7 Crown Circus, Dowanhill.

[6] Measom 1859, 328.

[7] Managers Minutes, 29 Aug 1864, DCR CH3/1267/7, at which an extract of the Missionary Committee Minutes was read.

[8] He ended up living in Athole Gardens off a small annuity provided by the super-wealthy Edinburgh brewer, McEwan, whom he had once employed in Alloa.

[9] George Thomson, Preses, Open Letter to Members of Partick East UP Church, 26 Nov 1864, DCR CH3/1267.

[10] George Thomson, 26 Nov 1864, DCR CH3/1267.

[11] On the day the church was opened a note was pinned to the door reading: 'This church is not for the poor and needy/ But for the rich and Doctor Eadie, / The rich step in and take their seat, /But the poor walk down to Cambridge Street' (quoted in Jeans, 1963, 6).

[12] Drummond and Bulloch 1975, 45.

[13] Sprott 1882, 234-5. For the history of ecclesiology in Scotland, see Kelly 2006-7, 3-32.

[14] See McFadzean 1979, 192.

[15] Thomson, A 1864, 58. See also Thomson, A 1866, 368-71, when his prime target, however, was Gilbert Scott's design for the University of Glasgow.

[16] Eadie 1872, 172.

[17] The drawings were submitted under the names of Leiper and Melvin, but Leiper was clearly the driving force behind the conception and implementation of the design. The partnership folded as work began on the church and Melvin retired from architectural practice altogether.

[18] Godwin 1876, 320.

[19] The glass depicting the head of David was apparently broken by a boy throwing stones in 1875 and replaced by Messrs Kier of Glasgow who did their best to replicate the design working from what remained of the head and face. The head was re-named Peter.

[20] Managers Minutes, 24 Nov 1866, DCR CH3/1267/7, recording a letter from Cottier which was read at the meeting of the Board of Managers of the Church, 'stating that in the course of a fortnight, he expected to be able to show a drawing for, and give an estimate of the cost of window in Choir-room'.

[21] Letter from George Thomson, Preses, Managers Minutes, 1 Dec 1869, DCR CH3/1267/102.

# 3 THE AESTHETIC AND DESIGN CONTEXT
## Juliet Kinchin

**Plate IV**

*A* Noyon Armoire, E-E Viollet-le-Duc, 1858–75, *Dictionnaire raisonné du mobilier français.*

*C The Blue Bower*, DG Rossetti, oil on canvas, 1865. Courtesy of Barber Institute, Bridgeman Art Library.

*B* Page illustrating Assyrian Ornament, O Jones, 1856, *The Grammar of Ornament.*

*D* 'Example V & Example VI', DR Hay, 1847, *The Laws of Harmonious Colouring.* Courtesy of Juliet Kinchin.

## Uniting the 'Sister Arts'

In 1863, EW Godwin made an impassioned plea for a new reciprocal relationship between the 'sister arts' of architecture, painting and sculpture that reflected the desire of many Gothic Revivalists since AW Pugin to heal a perceived fissure between these art forms that was traced back to the Renaissance.[1] In the new kind of collaborative relationship that developed between Leiper and Cottier, and their integrated approach to the architecture and interior decoration, Dowanhill can be viewed as making a significant contribution to this debate. As the *Building News* noted when the church opened: 'The architect's aim has been to build a Presbyterian church which might have some claim to be reckoned artistic.' This concern with reuniting architecture, art and craft, and with the musicality of expression, was to culminate in the full-blown synaesthesia of Art Nouveau.

From the outside of the Church, the no-frills approach evident in its refined, stony forms communicated a sense of stability and solidity, an identification with spiritual and poetic rather than material values. It also provided a contrast to the explosion of colour and theatricality within. Between them Leiper and Cottier orchestrated the transition of worshippers from the greyness and monotony of mundane experience into an altered reality, an imaginative space that conjured up distant places and times while simultaneously communicating a sense of vitality and modernity. The spiritual message of the worship was potently emblazoned on the eyes and ears of members of the congregation, so as to prompt inner thought, and enveloping them in waves of song, colour and the preacher's rhetoric.

## Painted Decoration

The concept of the integrated interior was a feature of the nineteenth-century Gothic revival, and the technical issues and aesthetic principles of painted decoration were being widely aired in the 1850s and early '60s. In practice, however, 'there are few things in connection with the revival of Ecclesiastical art which have been more neglected than interior coloured decoration', wrote EW Godwin in 1865.[2] 'Few people who have mixed much in the society of architects can have escaped observing with what a grandiose contempt the English architect regards painted decoration', he continued in a further article.[3] Central to any modern revival was the painful process of redefining the respective roles and status of both architect and painter, but Godwin was optimistic that before long there would be wall paintings and monumental art 'second only in drawing to the best Greek work, and second only in vigour of composition and dramatic interest to the noblest work of the Middle Ages'.[4] The inter-relationship between the architectural forms and painted decoration at Dowanhill, the use of particular colour combinations, motifs and techniques, all suggest that Leiper and Cottier were tuning in to debates and cutting-edge practice in England and France as well as Scotland – whether directly or indirectly.

A hugely important influence on many of their generation was the architect GE Street, in whose office William Morris, Edward Burne Jones and Norman Shaw all trained, and to whom Cottier's friend (and for a time partner) Bruce Talbert, dedicated his influential Gothic Forms in 1867. One example was the painted sedilia in geometric Gothic style that Street designed for St James the Less, Pimlico, in London 1859-61. Street's views on the design and decoration of town churches were published in the *Ecclesiologist*, the English High Church magazine that also published the polychromatic experiments of William Butterfield and a series of articles by Gambier Parry on church decoration in 1858-60, as well as another by the same author promoting a new spirit-based technique that he was testing in 1862.[5] In terms of publications, still more relevant to Cottier and Leiper was Viollet-le-Duc's extensive essay on painted decoration that appeared in the seventh volume of the Dictionnaire raisonnée de l'architecture française in 1864 (fig 20), and Godwin's twelve-part series entitled 'Painted Decoration' that appeared in the Building News while Dowanhill was underway. In Scotland, the interior designer and aesthetician, DR Hay played an influential role in advocating painted and stencilled decoration through his books such as the Laws of Harmonious Colouring, first published in 1838, and his practice as an interior decorator. Hay had showcased his colour theories in the famous Architectural Exhibition, 1853-7, that took place in Glasgow, in Exhibition Halls designed by Thomson, while Leiper and Cottier were apprentices.

In the 1840s and '50s there had been moves to revive English wall painting on a grand scale through a series of large-scale murals at the new Palace of Westminster, based on the example of the Nazarene painters in Rome. The results were mostly disastrous, not least from a technical point of view, because the colours tended to fade and flake off. Apart from this, Godwin also objected to the apparent 'stand-alone' approach to mural art; wall painting had to be a relative art. It wasn't a question of good painting, but of good decoration.[6] Significantly, he looked to the artists with whom Cottier had studied:

> It is not in what is supposed to be the highest ranks of the profession that an architect must look for an artist to paint his walls and ceilings. Such men as Rossetti or Mr. F. Madox Brown […] are the only men we have that are capable of becoming painters in the strong broad architectonic sense […] Even one energetic, business-like, good-tempered man would be enough to gather round him a school for the exercise of painting as a monumental art […] What we want more than anything else – the first requisite in architectural and mural decoration – is a good colourist.[7]

Enter Daniel Cottier. At the same time an architect's work was something more artistic than to provide mere wall space or mere picture frames. Enter William Leiper.

**Fig 20** Viollet-le-Duc – Arcading and Painted Decoration.

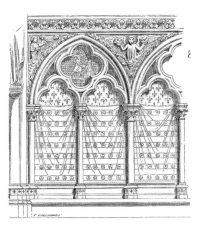

*A* Illustration from 'Arcature', E-E Viollet-le-Duc, 1854–68, *Dictionnaire raisonné de l'architecture française du XIe au XVIe siècle.*

*B* Illustration from 'Peinture', E-E Viollet-le-Duc, 1854–68, *Dictionnaire raisonné de l'architecture française du XIe au XVIe siècle.*

*C* Dowanhill Pulpit, W Leiper and D Cottier 1865. Courtesy Four Acres Charitable Trust.

**Plate V** Pre-Raphaelite Painting – *Work*, FM Brown, oil on canvas, 1852 – 65. © Manchester City Galleries.

This complex and painstakingly detailed view of labourers digging a drain was devised as an allegory of modern society giving pride of place to the workers. Affixed to the wall on the left is a poster for The Working Men's College in London's Red Lion Square while on the opposite side, leaning on the rail, are the 'brain workers', Thomas Carlyle and FD Maurice whose vision of society put the artisan centre-stage. The College, which was founded by Maurice and strongly supported by Ruskin, was a philanthropic enterprise aimed at providing access for artisans like Cottier to a liberal and rounded education. Ford Madox Brown (1821-93) taught at the College from 1857 often taking students to view this painting in progress in his studio. It is tempting to think he might have introduced a touch of his student Cottier into the red-haired navvies. Madox Brown was also a founding member of Morris Marshall, Faulkner & Co, the company established in 1861 (also in red Lion Square) that brought together such an inspiring group of architects and artists under the leadership of William Morris.

Cottier and his mentor shared a seafaring background, Madox Brown's father having been a ship's purser, and Cottier himself no stranger to international trade and travel by sea. His father was a sailor from the Isle of Man and his maternal grandfather a Master mariner at Greenock. Later in life Cottier used an anchor as his personal symbol. With his unruly mop of curly red hair, he apparently cultivated the air of an old sea-dog, looking 'more like an ideal coasting skipper than an artist'.

Madox Brown delivered one of the most wholehearted tributes on Cottier's Glasgow work. The interior of the Queen's Park UP church, on which Cottier was working with Alexander Greek Thomson at around the same time as Dowanhill (1867-69) was a revelation and demonstrated the extent to which Cottier had outstripped his London training with a 'range of performance beyond that of any other artist' as a colourist: 'Here line and colouring are suggestive of paradise itself', he exclaimed, 'well done Glasgow! I put[… ]this Thomson-Cottier church above everything I have seen in modern Europe'. (JK)

## An Artistic Collaboration: Leiper and Cottier

Both Leiper and Cottier presented themselves as 'artworkers' in the broadest sense, and theirs was a self-consciously 'artistic' collaboration that rejected the conventional hierarchical relationship between architect and 'tradesman'. Temperamentally they appear to have complemented one another. The Rev Dickie described Leiper as 'essentially an artist, and a man of fine imagination, with a passion for beauty of form which made his devotion to architecture a calling rather than a profession'.[8] Leiper emerges as something of a loner – shy, and introverted (to the point of paranoia if we are to believe Frank Worsdall).[9] He never married and never ran a large office. Some suggest he was 'difficult' and his initial partnership with Melvin in 1864-5 was certainly short-lived. On the other hand he clearly inspired complete devotion in his later assistant Hunter McNab. By contrast Cottier was phenomenally gregarious and outward-going, recruiting a talented workforce to sustain his operations on three continents.

The Dowanhill collaboration was more comprehensive than that between Cottier and Stevenson at Townhead Parish Church where Cottier's input was restricted to the painted direction (Morris Marshall Faulkner & Co provided some of the glass). It was also on a more equal footing than the Cottier-Thomson relationship at Queen's Park UP Church where one senses the older architect kept a fairly tight rein on Cottier, requiring a higher level of finish and stricter adherence to the lines of a predetermined scheme. At Dowanhill one cannot easily define where the creative input of Leiper ends and that of Cottier begins. This was perhaps closer to the spirit of artistic co-operation which Cottier had observed among William Morris and his friends, witnessing the way they set about the design and decoration of the Red House (1859-62) and the establishment of Morris, Marshall, Faulkner & Co (1861). In a circular advertising the latter firm in 1862, they claimed to take a newly integrated approach to the decoration of 'artistic' interiors, undertaking 'Mural Decoration, either in Pictures or in Pattern Work, or merely in the arrangement of Colours', and 'Stained Glass, especially with reference to its harmony with Mural Decoration'.

At a time when the cult of the artistic persona was gaining momentum, Cottier in particular 'laid himself out to be odd and remarkable', cultivating an earthy directness in his dealings with clients which extended to his style of painting. Andrew Wells describes how when surrounded by a sedate church committee, Cottier would cry out to him painting the ceiling such directions as 'Andra, slabber on some broon there, just beside the wibble-wobble'.[10] His unruly mop of red hair and bushy beard were in contrast to the soberly bourgeois self-presentation of the slightly older Alexander Thomson. Cottier's look had more in common with the fashionably romantic image of Pre-Raphaelite artists like Dante Gabriel Rossetti who literally projected themselves into their art in designs like the stained-glass cartoon of St George's wedding, 1860. Although such personal references would have been inappropriate in the context of a Presbyterian church, one cannot help noting the flaming red hair and beard of David in both the rose-window head and the larger Choir window. Cottier's imprint is certainly unequivocal in the boldly scripted signature at the bottom of the Miriam window that was to become his trademark over the next two decades. From the 1870's so-called 'Art manufacturers' used an association with individual artists and architects to add value to their products, a new marketing strategy that we now take for granted in designer labels. Like Cottier, Glasgow-born Christopher Dresser was to become a household name in the 1870s and '80s, and used a similar freehand signature on many of his mass-produced ceramics to suggest their artistic authenticity.

As if to emphasise that they were dealing with an artist rather than a business-man, on one occasion Cottier apparently wrote the tender for the painting of a church 'on the back of a soiled theatre bill'.[11] (Could this have been for Dowanhill one wonders?) Members of the congregation there were certainly mystified by his unconventionally artistic and experimental way of working: 'they used to come into the church to see him working on the walls. One day they saw one design and scheme of colour; next day they would find it all washed out. This process of rubbing in and washing out went on for weeks, till some of them began to think he was "not all there"'.[12] The ceiling design had not been lined out in red ochre as was customary, and from the stretches of ceiling that have recently been investigated one can see slight variations between the bays in terms of the disposition and form of certain motifs. Arguably Cottier was taking painted decoration to a new 'artistic' level. One cannot fail to be struck by the loose and painterly quality of the way the paint has been applied. This must have communicated the authentic 'handprint' of an artist rather than the impersonal perfection of a tradesman pricing his work by the yard, though some doubtless saw it as simply gauche. His empirical way of working might have been partly due to his exposure to Robert Scott Lauder's teaching at the Trustee's Academy in Edinburgh in the early 1860s during the period when he worked for Field & Allan. Unlike studies at the RA and Schools of Design where students were only allowed to progress to colour after developing linear drawing skills, Lauder encouraged his students to experiment and express themselves directly through colour in a looser, more expressive manner.[13] It was an issue that ran through much of High Victorian debate on art, decoration and taste. The essence of the libel trial of Whistler versus Ruskin in 1876 was about whether freely handled and apparently unfinished work could be viewed as 'art'.[14]

## Design Sources

Given the iconoclastic nature of the Reformation in Scotland, Leiper and Cottier had to look to architectural sources from further afield for inspiration, which in itself was a mark of the growing cosmopolitanism in Glasgow's economy and culture. Without the need to bow to precedent they arguably had greater freedom in creating an imaginative amalgam of styles than their English contemporaries. The archaising impulse in this amalgam expressed the search for a modern style that would communicate the noble simplicity and unaffected purity appropriate to Christian worship. At the same time there was growing interest in cross-cultural analyses of design looking at affinities of style in different periods and cultures. This was particularly evident in Owen Jones's influential *Grammar of Ornament* and Ralph Wornum's *Analysis of Ornament*, both published in 1856, and required reading in Schools of Design throughout Britain. Dowanhill's assured stylistic blend clearly related to the design reforms of figures like William Burges, EW Godwin, Viollet-le-Duc and Owen Jones, as well as influences nearer home such as Alexander Thomson, Scott Lauder and DR Hay. Cottier's exposure to Pre-Raphaelite painting and the work of Morris, Marshall, Faulkner & Co in London would also have been fresh in his mind.

## A Presbyterian Version of Early French Gothic

From the exterior the most obvious debt of Leiper's design for Dowanhill was to Early French Gothic. In his emphasis on clean-cut geometrical forms and simple volumes, Leiper followed the example of his mentors JL Pearson, William White and William Burges, and took his cue from the thirteenth-century village churches and cathedrals of Normandy. Above all, the octagonal spire, clasped to the tower with open corner pinnacles, is reminiscent of churches around Caen such as those illustrated by WE Nesfield in his *Specimens of Mediaeval Architecture*, 1862. The spate of books and drawings published in the architectural press at this time emphasises the currency of these Early Gothic sources in the late 1850s and '60s, and their perceived modernity.

**Plate VI** WE Nesfield and Normandy Gothic.

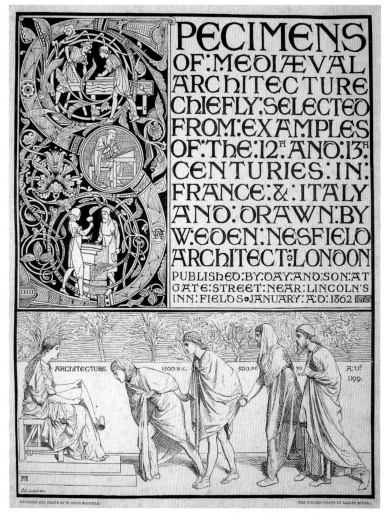

Nesfield (1835-1888) was a London-based architect with strong connections to Scotland and Glasgow: he had trained in the office of William Burn (1851-3) where he met Richard Norman Shaw, the two becoming collaborators on a detailed study of Gothic architecture in 1854, when they travelled extensively in France and met Viollet-le-Duc. The partnership between the two ran from 1862-8, though they continued to share an office until 1876. Nesfield's eclectic tendencies were already apparent in the early 1860s and he was soon pioneering Aesthetic tendencies in architecture and design, being a good friend of EW Godwin and of the artists Albert Moore and James McNeill Whistler. He was a model of the 'art-architect', his office being described as 'the studio of an artist rather than the business room of a professional man'. This was the recollection of the Glaswegian architect John McKean Brydon (1840-1910), who became Nesfield's chief assistant, having previously worked for Campbell Douglas Sellars in Glasgow before entering a partnership with Cottier and Bruce Talbert in London, *c*.1870-2. (JK)

*Title Page,* illustrated in WE Nesfield, *Specimens of Medieval Architecture,* 1862, photograph courtesy of Juliet Kinchin.

There had been a shift away from the more decorative fifteenth-century Gothic forms advocated by Pugin and the Ecclesiologists in the preceding decade. Despite the debt, frankly acknowledged, to archaeological and published sources, the Dowanhill scheme was no pedantic or 'archaeologically correct' exercise, however. Both Leiper and Cottier took from what they saw in Early French Gothic and made it their own. As in the work of William Burges and E W Godwin, the muscular, archaising forms of the style provided the framework for a new eclecticism, and was infused with both a more classical sensibility and more 'exotic' touches than would have been tolerated in the designs of A W Pugin, the Ecclesiologists, or the any of the 'Academic Goths'.

From the mid-1850s France had become a regular summer destination for British architects, particularly those of a Gothic persuasion, and Burges's winning design for the Lille Cathedral competition in 1856 stimulated interest in Normandy in particular. High profile commissions in an early Gothic style that had a direct bearing on the exterior and interior design of Dowanhill were Godwin's two Town Halls at Northampton (1861) and Congleton, Staffs (1864) (fig 21A). (Note in particular the parallels in the external gablets and interior spandrels.) Concurrent with Dowanhill, Leiper's French Gothic design for Dumbarton Burgh Hall in 1865 (fig 21B) also bore a marked similarity to these buildings. Given the cheapness of travel by steamboat and rail, and the circles in which they moved, it is possible that both Leiper and Cottier had already travelled to Northern France during their spell in London c.1858–62.[15] Both designers were certainly to do so in the years that followed Dowanhill. In a letter of 1875, for example, written to William Smith in Aberdeen about decorating the ceiling of the St Nicholas West Kirk there 'in good blue' studded with gold stars, Cottier remarked 'I have often seen it abroad',[16] and Leiper's obituary noted that he had travelled to Normandy to make a special study of Caen in preparation of his design for Camphill UP Church, Glasgow in 1875.[17]

By the late 1850s the French architect Viollet-le-Duc was replacing John Ruskin as the Gothic Revival's leading pundit, not least on account of his profusely illustrated *Dictionnaire raisonnée de l'architecture française du XIe au XVe siècle* which appeared in twelve parts between 1854 and 1876. 'We all crib from Viollet-le-Duc,' William Burges once admitted, 'although probably not one buyer in ten ever reads the text'.[18] Viollet-le-Duc

**Figure 21** Godwin and Leiper.

*A* Congleton Town Hall, E W Godwin, 1864.

*B* Dumbarton Burgh Hall, W Leiper, 1865. Item 196708 courtesy of RCAHMS. Licensor www.rcahms.gov.uk

took his inspiration from medieval models but believed that objects should be beautiful and modern; forms should correspond to uses. He studied secular furniture from manuscript sources, but was also interested in prefabrication, and saw the potential of new materials to create a new architecture. His approach validated Leiper's use of cast-iron columns and his bold adaptation of Early Gothic to the prefabricated railings around the Church. Of particular relevance to Dowanhill were also the illustrations of thirteenth-century painted furniture in the cathedrals of Bayeux and Noyon that appeared in Viollet-le-Duc's *Dictionnaire du mobilier francais* (1857) (fig 22A). The impact is unmistakable on the painted furniture designed by Burges in 1858-62 which appeared at the London International Exhibition in 1862. The architectonic arcading, ringed shafts and miniature roofs of a piece like Burges's Yatman cabinet (fig 22B) all in turn reappear in the Dowanhill pulpit (figs 22C-22D).

**Fig 22** Painted Furnishings.

*A* Noyon Armoire, E-E Viollet-le-Duc, 1858-75, *Dictionnaire raisonné du mobilier français.*

*B* Yatman Cabinet, W Burges designer, EJ Pointer, painter, 1858, Courtesy of the Victoria & Albert Museum.

*C* Painted Pulpit Canopy Roof, Dowanhill Church, D Cottier, 1865. Courtesy of Historic Scotland.

*D* Painted Pulpit Canopy Front, Dowanhill Church, D Cottier, 1865. Courtesy of Historic Scotland.

**Plate VII** Viollet-le-Duc.

*A* Three illustrations of painted decoration, E-E Viollet-le-Duc, 1854–68, *Dictionnaire raisonnée de l'architecture française du XIe au XVe siècle.*

*B* Painted Spandrel in Dowanhill Church, D Cottier, 1865. Courtesy of Historic Scotland.

*C* Measured Drawing of Painted Spandrel in Dowanhill Church. Courtesy of Groves-Raines Studio.

Viollet-le-Duc – Painted Decoration. *(A)* Three illustrations from Viollet-le-Duc's 1864 essay on painted decoration, demonstrating how colour and ornament could be used both to shape perceptions of architectural space, and enhance the character of architectural features.

'Decorative painting is above all a question of harmony and there is no system of harmony that cannot be explained. Decorative painting is, however, one of the most difficult elements of architectural art to deploy, precisely because the laws vary according to the nature of the place and object being decorated.' *(A)* demonstrated his point that 'Decorative painting can enlarge or diminish a space, make it light or dark, bring it near or far, create a pleasing or tiring effect.' (Viollet-le-Duc 1864, 79). Quite apart from working as a harmonious system in its own right, therefore, it was important that the decoration was relative to the place it occupied within the overall architectural scheme; ascending and rigid patterns such as those in the right hand illustration were suitable for vertical, load-bearing elements, while the examples in the central illustration enhanced the cylindrical surface of features like columns. Elsewhere he illustrated the twelfth- and thirteenth-century practice of 'lining' out walls that symbolically alluded to string-courses and the horizontality of the walls' structure.

The disposition of colours and motifs in the Dowanhill interior *(B&C)* suggest that Leiper and Cottier were following the kind of principles outlined in Viollet-le-Duc's essay, whether they were picking them up directly from this source or via one of the other designers like Godwin or Burges who were attuned to this way of thinking. (JK)

Leiper was not constrained by a rigid adherence to thirteenth-century Gothic examples but skilfully adapted the historical style to the requirements of Presbyterian worship and a modern urban context. Like Alexander Thomson, he was steeped in the Old Testament and his architecture was informed by an intimate understanding of Presbyterian theology. In the interior, the whole space was spanned by a hammer-beam roof with a plaster rather than timber finish as in most comparable English Gothic and Gothic Revival churches. Any concept of archaeological correctness was further compromised by the need to rework the traditional Gothic plan, doing away with a chancel and aisles. Above all it was important that the entire congregation could see and hear the Minister. 'The interior of such a church should be practically an auditorium of the best construction', declared James Cousland in his 'Remarks on Modern Church Architecture', addressed to the Glasgow Architectural Society in 1862.[19] As in many other Presbyterian churches at the time Leiper freed up the sightlines within the body of the church by designing galleries on three sides supported on slender cast-iron rather than masonry columns. It is possible that in 1855 while apprenticed with Boucher & Cousland he worked on the Free Church in Renfield Street, the first church in Glasgow to use this form. As an assistant with Campbell Douglas and Stevenson he had also presumably observed the design and construction of Stevenson's bold Kelvinside Parish Church, 1862-4, that punctuated the junction between Byres and Great Western Roads. The interior was designed with cast-iron arcades in a punchy Italian Gothic manner.

### The Pulpit Wall

Undoubtedly one of Leiper's most imaginative contributions to the reconfiguration of the traditional Gothic church was his treatment of the pulpit wall, and it was here that Leiper appears to have looked most closely to the example of Alexander Thomson in terms of creating a theatrical focus within the body of the church. The renting out of pews at different prices also resonated with the design of a theatre. The importance attached to preaching and the personality of the preacher was reflected in the enclosure of a portrait of the first Moderator, Rev Thomas Lawrie, within the Foundation Stone, and his name appeared on the 'David' window in the Choir gallery.

Ingeniously, Leiper contracted the conventional chancel that one would expect to find in a Gothic church into a dramatic, arcaded pulpit-feature on the end wall (fig 23A) that combined the visual and decorative emphasis normally associated with a chancel screen, altarpiece and sedilia all in one. The architectural drama of this preaching gallery was engineered by providing access from stairs to the rear so that the Minister magically 'appeared' before the congregation, beneath a flaming canopy (fig 20C), without breaking the visual integrity of the wall. There is a marked similarity between the arcaded form of the gallery and that of sediliae designed by GE Street and EW Godwin, the difference being that these features were located, following Gothic convention, on the side wall of a chancel.

With no altar-cloth or elaborate vestments there was little call for textiles in a Presbyterian church. Leiper used a single piece of embroidery to great effect, however, in the seat-back of the pulpit (fig 23A). According to the Rev Dickie, 'this beautiful piece of crewel work behind the pulpit was sewed to his [Cottier's] design by the hands of his sister, Miss Cottier, who shared her brother's love of artistry'.[20] Miss Cottier's collaboration with her brother at Dowanhill can be compared to that of Jane Burden with her husband William Morris. Jane Morris described working 'daisy' curtains in this manner for the master bedroom at Red House, the first married home of the Morrises, in 1860: 'The first stuff I got to embroider on was a piece of indigo dyed blue serge [...] I took it home and he [Morris] was delighted with it, and set to work at once designing flowers – these were worked in bright colours in a simple, rough way – the work went quickly.'[21] The pulpit seat-back was a needlework equivalent of Cottier's painterly technique in the wall decoration. The style of Miss Cottier's embroidery was also similar to that of two altar frontals, one designed by Street in 1850 (and described by him in the *Ecclesiologist* in 1863), and a related piece produced by Morris & Co in 1862 for the church of St Martin-on-the-Hill, Scarborough.[22] The latter was probably exhibited at the London International Exhibition in 1862 where Cottier could have seen it.

**Fig 23** Pulpit Interior.

**A** Painted Pulpit Seat, Dowanhill Church, W Leiper & D Cottier, 1865, with crewelwork by Cottier's sister, reconstructed by Michael Donnelly. Courtesy of Four Acres Charitable Trust.

**B** Painted Decoration within the Pulpit Canopy, Dowanhill Church, D Cottier, 1865. Courtesy of Historic Scotland.

The red ground of the embroidery picked up the flaming painted decoration above. 'The need for the descent of the Holy Spirit upon God's ministering servant when proclaiming the gospel is beautifully symbolised by the tongues of fire descending from the blue of heaven' wrote Rev Dickie (fig 23B).[23] The whole wall embodied a symbolic mediation between earth and heaven, sending upwards the prayers and praise of the Congregation and drawing down divine inspiration upon the Minister. This was picked up in the interlocking triangles of the star in the window above that pointed up and down simultaneously. Originally a font was incorporated in the stonework of the pulpit, but the process of Baptism became a little too theatrical for many of the parents standing down below who saw their offspring raised dangerously on high in a gesture approaching that of a ritual sacrifice. To avert a tragedy Leiper was commissioned in 1868 to design a separate font in the style of the building costing £10 to stand in the body of the church.[24]

## Veiling the Holy of Holies and the Masonic Connection

The resonance between the Dowanhill pulpit and Viollet-le-Duc's image of a thirteenth-century painted and curtained arcade from the Abbaye Fontfroide, published in 1864, suggest that Leiper and Cottier had at least leafed through this volume of the *Dictionnaire raisonée de l'architecture française*, and internalised some of the visual ideas. EW Godwin had incorporated similar painted curtains both in the Council chamber of his Northampton Town Hall (1861) and Congleton Town Hall (1864), and illustrated a range of conventions for the representation of painted curtains based on Gothic examples in one of his articles on 'Painted Decoration' that appeared in 1866-8 (fig 24A). Both Viollet-le-Duc and Godwin emphasised that such motifs were not naturalistic representations but functioned as kinds of hieroglyphs for a symbolic idea. Such sources may have provided the original idea, but in Dowanhill the 'curtains' were deployed in an innovative way which picked up on the symbolism implicit in Alexander Thomson's impressive treatment of the pulpit features in his UP churches. 'This grand design seems to celebrate a transitional line, and is expressed as a ceremonial entrance to some inner sanctuary', writes Edward Taylor of the St Vincent Street pulpit screen, and goes on to convincingly argue that its symbolic purpose was to commemorate the 'veil' across the inner shrine of Solomon's Temple which housed the Ark of the Covenant.[25] (Masonic symbolism was believed to derive from the Temple of Solomon.) What better way of symbolising such a 'veil' within a Gothic-style church than by means of painted curtains? This is borne out by the presence of apparently Masonic references in the stained glass above the pulpit, such as the Star of David, the triangular motifs enclosing circular dots, and Jonathan's fabric hat (fig 25). The head at the top of the rose window is that of Moses, the prophet to whom 'Freemasons of the present day' traced the secrets of their knowledge, according to DR Hay.[26] Such motifs and references were openly and speculatively discussed at the time, and do not necessarily imply affiliation to the Masonic brotherhood, although William Burges, Leiper's sponsor for entry into the RIBA, is known to have been an active member. There are certainly well documented connections between the Partick East congregation and the Masons, prior to the building of the new church. The local Masonic Lodge, St Mary's, was even used as a temporary place of worship when the congregation was first being established. According to the Rev Dickie, the foundation stone of Partick East Church was laid with Masonic honours. The Masons wore their regalia and brought their brass band for the occasion, but the Rev Smart, who had been secured to preach at the ceremony, was so astounded by this 'innovation', that he 'declined to preach, and departed'. A Mr Miln, however, was 'commandeered' to deliver the sermon.[27] Although the evidence is not conclusive, the recent researches into the sacred geometry and aesthetic principles of Alexander Thomson, and their relationship to Masonic culture also suggest that this was likely to have been a dimension in Leiper's architectural design.[28]

## Assyrian and Egyptian Influences

The boldly exotic and archaising imagery of Cottier's David and Miriam window chimed with the commercial and imperial character of Glasgow in a way that would have seemed inappropriate in the more narrowly defined classicism of Edinburgh, and it clearly related on one level to the stylistic and decorative vocabulary developed by Greek Thomson. It is possible that Cottier had been directly involved in the decoration of the Caledonia Street Church during his apprenticeship with Cairney's in the 1850s, and he was certainly moving in Thomson's orbit again in the mid-1860s. We know that Thomson made reference to sources like Sir John Gardner Wilkinson's Manners and Customs of the Ancient Egyptians which provided an accessible source for the kind of accessories and motifs that also appear in Cottier's designs (fig 26). Austen Henry Layard's excavations in Assyria in the 1840s and his published reconstruction of interiors like Ashurbanipal's throne-room at Nineveh in 1851 emphasised their strongly coloured painted decoration. Layard's publication and related French and German sources were all accessible through the library of the Architectural Section of the Glasgow Philosophical Society that was catalogued in 1865.[29]

**Fig 24** Painted Curtains.

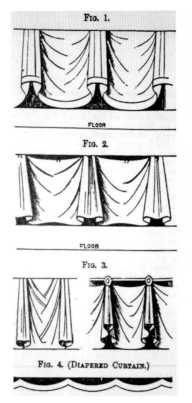

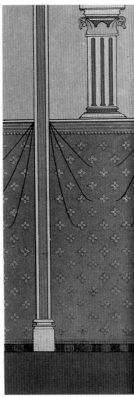

*A* 'Designs for Painted Curtains', EW Godwin, 1866-7, *Building News.*

*B* Illustration of Medieval Painted Curtain Design, E-E Viollet-le-Duc, 1870, *Les Peintres de Notre-Dame de Paris.*

*C* Painted Curtains on the Rear Panel of the Pulpit, Dowanhill Church, D Cottier, 1865. Courtesy of Four Acres Charitable Trust, photograph Jane Davies.

Painted Curtains. Similar themes reappear in Godwin's domestic scheme for the Great hall in Dromore Castle, Ireland, built for the Earl of Limerick, and in illustrations to the series of twelve articles written for the Building News, 1866-67, on the subject of painted decoration. (JK)

**Figure 25** Masonic References.

*A  Star of David*, Rose Window, Dowanhill Church, D Cottier, stained glass, 1866/7. Courtesy of Tom Donald.

*B  Jonathan*, Rose Window, Dowanhill Church, Daniel Cottier, stained glass, 1866/67. Courtesy of Tom Donald.

**Fig 26** Egyptian and Assyrian Influences.

*A* 'The Almeh', E W Lane, 1836, *Manners and Customs of the Modern Egyptians.*

*B* 'Sagat' and 'Tar', E W Lane, 1836, *Manners and Customs of the Modern Egyptians.*

*C Miriam*, Dowanhill Church, D Cottier, stained glass, 1867. Courtesy of Tom Donald.

In *The Grammar of Ornament* Owen Jones presented Ancient Egyptian and Assyrian ornament as a pure original style derived directly from nature (fig 27). Thomson talked in similar terms of the first creative use of man's aesthetic faculty, which he traced in his second Haldane lecture: having satisfied his need for shelter man begins to 'draw directly upon his aesthetic faculty. He begins with lines and spots, simple circles, intersected circles, stars, either single or in rows, straight lines, zigzag lines, wave lines and spiral lines, in every conceivable combination. He shows his sense of proportion in dividing spaces with noticeable degrees of relationship to each other, and probably colours the whole in harmonious contrasts'.[30] This reads like a description of Cottier's Dowanhill scheme.

Following on from the widespread interest in archaeological excavations in Assyria and Egypt during the 1850s, there was a concern among fine artists to depict Biblical subjects with authentic detail. In addition, the Scottish artists David Wilkie and David Roberts had both travelled to the East in the 1840s. Of particular relevance are a group of drawings and paintings produced for an ambitious publishing project in London for an Illustrated Bible that was started by the Dalziel Brothers in 1863. Lord Leighton, Sir Edward Poynter and Simeon Solomon participated with Egyptian and Assyrian scenes, including images of Miriam with her tambourine and David playing his harp. Ford Madox Brown was commissioned to produce three of the images, including the drawing and painting 'The Coat of Many Colours', 1864-6. The handling of Jacob's head and the assistant's harp are comparable to details in Cottier's

**Fig 27** Page illustrating Assyrian Ornament, O Jones, 1856, *The Grammar of Ornament.*

glass (fig 28). When the drawing was exhibited in 1865 at the Piccadilly Gallery, Madox Brown explained in the accompanying catalogue how he had taken details of the costumes and accessories from Assyrian and Egyptian sources 'which, alone, it seems to me, should guide us in Biblical Subjects'.[31] Cottier was working in Edinburgh by this time but he may have visited London in connection with the 1864 South Kensington Exhibition of Stained Glass to which he contributed a panel. In any case he would surely have followed the reviews of his former teacher's work whose subject matter reflected his own stylistic preoccupations in Glasgow.

**Fig 28** Cottier and Ford Madox Brown.

*A Abraham*, Rose Window Dowanhill Church, Daniel Cottier, stained glass, 1866/67. Courtesy of Tom Donald.

*B* 'Jacob', Detail from *The Coat of Many Colours*, FM Brown, oil on panel, 1866. Courtesy of the National Museums Liverpool.

*C David*, D Cottier, stained glass, 1867. Courtesy of Tom Donald.

*D* 'Attendant' Detail from *The Coat of Many Colours*, FM Brown, oil on panel, 1866. Courtesy of the National Museums Liverpool.

The uncorseted dress and bull-necked, thick-waisted form of Miriam (fig 26C) pointed to a new ideal of feminine beauty that was to become associated with mainstream Aesthetic taste in the 1870s. It was certainly in contrast to any conventional representations of ideal womanhood or wilting femininity, and to the pinched waists of contemporary fashions. Apart from the 'Grecian' fillet around her hair that dominated fashions in 1869, the 'Assyrian' fringe of Miriam's dress was to become a signifier of 'artistic' dress in the 1870s, and was viewed as a more rational alternative to the flounces and beribboned trimmings of more conventional dresses. Similarly the red-headed and blond beauties of the stained glass heads beneath the Galleries are redolent of the modern 'Aesthetic' looks popularised in Pre-Raphaelite painting of the time (fig 29).

**Divine Harmonies**

*Song*

The medium through which the liturgical, the spiritual and the architectural converged was music. Psalmody, the singing of a choir led by a Precentor, played an important part in traditional Presbyterian worship. As Rev Dickie remarked, 'every good Presbyterian regarded himself as an authority upon the music of the church'.[32] The auditioning and election of the Precentor was in itself an important musical event in the community. At Dowanhill a dialogue in sound was set up between the preaching of the Minister from the pulpit and the waves of music that spread through the congregation towards him from the Choir in the South Gallery. The Music Committee had appointed a 'Conductor of Praise' and a professional soprano whose combined salaries in 1867 came to £51 per annum. Cottier's windows in the Choir Gallery representing David with his lyre ('Praise ye the Lord') and Miriam with her tambourine ('Sing ye to the Lord'), provided a literal and figurative invocation to worship through song.

*Instrumental Music*

Despite an emphasis on song, the introduction of instrumental music was another matter altogether, and one hotly contested within the United Presbyterian Church. The congregation of Glasgow's Claremont Church, opened in 1856, had attempted to press the issue by equipping themselves with an organ, but the Church Synod refused to sanction its use in public worship for the next sixteen years! At Dowanhill, the Music Committee's request in 1867 to 'buy or rent a harmonium' for choir practices was the thin end of the wedge, and by 1875 the Committee announced that it had sufficient funds to purchase an organ.[33] When the Kirk Session put this contentious proposal to the Congregation, there were 209 in favour, but a substantial number remained opposed or at best neutral, raising the spectre of desertion which the Church could ill afford. After a further year of negotiations and enquiries, however, it was decided to accept a tender from the pre-eminent firm, H Willis & Son of London, to build an organ for £975 (considerably more than the combined cost of the original painted scheme and stained glass). Willis had also supplied an organ to the Townhead Church on which Cottier worked with JJ Stevenson, and thereafter also to Glasgow Cathedral. Leiper advised on the installation at Dowanhill, and in 1876, a 'brilliant' organist was appointed followed by the addition of a second paid singer to support the choir.[34]

On a more abstract level, the proportions and colouring of the church interior were orchestrated to reinforce the notion of divine musical harmonies. Cottier's ornamental designs set up rhythmic patterns, with the geometrical elements offset by the motion and curving grace of his 'wibble-wabble' pattern. Between them, Cottier and Leiper created a complete melody of colour and harmony of form that can be viewed as an early expression of the Aesthetic preoccupation with synaesthesia in the arts and the multi-sensory nature of

**Fig 29** Female Representations.

*A Ruth*, Dowanhill Church, D Cottier, stained glass, 1866/67. Courtesy of Tom Donald.

*B The Blue Bower*, DG Rossetti, oil on canvas, 1865. Courtesy of Barber Institute, Bridgeman Art Library.

*C Helen of Troy*, FA Sandys, oil on canvas, 1867. Courtesy of National Museums Liverpool.

*D Lydia*, Dowanhill Church, D Cottier, stained glass, 1866/67. Courtesy of Tom Donald.

perception. Walter Pater's famous 1877 dictum that 'All art constantly aspires towards the condition of music' was to become a touchstone of Aesthetic art and design, expressed most famously, perhaps, in Whistler's series of paintings of 'Harmonies' 'Nocturnes' and 'Symphonies' of the 1870s.[35]

*Musical Colour*

Colour was said to address the eye in the same way as music addressed the ear. A catalogue of the Library belonging to the Architectural Section of the Glasgow Philosophical Society drawn up in the mid-1860s, includes several key works on colour by George Field, Michel-Eugène Chevreul and DR Hay. The leading chemist, and natural philosopher George Field wanted to transform his knowledge into an 'aesthetical science' reconciling materialism and idealism. His theories drew an analogy between colour, line, sound, language and the structure of the universe. His views were reiterated in Owen Jones' Grammar of Ornament (1856), publications by Christopher Dresser, and summarised in books by Hay. In The Laws of Harmonious Colouring, for example, that appeared in seven editions from 1836-47, DR Hay explored the idea that related colours reverberated like harmonic tones in a chord (fig 30). His aim was to disseminate scientific ideas about harmony of colouring that were already familiar to some fine artists in a simple and popular form that could be used by designers and decorators. In composing a scheme Hay stressed the need to reflect the intended function and natural lighting of the interior, and advocated that the tone of any scheme should be set by the general colour of the furniture and woodwork, principles that Cottier followed at Dowanhill (fig 31), much as Thomson had done in his schemes. At Dowanhill the ground tones of the woodwork and walls were offset by the emotional intensity of the decorative elements in the coloured paintwork and glass. Within the overall harmony there were fluctuations between the joyous explosion of colour in the Choir Gallery, the celestial blue ground of the starry ceiling above, and the hotter fiery intensity emanating from the pulpit. At the

time of Thomson's death in 1875, Cottier still had on loan from his friend a book worth £16. In view of their collaboration on Queen's Park Church and Thomson's preoccupation with coloured decoration, it is tempting to speculate that this considerable sum represented a luscious chromo-lithographed publication like the first edition of Owen Jones's Grammar of Ornament (1856), the production of which virtually bankrupted the author. Hay, Field and Jones all stipulated that for an harmonious arrangement of colours all three primary colours needed to be present 'either in simple or mixed state', and that the distinctions of harmony depended on the dominance of one of these three. On this principle, Field and Hay worked out a system of 'chromatic equivalents' that enabled decorators to systematically balance combinations of primary, secondary and tertiary colours. The balance could be further tweaked by adjusting the tones shades and hues.

*Sacred Geometry and Ideal Proportions*

Alexander Thomson held mathematics to be the key to rational thought, and the search to create a system of ideal proportions was implicit in all his work, as several recent studies have convincingly demonstrated. For him, geometry was not only a stylistic exercise but almost an article of faith. Although he departed from the Greek models which Thomson viewed as the most ideal architecture of proportions, Leiper was coming from the same religious background and the analysis of recent measured drawings suggests that he too was committed to expressing a system of harmonic proportions in his design for Dowanhill (see below, **Chapter 8, Dowanhill Church And Numeric Proportion**).

In a Scottish context this resonated with earlier explorations of the consonance between art, proportions and music in the writings and practice of the Scottish decorator and aesthetician, DR Hay, most notably in his books *Proportion, or the Geometric Principle of Beauty Analysed*, *The Science of Beauty*, and his study relating to the Parthenon's geometry. It was a period of increased

**Fig 30** DR Hay Examples.

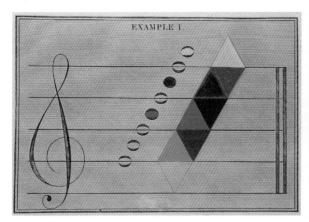

*A* 'Example I', DR Hay, *The Laws of Harmonious Colouring*. Courtesy of Juliet Kinchin.

*B* 'Example II', DR Hay, *The Laws of Harmonious Colouring*. Courtesy of Juliet Kinchin.

*C* 'Examples VI1 & VIII', DR Hay, *The Laws of Harmonious Colouring*. Courtesy of Juliet Kinchin.

insight into the geometry and aesthetics of ancient art. Theories of harmonic proportion were not however confined to the 'Classic' party. RW Billings (most famous for *The Baronial and Ecclesiastical Antiquities of Scotland*, 1852) tried to unlock the sacred principles of Scottish antiquities in his study, *The Infinity of Geometric Design Exemplified* (1849).

The symbolic use of numbers and proportions was often associated with Freemasonry, a topic frequently discussed in books and journals of the mid-nineteenth century. 'Although its practical secrets have long been lost', wrote Hay, 'the Freemasons of the present day trace the original possession of them to Moses, who, as they say, "modelled masonry into a perfect system".' As Moses

was educated in Egypt, Hay argued, 'where Pythagoras is said to have acquired his first knowledge of the harmonic law of numbers, it is highly likely that this perfect system of the great Jewish legislator was based upon the same law of nature which constituted the foundation of the Pythagorean philosophy'.[36] The idea that the fundamental musical relations in the octave could be represented by simple numerical ratios was fundamental to the Pythagoreans. Number, proportion & harmony underlay ideas of Pythagorean philosophy, and the application of number theory to music was a central preoccupation. Harmony had for the Pythagoreans a cosmic significance. In this view, architectural proportions were part of a larger system in which everything was held in balance.

**Fig 31** Harmonious Colouring and Wall Painting at Dowanhill Church.

*A* 'Examples III & IV', DR Hay, 1847, *The Laws of Harmonious Colouring*. Courtesy of Juliet Kinchin.

*B* Nave Wall Painting Dowanhill Church, D Cottier, 1865 – 6. Courtesy of Historic Scotland.

**Plate VIII** *Moses.*

*A Moses,* Rose Window Dowanhill Church, D Cottier, stained glass, 1866-7. Courtesy of Tom Donald.

*B Moses in Gratitude,* First Presbyterian Church, New York, Cottier & Co, stained glass, 1887. Courtesy of Ezra Shales.

DR Hay read the following to the Royal Institute of British Architects on 13 November 1854:

*There really does exist a mathematical law coinciding with the harmony always found in nature and that this law can be applied in imparting orthographic beauty to architectural structures of any order or style as also to explain the nature of this law and the system by which it can be applied. Hay 1854, 9*

*When any two figures or forms are placed in juxtaposition, in order to produce a pleasing and harmonious effect it is requisite that there exist between them a distinct and definite degree of contrast, that is, that their respective proportions must bear a very simple ratio to each other. Hay 1854, 12*

*The probability exists that a system of applying this law of nature in architectural constructions was the only great practical secret of the Freemasons, all their other secrets being connected, not with their art, but with the social constitution of their society'. It can scarcely be doubted that there was some such practically useful secret amongst the Freemasons or early Gothic architects, for we find, in all the venerable remains of their art which exist in this country, symmetrical elegance of form pervading the general design, harmonious proportion amongst all the parts, beautiful geometrical arrangements throughout all the tracery, as well as in the elegant symmetricised foliated decorations which belong to that style of architecture. Although the practical secrets of their art have been lost, the Freemasons of the present day trace the original possession of them to Moses, who, they say, 'modelled masonry into a perfect system, and circumscribed its mysteries by landmarks significant and unalterable'. Hay 1854, 21-2*

[1] Godwin 1863, reprinted in Godwin 2005, 35-9.
[2] Godwin 1865, 5.
[3] Godwin 1866-8, 22 Jun 1866, 405.
[4] Godwin 1866-8, 19 Jul 1867, 491.
[5] Godwin 1866-8, 3 Jan 1868, 6.
[6] Godwin 1866-8, 16 November 1866, 757.
[7] Godwin 1866-8, 22 June 1866, 405.
[8] Dickie 1926, 71.
[9] Worsdall 1966, 30.
[10] Wells 1902, 145.
[11] Gould 1969, 2.
[12] Dickie 1926, 73.
[13] See Errington 1983, 27-44.
[14] For the Whistler versus Ruskin trial, see Merrill, 1992.
[15] Cottier's mentor, Ford Madox Brown had been born in Calais and had studied in France; Pearson, White, Burges, Nesfield and Godwin had all travelled and sketched extensively in France by the early 1860s.
[16] ACLA 8, 14 June 1875. I am grateful to Max Donnelly for providing access to his transcript of this.
[17] See McNab 1916, 303, who states that the spire was modelled on that of Saint-Pierre, Caen.
[18] Crook 1981, 120.
[19] Cousland 1862.
[20] Dickie 1916, 9. See also Dickie 1926, 73.
[21] See Parry 1996, Cat M.6, 236.
[22] See Street 1863, 255-80; and Parry 1996, Cat. M.3, 234.
[23] Dickie 1926, 73. The Biblical reference is to Pentecost, in *Acts*, 2, 1-4, which mentions 'cloven tongues, like as of fire' which descended on each of the Apostles, 'fill[ing] them with the Holy Ghost'.
[24] Dickie 1926, 81.
[25] Taylor 27 (2000), 19.
[26] Hay, 1854, 20-22.
[27] Dickie 1926, 23-4. This difference of opinion over the appropriateness of Masonic involvement was noted, with the comment 'times change', in the *DCMR* (Dec 1951), when Rev William Baxter was called to the Chair of the Trades House of Glasgow Lodge on 12 Nov 1951 at the hand of the Grand Master Mason of Scotland.
[28] See Taylor 26 (2000), 7-14.
[29] The Library was dispersed in the 1960s. For the catalogue of the Architectural Section, see Stamp 1998, 9.
[30] Thomson 1999, 128.
[31] Brown 1865, 31.
[32] Dickie 1926, 67.
[33] Dickie 1926, 83.
[34] Dickie 1926, 84.
[35] Pater 1877, 284.
[36] Hay 1854, 20-22.

# 4 BEYOND DOWANHILL
## Juliet Kinchin

**Plate IX**

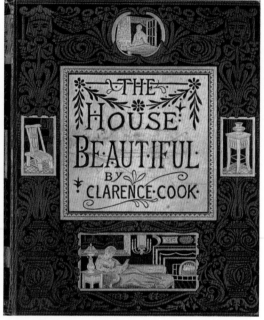

*B* Cover designed by D Cottier for C Cook, 1878, *The House Beautiful*. Photo: John Hammond.

*A* Jean-Baptiste-Camille Corot, *Orpheus Greeting the Dawn (or Hymn to the Sun)*, 1865, Oil on Canvas, Chazen Museum of Art, University of Wisconsin Madison, Gift in Memory of Earl William and Eugenia Brandt Quirk, Class of 1910, by their children (E James Quirk, Catherine Jean Quirk & Lillian Quirck Contley). Photo Credit: Eric Tadsen.

*C* Painted Ceiling, Cairndhu House, W Leiper and Cottier & Co, 1872. Courtesy of Juliet Kinchin.

## Introduction

In this chapter, selected schemes and associates of Cottier and Leiper are discussed to demonstrate their wider impact on household taste and collecting of the 1870s and 1880s.

Like William Morris, with whom he was frequently compared, Cottier's business initially depended on ecclesiastical work, but both he and Leiper were to make their names in the domestic market (fig 32), designing turreted retreats for Glasgow's industrial and mercantile elite and art lovers' houses in Aberdeen. This market, and this integrated approach to interiors was further developed in the 1880s by a group of Cottier's associates in Glasgow –Andrew Wells, Hugh McCulloch and Charles Gow. Meanwhile Cottier moved from working for a small group of select patrons in Scotland to producing and retailing a combination of 'art' manufactures, paintings, prints and antiques on three continents, to a broader, more anonymous market with 'artistic' aspirations.

**Fig 32** Leiper – Domestic Architecture.

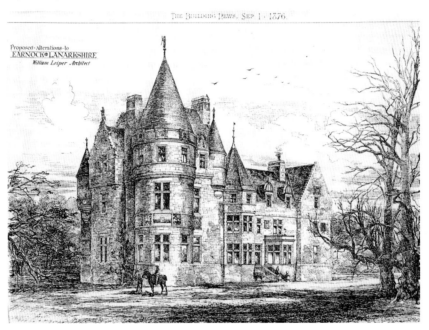

*A* Earnock, Lanarkshire, W Leiper, 1876.

*B* Interior of Kinlochmoidart House, Inverness-shire, W Leiper, 1883.

## Seaton Cottage, the Aberdeen Connection, and The Elms, Arbroath

The earliest documented interiors by Cottier were in Aberdeen, for the miller collector and art critic Dr James Forbes White with whom the gregarious designer had apparently struck up a friendship in the course of a train journey. Some time around 1862-3, Cottier added a drawing room and dining room to White's villa, Seaton Cottage, Bridge of Don (fig 33), not far from St Machar's Cathedral in Old Aberdeen where Cottier executed a window for White in 1864. He also added a drawing room to Bridgefield, Bridge of Don, for White's mother. At Seaton Cottage, in the recently revealed tertiary colour combinations and stylised ornament of the painted schemes, coordinated with stained glass and painted tiles, one gets a hint of what was to come at Dowanhill. The colours were unusual, and according to his daughter, White recalled thinking at first how terrible they were when he saw them going on, despite his pleasure at the end result.[1] The glass roundels, depicting Old Masters from Raphael to Rembrandt in the dining room, and literary women in the drawing room, reflected White's artistic and cultural preoccupations. Not only as a patron, but as a critic and collector he exerted a profound influence on Cottier and Leiper, not least in his passion for contemporary French and Dutch painting, and recent research by scholars in Aberdeen is bringing to light his impact on the wider course of Scottish painting and collecting.[2]

Cottier was to convert the knowledge he absorbed from White into collaborations with artists like Hugh Cameron and Matthew Maris, and perhaps more importantly into his lucrative business as an art dealer. Indeed it seems likely that Cottier channelled some of White's collection onto the international market when White was forced to sell in the late 1870s. Leiper appears to have had some family connection with Aberdeenshire, but was probably drawn into White's orbit through Cottier. It was possibly at Seaton Cottage that Leiper first became friendly with Arthur Melville with whom he studied at the Academie Julian in Paris c.1878-9. Another prominent artist in White's circle was George Reid (later knighted and President of the Royal Scottish Academy) for whom Leiper designed a studio-house, 'St Luke's', and Cottier designed a window in St Machar's commemorating his brothers. Cottier furnished and decorated the interiors of several other houses for the Aberdeen elite, including 'Kepplestone' (fig 34), the house next door to Reid's, for the prominent granite merchant and collector, Alexander Macdonald, and 'Garthdee' (now part of the Scott Sutherland School of Architecture) for another merchant, John Moir Clark as well as the Elms, Arbroath for Provost Corsar (fig 35). Together these commissions, spanning the period immediately before and after Dowanhill, amounted to a revolution in domestic taste. As the Aberdeen lawyer Lachlan Mackinnon recalled, 'The change-over to the "severe Cottier" style of house decoration took place in the 'seventies'.[3]

## Colearn, Cairndhu and Cornhill

This trio of substantial houses in Scotland were in a similar style and all date from 1869-73. The first was the substantial Colearn house in Auchterarder, Perthshire, designed by Leiper in 1869. By the time Cottier came to furnish the interiors, he had been joined in his London partnership by old Glasgow friends Bruce Talbert and John McKean Brydon, and had Rhoda and Agnes Garrett as apprentices (see below). The geometric and eclectic Gothic of Dowanhill and Talbert's Gothic Forms (1867) was from this point on lightened and modified by the fashionable influence of Japan. The restrained outline of the furniture was enhanced by the incorporation of painted panels and tiles. In 1871 Leiper and Cottier & Co received a further high profile commission for a house in Helensburgh from John Ure, a grain miller who became Lord Provost of Glasgow, and whose son became Lord Strathclyde. With clients this influential their longer-

**Fig 33** Cottier and John Forbes White.

*A* Interior of Seaton Cottage, Bridge of Don, D Cottier, 1863–7. Courtesy of Aberdeen Art Gallery & Museums Collection.

*B* Interior of Seaton Cottage, now Glenseaton Cottage, Bridge of Don after restoration. Courtesy of Bill Church.

term success was assured. Leiper designed Cairndhu, an art lover's house with a large gallery decorated in the most advanced Aesthetic taste by Cottier and Andrew Wells (fig 36A). Ure was a musical enthusiast (he had an organ built into the hall), and kept the company of artists. A book of Glasgow Art Club sketches published in 1881 was dedicated to him, and by this time the interior of his new house had apparently 'already formed the subject of paintings by Mr. Lockhardt and other artists'.[4] The British Architect described the house as 'carried out under [Leiper's] close supervision, down to almost every detail of the furnishing', and noted the elaborate and rich colouring of the interiors; 'The decoration of the whole house is strong and picturesque in style'.[5] Work on the house continued till 1875-6 and cost much the same as the whole of Dowanhill Church, totalling about £8,000. As already mentioned, in 1873 Alexander Kay, one of the moving forces behind the Dowanhill Church, commissioned the Leiper-Cottier duo to build and decorate Cornhill, his house in Biggar.

**Fig 34**  Interior of Kepplestone House, Aberdeen, Cottier & Company, 1875. Courtesy of Aberdeen Art Gallery & Museums Collection.

**Figure 35**  Painted Ceiling, The Elms, Arbroath, W Leiper, D Cottier, 1867–9. Ref SC7007613 courtesy of RCAHMS. Licensor www.rcahms.gov.uk

## Wells, McCulloch and Gow in Glasgow

Through the work of his assistants Andrew Wells, Hugh McCulloch and Charles Gow, Cottier continued to make his presence felt in Glasgow. Following Cottier's departure from Glasgow Wells continued to work with Leiper and Cottier & Co (fig 36) until 1886, when poor health caused him to leave Scotland and join the Lyon and Cottier partnership in Australia for ten years. In 1897, having recently returned to Glasgow, he entered into an agreement with William Guthrie who had bought out his brother John's share of the family house-painting business. The new company of Guthrie and Wells Ltd supplied stained glass to churches and homes throughout the city, winning an award for their stained glass at the Paris Exposition Universelle in 1900, and have since come to prominence through their connection with Charles Rennie Mackintosh, for their furniture designs and for decorative schemes.

On several occasions Leiper worked with other decorators and stained glass artists formerly employed by Cottier, notably Hugh McCulloch and Charles Gow, for example the decoration of the Banqueting Hall in the Municipal Chambers (now City Chambers), in Glasgow. Gow left their partnership in 1892 to once again work for Cottier, this time in Adelaide, Australia. McCulloch continued to supply decorative painting work and stained glass in the West of Scotland, working with Glasgow Style artists and designers like David Gauld, John Ednie and EA Taylor. He remained closely involved with issues of design education and the Glasgow School of Art, training a large number of apprentices as 'decorative artists in the real sense and not merely producers of "first class painted surfaces"'.[6] In 1915 he became a bailie.

## Kelmscott House and Cottier & Co in London

Kelmscott House on the banks of the River Thames is best known for its association with William Morris. In 1878 Morris took on the remaining lease of 'The Retreat' as it was then known, from an acquaintance of his, George Macdonald, the Aberdeenshire-born poet, writer and preacher who had lived there since 1867 with his large family. It is possible that Cottier encountered Macdonald through his Aberdeenshire connections, but the link is just as likely to have been through the Working Men's College in London that was supported by Macdonald's close friends FD Maurice and John Ruskin. The latter described Macdonald's sermons as the best 'beyond all compare – I have ever read'.[7] The commission came at around the time of Cottier's removal back to London in 1869, and deployed the familiar combination of red walls stencilled with black fleur-de-lys, and a dark blue ceiling with scattered stars in silver and gold, and a silver crescent moon. Cottier & Co were beginning to make their mark among London clients and architects. In a letter to Stevenson in March 1870, George Gilbert Scott Junior noted:

> I saw 'Cottier & Co' upon a door today in Langham Place. I hope he will do good work. There is a danger of giving in too much to the tone and general moral effect of a modern house even when improving the details. Effeminacy – commonly called comfort – and desire of display never produced good art and never can. A certain masculine character and a feeling of reality and a self-respect which does not heed the assistance of puffery are essential to good domestic work. Otherwise we are but pandering to rich snobs.[8]

## Supporter of Women Artists

Cottier, Stevenson and Brydon were all to play a role in debates around the nature and value of women's role in the context of architecture. Cottier's involvement of his sister in the interior decoration of Dowanhill (see above, **Chapter 3, The Pulpit Wall**) was an early instance of the practical way in which Cottier challenged patriarchal attitudes to architecture and design that sought to limit women's activities to the home and unpaid domestic duties. His wife, Marion Field, whom he married in December 1866, just after the opening of Dowanhill

**Fig 36** Domestic and Ship Interiors.

*A* Painted Ceiling, Cairndhu House, Helensburgh, W Leiper and Cottier & Co, 1872. Courtesy of Juliet Kinchin.

*B* Dining Room of the *Livadia* Steam Yacht, W Leiper designer, A Wells decorator, 1875.

Church, may also have collaborated with him on artistic projects. Being the daughter of his former employer in Edinburgh, she would have known all about the business of colour, stained glass and interior decoration. However, we know tantalisingly little about her beyond the fact that she modelled for various artists within her husband's circle, notably Hugh Cameron and later, Pinkham Ryder. At a time when educational and professional opportunities for women were still minimal, Cottier also took on the training of two women who were to become the most famous female interior designers of the 1870s and '80s in the English-speaking world – the cousins Rhoda and Agnes Garrett. The initial introduction to Cottier was possibly through their relation JJ Stevenson, with whom Cottier had worked on the Townhead Parish Church in Glasgow. In 1867 Cottier had also carried out stained glass for the house of Stevenson's brother in South Shields. The Garretts (fig 37) had originally wanted to train as architects, but found it impossible to get taken on in an architect's office. Women were in fact barred from the RIBA until 1898. It was Cottier who first gave them a break with the offer of space in his London studio, and when he departed for New York they entered a formal apprenticeship with his partner and former colleague from Glasgow, JM Brydon. The two cousins thereafter established an independent firm in Gower Street, London, achieving international prominence through their displays at the Paris International Exhibition of 1878. Their domestic commissions included Aesthetic furnishing schemes for Agnes's sister, the pioneering doctor Elizabeth Garrett Anderson, for the educational reformer Dorothea Beale, and work in many of the women's colleges in Oxford

**Fig 37** Interior illustrated in R and A Garrett, 1876, *Suggestions for House Decoration in Painting, Woodwork and Furniture.*

**Plate X** Cottier in London – Regent Canal Explosion, *Illustrated London News*, 1874. Courtesy of Mary Evans Picture Library.

In London Cottier lived in the artists' enclave near St John's Wood with a house at 3 St James Terrace, Regent Park. In October 1874 there was a huge explosion on a barge passing under a bridge on the Regent Canal. The bridge was entirely destroyed; several of the neighbouring houses were half-ruined. Among these was the house of the artist Alma-Tadema who was travelling back from Glasgow when it happened. The artist John Pettie wrote to Alexander Macdonald of Kepplestone 'On our way through Glasgow we heard of this dreadful explosion', Mac and his wife have lost in it, and Cottier has lost money.' (DR)

Sources:
*Illustrated London News*, October 1874
V G Swanson *Sir Lawrence Alma-Tadema*, Doctoral Thesis 1994
*The Papers of Alexander Macdonald of Kepplestone and his trustees, c.*1852-1903.

and Cambridge. Examples of their furniture can be seen at Standen, a Sussex house designed by Philip Webb now run by the National Trust. They also wrote a bestseller, the moderately priced *Suggestions on House Decoration in Painting, Woodwork and Furniture* (1876) in Macmillan's 'Art at Home' series. Arguably this popular publication addressed a wider audience than the more upmarket publications by their cousin JJ Stevenson, such as the two-volume *House Architecture* (1880), also published by Macmillan. Not only were the Garretts high profile authors and designers, but Rhoda in particular was an active feminist, campaigning tirelessly for women's rights and the struggle 'for the successful removal of intolerable grievances'.[9] This important access between design and women's suffrage was to come to the fore in the generation of the Macdonald sisters and Jessie Newbery at the Glasgow School of Art in the 1890s.

## 'The London Brethren'

The interior of Dowanhill in particular was comparable to the style in which Bruce Talbert, John McKean Brydon and subsequently John Moyr Smith were working (fig 38). By 1867 all three had left Glasgow and were gravitating to London, but remained closely in touch with their former Glasgow colleagues. The framework in which these three connected with Cottier and Leiper was probably the office of Campbell Douglas and Stevenson where Talbert, Brydon and Moyr Smith had all worked; also through the Glasgow Architectural Society. All these designers formed part of a loose group of Scottish artists and architects in London whom Alexander Thomson once referred to as the 'London brethren' in a letter to his brother.[10]

**Fig 38** Cottier and Bruce Talbert 1867-9.

*A* Quatrefoil, Dowanhill Church, D Cottier, stained glass, 1867-9. Courtesy of Historic Scotland.

*B* Quatrefoil, Bruce Talbert, 1867, *Gothic Forms*.

*C* Quatrefoils, Dowanhill Church, W Leiper, architect, D Cottier, decorator, painted timber panels, 1865-6. Courtesy of Historic Scotland.

In 1867, shortly after the completion of Dowanhill, Talbert published his influential folio entitled *Gothic Forms* that showed the application of a muscular Gothic language to domestic interiors and furniture. It was avidly taken up by a lay audience, although primarily directed at the trade:

*The originality of the design was as marked as its vigour. His style became immediately the fashion, and more than fashionable; it was exaggerated by some, and watered down by others. Who does not remember the ebonised wood, the gold panels, the painted flowers, the spindles, and the rest? There was a rage for what was ignorantly miscalled 'Early English' furniture; to be succeeded at such quick intervals by other rages, that it is difficult to realise how short a while ago it is since Talbert was out-*

*Talberted by Mr. Moyr Smith, the most vigorous of his disciples [...] It was in furniture that Talbert's influence told most effectually, but it was not confined to that; he furnished some of the most characteristic designs that were brought out between the years 1870 and 1880.*[11]

John Moyr Smith initially served an apprenticeship with James Salmon I, an influential and respected Glasgow architect and a co-founder with Alexander Thomson of the Glasgow Architectural Society in 1858. Leiper and Cottier also attended the Society meetings. Smith was to work for Christopher Dresser and architect-designers like Thomas Collcutt and EW Godwin in London, but he became best known for the tile series he produced for firms like Minton's that were exported all over the

**Fig 39** Jean-Baptiste-Camille Corot, *Orpheus Greeting the Dawn (or Hymn to the Sun)*, 1865, Oil on Canvas, Chazen Museum of Art, University of Wisconsin Madison, Gift in Memory of Earl William and Eugenia Brandt Quirk, Class of 1910, by their children (E James Quirk, Catherine Jean Quirk & Lillian Quirck Contley). Photo Credit: Eric Tadsen.

**Plate XI** Cottier & Co London, Ceramics.

*A* Floral Charger, Cottier & Co London, ca. 1884. Courtesy of Four Acres Charitable Trust.

*B* Portrait Charger, Cottier & Co London, ca. 1884. Courtesy of Four Acres Charitable Trust.

world, and for his numerous illustrated publications such as *Ornamental Interiors*, 1887. Throughout the 1880s in London he edited his own journal, *Decoration*, which featured the work of various Glasgow contemporaries like Thomson, Talbert and Andrew Wells.

### Collectors and Collecting

The support of local dealers and individual collectors or patrons was vital to the establishment of a distinctive 'Glasgow style' of art and design. As both an independent art dealer and collector Cottier participated in the early expansion of the gallery-based art market in Glasgow, linking associates like the Glasgow dealer William Craibe Angus to an international network of dealers including EJ Van Wisselingh (the Hague and London), Duveen and Goupil (Paris), Inglis and Avery (New York). During frequent trips to the Continent he began dealing in contemporary Dutch and French painting (fig 39), and

**Fig 40** *Collection Cottier Catalogue,* Durand-Ruel, auction catalogue with a memorial by WE Henley, 1892. Courtesy of Four Acres Charitable Trust.

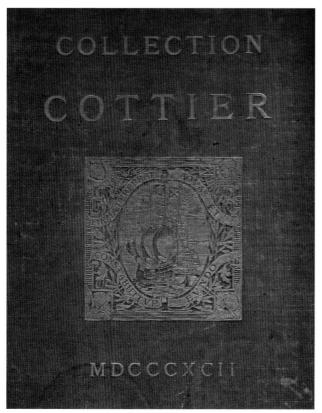

COLLECTION

COTTIER

CATALOGUE

PARIS

DURAND-RUEL: 16 Rue Laffitte

New York: 315 Fifth Avenue

1892

persuaded the dealer Van Wisselingh to become manager of the London gallery. Through this connection the Dutch artist Matthijs Maris came to live with Cottier in 1877, producing both paintings and stained glass for the firm's various outlets. Cottier introduced receptive audiences in Glasgow, New York, Montreal, Sydney and Melbourne to the paintings of contemporary French and Hague School artists, and maintained his Scottish connections through loaning considerable numbers of pictures to the international exhibitions held in Edinburgh in 1886 and in Glasgow in 1888. The major sale of his collection following his death in 1891 was held in London, New York and Paris (fig 40), and attracted Scottish collectors like WA Anderson, whose Park Circus house Leiper and Wells had recently remodelled, as well as those like the New York collector Henry Clay Frick, and Sir William Van Horne in Montreal.

The Glasgow dealer Alexander Reid has been the subject of an exhibition and several publications, but eleven years before he painted Reid's portrait in 1887, Van Gogh was visiting Cottier's showrooms in London. In 1883 he sent some drawings to his brother Theo noting:

*I thought perhaps these drawings would be something for Cottier. I imagine they would look well placed in the panels of a large cabinet, over a mantelpiece, or in a wainscot – in short, framed in woodwork as they do in England, and elsewhere too. But you know how it is with Cottier, when there is a certain degree of style in a drawing he likes it well enough, but, alas, he generally pays little. Still, I believe he is*

*one of those who would care for them; and besides, he could display the drawings favourably.[12]*

Similarly one of Reid's clients, William Burrell, now the best known of the Glasgow collectors, was only one of many individuals in the city interested in contemporary French and Dutch painting. Moreover Burrell did not buy Matthijs Maris' *Butterflies* until 1901, although Cottier had been employing Maris and selling his work since the 1870s (fig 41).

From New York, Cottier & Co also furnished the homes of art lovers in Montreal, then the economic capital of Canada. The Montreal Museum of Fine Arts was established in 1860, and the most significant Canadian collectors in the decades leading up to World War I, like Van Horne, were to be found in that city. As their names indicate – Ross, Angus, Lord Strathcona, Drummond – many of the others had Scottish connections, and socialised around the Presbyterian Church of St Andrews in Montreal. Writing in the Studio in 1907, Croal Thomson commented:

*It is not yet generally recognised, yet it is a fact which will have considerable weight in the art markets of the world in days to come that, after London, Paris and New York, Montreal is the most important artistic centre for art of the finest quality. For thirty years or more there have been growing in Montreal collections of pictures which can hold their own with the very best.[13]*

**Figure 41** Cottier and Matthijs Maris.

*A Lady of Shalott,* Matthijs Maris, stained glass panel manufactured by Cottier & Co. London, ca. 1872. © Glasgow Life (Museums).

*B Lady of Shalott,* Matthijs Maris, oil on canvas, ca. 1875. © Glasgow Life (Museums).

**Plate XII** *Dancing Girl,* Matthijs Maris, oil on canvas and wood, 1879. Courtesy of Rijksmuseum.

*Dancing Girl,* four panels, 1879, Matthijs Maris, oil on canvas.

These panels were presented to the Rijksmuseum in 2000. According to the information provided by the museum they were originally purchased in Paris in 1878 by EJ van Wisselingh who was at that time employed by Cottier. They were purchased on the advice of the painter Matthijs Maris but Cottier was displeased and had Maris undertake work on the panels. He subsequently sold them as genuine Maris paintings to a Scottish collector. A Dutch collector bought them in 1913 for the enormous sum of 38,000 guilders. The panels disappeared from public view until they were recently presented to the Rijksmuseum. (DR)

Source: The Rijksmuseum website

Like collectors in Scotland, those in Montreal demonstrated a marked preference for contemporary French and Dutch work, stimulated in part by the efforts of Cottier.[14]

## Cottier Abroad: Australia and North America

Having been born into a seafaring family in the west of Scotland, Cottier was no stranger to international trade and travel, and throughout his life cultivated the air of an old sea-dog, apparently looking 'more like an ideal coasting skipper than an artist'.[15] He took advantage of rail and steamer routes to expand his affairs into an international market, and in 1873 set up an Australian operation, Lyon & Cottier, with branches in Sydney and Melbourne (fig 42). The ground had been prepared by John Lamb Lyon (1853-1916), a fellow apprentice in Glasgow and London who had emigrated in 1861. Although Cottier made at least three trips to Australia, the operation of Lyon, Cottier & Co was largely Lyon's concern. Lyon also visited Cottier in New York and Europe, and maintained contact through several of Cottier's Glasgow assistants who had worked on Downhill. Andrew Wells, for example, joined the Australia branch as a partner in 1880 and worked there for about a decade before returning to Glasgow. Charles Gow spent a brief spell there in the mid 1870s, returning to work in Glasgow with another former Cottier employee, Hugh McCulloch, before emigrating properly to Australia in 1891 as a partner in the firm in Adelaide. From its inception the firm was instantly successful and an extensive folio of designs now in the Mitchell Library, Melbourne, suggests that they virtually monopolised high-class commissions for decorative work there during the 1870s and 1880s.

Cottier's New York branch, established in 1873, was also a runaway success, helped by the association with Talbert, whose work was already highly in demand there, and by the prominent critic Clarence Cook as publicist. In a series of magazine articles subsequently published as a best-selling book on household taste, *The House Beautiful*, 1881 (fig 43A), Cook repeatedly praised the firm's Artistic fabrics, furniture (fig 43B) and stained glass. Some designs were in fact versions of Godwin's furniture which Cottier had initially imported and later manufactured in New York. On significant Aesthetic interiors like the Boston Trinity Church (1878) and the New York Union League Club, Cottier worked alongside American designers John La Farge and Louis Comfort Tiffany. The North American operation was managed and subsequently owned by James Smith Inglis who had followed Cottier from Glasgow in 1873.

**Figure 42** Australia.

The Red Drawing Rooms, Lyon, Cottier & Co, 1879, Government House, Sydney, NSW, photograph courtesy of the Historic Houses Trust.

In 1879 colonial architect James Barnet commissioned the firm Lyon, Cottier & Co to decorate the state-room interiors of Government House as part of a refurbishment programme.

The drawing room ceiling incorporated hand-painted medallions of allegorical portraits of the four seasons and night and day, within compartments of stencilled stylised naturalistic designs. According to the Australian Historic Houses Trust the decorative schemes for the stencilled wall friezes, fillings and dados were inspired by neo-Egyptian, neo-Grecian and Anglo-Japanese ornamental styles. To complement the painted decoration, the firm coordinated the refurbishment of all the soft furnishings. (DR)

Source: Historic Houses Trust website.

**Plate XIII** Andrew Wells.

**A** Lily Design, Booloominbah NSW, A Wells, painted panelling, ca. 1889. Courtesy of the University of New England.

**B** *Pomona*, A Wells, wall painting for W Pearce at 10 Park Terrace, Glasgow, ca.1888. Courtesy of Gordon R Urquhart.

With the establishment of Lyon, Wells, Cottier & Co, John Lamb Lyon and Daniel Cottier brought Cottier's first pupil Andrew Wells who had originally been involved in the decoration of Dowanhill Church into the Australian branch of Cottier's business where he concentrated on the decoration with Lyon overseeing the stained glass. Prior to this Wells had been working independently of Cottier in Glasgow, notably on Sir William Pearce's house at 10 Park Terrace where examples of his mature style survive. (DR)

**Plate XIV** Lyon, Cottier & Co.

*A* Window from Joylen, Birchgrove, NSW, John Lamb Lyon, stained glass, ca. 1884. Collection: Powerhouse Museum, Sydney. Photo: Sotha Bourn.

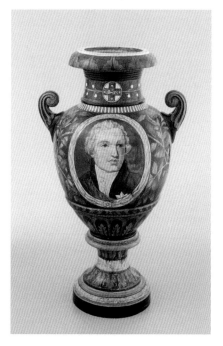

*B* Portrait Vase of Sir Joseph Banks. Lyon Cottier & Co, painted clayware, ca.1880. Collection: Powerhouse Museum, Sydney. Photos: Sotha Bourn.

**Fig 43** Cottier and *The House Beautiful.*

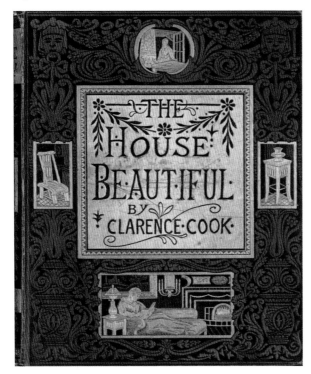

*A* Cover designed by D Cottier for C Cook, 1878, *The House Beautiful.* Photo J. Hammond.

*B* Cabinet by Cottier & Co decorated with figures of Amor, Mars, Fama and Fortuna, Greek masks, and urns, 1870–80. © National Museums of Scotland. Licensor www.scran.ac.uk

A decade on from Dowanhill we find Cottier travelling to Europe and North Africa with American friends, the painter Albert Pinkham Ryder and sculptor Olin Warner, whom he had taken under his wing in 1875 by exhibiting a Salon des Refusés in his New York showrooms. Their arrival in Paris coincided with that of Leiper and Arthur Melville from Scotland, and possibly that of John Lamb Lyon from Australia indicating the internationalism of a network which can be traced back to Glasgow in the 1860s.

**Plate XV** American Painting.

*A Stag Drinking,* AP Ryder, oil on leather, ca. 1880. Courtesy collection Spanierman Gallery, LLC, New York.

*B Stag and Two Does,* AP Ryder, oil on leather, ca. 1880. Courtesy collection Spanierman Gallery, LLC, New York.

Caption - Cottier commissioned the American artist Albert Pinkham Ryder to decorate a number of designs made by his craftsmen. In all likelihood, these vignettes were done in the early 1880s for Cottier & Co. New York. In 1877 Ryder travelled to London for about a month with Cottier. That same year he was a founding member of the Society of American Artists, where he exhibited Barbizon-influenced landscapes. Ryder again went to England with Cottier in 1882, the two joined sculptor Olin Levy Warner in Paris, then toured Holland, Italy, Spain and Tangier. (DR) Collection: Spanierman Gallery, LLC. New York.

**Plate XVI** Spring

*Spring*, Cottier & Co, *c.*1873-1885, stained glass, New York, The Metropolitan Museum of Art, photograph courtesy of The Metropolitan Museum of Art

This panel was acquired by the Metropolitan Museum of Art in 2007 and represents Spring. According to the Museum Bulletin the panel is an iconic example of his work and was originally owned by a member of Cottier's family possibly his son William Field Cottier. (DR)

Source: *The Metropolitan Museum of Art Bulletin,* Fall 2007

**Plate XVII** American Sculpture.

*Daniel Cottier*, Olin Levi Warner, bronze, 1878, overall size 11 x 6 x 6 inch. National Academy Museum, New York (128-S).

This bust of Daniel Cottier was a significant stepping stone towards recognition for American Sculptor Olin Warner. Having studied at the Ecole des Beaux Arts in Paris, he returned to the United States in 1872 and established a studio in New York but was at first discouraged by the lack of commissions. The patronage of Cottier among others brought an end to this period of struggle in about 1876 when Warner began to receive a number of portrait commissions. (DR)

Source: National Academy of Design, New York

[1] Gould 1969, 2.
[2] See especially Melville 2001.
[3] Mackinnon 1935, 67.
[4] Davison 1882, 452.
[5] Davison 1882, 453.
[6] 'Men you know', The Bailie, 1919.
[7] Quoted in MacDonald 1924, 337.
[8] Quoted in Stamp 2002, 255.
[9] Walker 1995, 98.
[10] Thomson 1994, 11.
[11] Day 1887, 194.
[12] Written between March and September 1883. See Van Gogh 1958, 46-7.
[13] Thomson, DC 1907, xxiv.
[14] See Brooke 1970. This kind of detailed research into the provenance of late nineteenth-century collections is beginning to reveal the extent of Cottier's influence and the network of which he was part.
[15] Henley 1892, ix.

# 5 DOCUMENTING THE CONGREGATION: MINISTRY AND MISSION

## Hilary Macartney

**Plate XVIII**

The Reverend W Dickie in Later Life. Courtesy of Partick Trinity Church.

## Introduction

As a context for the graceful Gothic Revival architecture and innovative scheme of decoration of Dowanhill United Presbyterian Church, this chapter presents a preliminary examination of the people most closely associated with it: the congregation and its ministers, and their relationship to the building itself and to the wider community. It begins with a brief account of the ministers who served Dowanhill Church and discusses, in particular, the key role of preaching in the relationship between minister, congregation and the Church. Through the study of the nineteenth-century records of the Church, held in Glasgow Archives, it also offers an insight into the social and moral values and mindset of the congregation which commissioned and worshipped in Church. Thus, it uses the records to examine the role of the Kirk Session, particularly during the period 1855-60 immediately before the building of the present church, when the father of the architect, William Leiper, was Session Clerk. A second strand explores the relationship between the Dowanhill Church congregation and its Mission congregations in poorer areas of Partick and Whiteinch. These brief studies are presented as examples of the kinds of ways in which further research might enrich our understanding and present-day experience of nineteenth-century church architecture and decoration in general, and Dowanhill Church in particular.

## The Special Relationship: Congregation and Ministers at Dowanhill

'Without mutual confidence between minister and people no congregation can prosper', observed the Rev Dickie in his sermon on the Jubilee of the Church in 1916.'[1] The relationship between ministers or priests and their flock in any denomination of the church at any period has always been of primary importance. That relationship is clearly highlighted in the Presbyterian churches, where the simplicity of the liturgy emphasises the minister's role in the teaching of the Bible as the Word of God. It was further strengthened in the United Presbyterian and Free Presbyterian churches in Scotland in the nineteenth century by the fact that ministers were directly chosen by their congregation. Indeed the refusal to allow anyone else, such as local landowners or a national establishment or hierarchical body, to influence the selection was a key principle in the foundation of the Secession churches in the eighteenth and nineteenth centuries, predecessors of the United Presbyterian Church, and in the Disruption of 1843, when many of the ministers walked out of the General Assembly of the Church of Scotland to form the Free Church.

The contract between congregation and minister was regarded by both sides as a calling, though in common with other UP churches, Dowanhill sought to offer generous remuneration in return for spiritual guidance. The special value placed on the bond between congregation and minister no doubt helps to explain the fact that, in the whole history of Dowanhill Church and

its predecessor, Partick Secession Church, from 1823 to 1984, there were just six ministers. The printed leaflet of the centenary celebrations in 1923 includes photographs of the two churches, Partick Secession and Dowanhill, and portraits of the four ministers up to that date: John Skinner, Thomas M Lawrie, William Dickie and William J Baxter (fig 44). The booklet of the centenary celebrations of Dowanhill Church in 1966 is likewise illustrated with portraits of just four ministers, this time Lawrie, Dickie, Baxter and the Rev Henry Chisholm, celebrating a hundred years of preaching at Dowanhill (fig 45).

In his book on Dowanhill, the Rev Dickie considered the advantages of the long service of ministers with one congregation. Short ministries, he acknowledged, could be helpful in the early stages of a minister's career, 'as a change enables him to avoid, or outlive early mistakes'. On the other hand, he concluded that long ministries were of particular value 'because of the intimacy which a prudent and sympathetic minister begets with the families of his people and because of the accumulative influence which can only be acquired by years of patient service'.[2] This was certainly the case with regard to the reverends Lawrie, Dickie and Baxter, whose combined service covered over 120 years of the history of Partick

**Fig 44** Rev John Skinner, Rev Thomas M Lawrie, Rev William Dickie DD, Rev William J Baxter MA, illustration from W Dickie, 1926, *History of Dowanhill Church 1823-1923*. Courtesy of Four Acres Charitable Trust.

REV. JOHN SKINNER
REV. THOMAS M. LAWRIE    REV. WILLIAM DICKIE, D.D.
REV. WILLIAM J. BAXTER, M.A.

**Fig 45** *100 years of Preaching*, illustration from Dowanhill Parish Church Centenary Celebrations Pamphlet, 1966.

**Fig 46** Map of Partick, ca. 1860, showing the location of Partick East United Presbyterian Church, predecessor of Dowanhill Church. Courtesy of the National Library of Scotland.

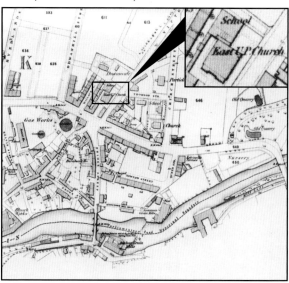

**Fig 47** Interior, Partick East United Presbyterian Church, Glasgow, predecessor of Dowanhill Church, illustration from W Dickie, 1926, *History of Dowanhill Church 1823-1923*. Courtesy of Four Acres Charitable Trust.

**Fig 48** Exterior, Partick East United Presbyterian Church, Glasgow, predecessor of Dowanhill Church. Courtesy of Glasgow University Library SK100 AIK.

Secession/Dowanhill. The relatively few changes of minister clearly contributed to the congregation's sense of the continuity and identity of their church, in spite of change – including several name changes, from its origins as Partick United Secession Church in 1823 and the building of its first church near the corner of Byres Road and Dumbarton Road (figs 46–48), through the union of the Secession and Relief churches in Scotland to form the United Presbyterian Church in 1847, the building of the new church at Dowanhill in 1865-6, the setting up of the daughter churches of Partick East UP and Whiteinch – later Victoria Park – UP later in the century (fig 49) (see below **The Congregation and its Missions**), the union of the United Presbyterian and Free Churches in 1900 to form the United Free Church of Scotland, and the union of the latter with the Church of Scotland in 1929.[3]

### Rev John Skinner

John Skinner, a descendent of Ralph and Ebenezer Erskine, two of the founders of the Secession Church in Scotland, was ordained as minister of Partick Secession Church in 1827, at the age of 23. He was clearly a colourful character who was very much involved in the hotly debated issues of his time. He championed the cause of the Voluntary or independent churches in public debates against the Established Church of Scotland, and became known for his 'fearless bearing' and 'fiery vehemence in controversial discussion'. In his book, *The Scottish Endowment Question* (1838), which likewise opposed the influence of landowners through the endowment of churches and educational establishments, he was considered by one reviewer to have allowed

himself to 'run wild in all kinds of playfulness, invective, sarcasm, irony, indignant reprehension, broad and almost reckless humour'.[4]

**Fig 49** Whiteinch United Presbyterian Church, later Victoria Park United Presbyterian Church, Glasgow. Courtesy of Richard Stenlake.

Skinner's freedom from the ties of establishment and endowment, however, also served to highlight the precariousness of his position and his dependence on the congregation to provide for him. His ordination involved an extraordinary display of his new congregation's wealth. The lavish dinner to celebrate the occasion was prepared according to the instructions of the ladies of the congregation. The accounts included the following:

> *Four pair of Fowls @ 4s pr; Four Ducks @ 6s.6d;*
> *23½ lbs Turbot @ 8d;*
> *3½ lbs Trout @ 1s.*
> *Account of Peter Dodd & Co: 21 lbs Round Beef @ 8d; 24 lbs Bacon Ham @ 8d; 12½  Salt Tongues @ 10d; 3 lbs Salt Butter @ 1s; 3½ lbs Cheese @ 10d; Salt Basket 8d.*
> *Account of Robert Rankin: 33 lbs Rost Veil @ 9d; 37½ lbs Mutton @ 9d.*
> *Glass and Crockery £1.4s.4d; Water waiter attending 7s6d.*
> *Account of Lamond & Co: 1½ doz Port Wine 26s, £1.19.0d; 1½ doz Sherry 30s, £2.5s.*
> *2 days' cooking by Mr John Wright 10s, paid by Mrs Lamon.*[5]

It is not clear how many actually sat down for dinner but fifty tickets were sold, and the rest were supplied to members of the presbytery and friends as guests.

The Rev Skinner's stipend was also very generous at £130 per annum, to which £10 was added for 'sacramental and other expenses'.[6] The Church began to develop under Skinner's ministry: membership was increased, and organisations and activities such as Prayer Meetings, Sabbath Schools and a Missionary Fund were instituted. However, growth was not sufficiently rapid to avoid serious financial difficulty which resulted in continual arrears in the payment of Skinner's stipend. Skinner himself generously proposed that his stipend should be paid at a variable rate of between £110 and £130, according to the number of sittings let in the Church – an interesting example of performance-related pay. However, the problem of arrears in stipend eventually led to Skinner's resignation at the end of 1839 and he and his family left for America in 1840. Despite the financial difficulties that led to this situation, the congregation presented him with a gold watch with eight jewels, valued at 30 guineas and inscribed 'as a parting gift of their enduring love from a few friends in the city of Glasgow for his talented exertions in the cause of religious liberty'.[7] He was minister of several Presbyterian churches in Virginia and Pennsylvania. Later, he published a recantation of his Voluntaryist principles and became minister of the Church of Scotland in London, Canada. He died in 1864, in his 60th year, from a large carbuncle on the back of his head 'which paid no heed to the lance of the surgeon'.[8]

### Rev Thomas M Lawrie

The Rev Lawrie was ordained in March 1841. His initial basic stipend was less than Skinner's, at £100 per annum, plus £10 sacramental expenses, and 'bonuses' in the form of additional sums collected by the congregation. A house was also taken for him, at a cost of £16 per annum. Lawrie's ministry, which lasted to his death in 1895, coincided with the rapid development of Dowanhill, and the new church, which opened in 1866 with over a thousand 'sittings', was ideally placed within the wealthy new suburb. By the time of his Jubilee in 1890, the total income of the Church had risen to £2000. The Rev Dickie had been appointed as his colleague the previous year, and their joint stipends totalled £800 per annum.[9] Dickie referred to the warmth of Lawrie's relationship with the congregation, describing him as 'in a very true sense the father of his people', and as having 'won the affections of the people by his friendliness, his geniality [and] his steady devotion to the highest interests of the Congregation.[10] His *Notices of Dowanhill Church, 1825-1888* (1891) were one of the main sources for Dickie's work on the history of the Church.

The programme and reports on the celebration of Lawrie's Jubilee reflect the combination of spiritual intensity and worldly remuneration which characterised the bond between minister and his congregation. It consisted of a 'soirée' held in Partick Burgh Hall. The congregation and guests sang verses from Psalms 90 and 100 which include references to praise as an approach to Heaven and the revelation of God's work to his servants. The choir also sang Mendelssohn's *How Lovely are the Messengers*. Material gifts from the congregation included a silver salver and a cheque for 1300 guineas. After his death in 1895, a memorial tablet incorporating a relief medallion of Rev Lawrie, was sculpted by J&G Mossman and unveiled in the vestibule of the Church (fig 50).

**Fig 50** Memorial Tablet with a Medallion Profile of Rev T Lawrie, executed by J&G Mossman and unveiled in Dowanhill Church vestibule 18 October 1895. Courtesy of Historic Scotland.

### Rev William Dickie

The Rev Dickie was ordained as a minister at Rosehearty, Aberdeenshire in 1878, and spent eight years at the United Presbyterian Church in Perth, the historic church of one of the Four Secession Fathers, William Wilson, before he joined the ministry of Dowanhill in March 1889 as the colleague of Rev Lawrie. In 1905, he was given an Honorary Doctorate in Divinity from the University of Glasgow 'in recognition of his successful ministry, his position as Churchman in the city, and his literary work'.[11] His books *The Christian Ethics of Social Life, The Culture of the Spiritual Life* and *Life's Ideals* expanded the themes of his sermons. He was also a gifted painter and exhibited in Glasgow, Paisley and elsewhere. According to the Rev Baxter, who was appointed as Dickie's colleague in 1923, 'a warm appreciation of his work' as an artist was published by a Paris art journal.[12]

Our knowledge and understanding of the history of Dowanhill Church, including its architecture and decoration, owe much to Dickie's book on the Church, his article on Cottier in the monthly newsletter of the Church in 1930, and his sermons preached on the Jubilee of the Church in 1916 (see below). Although he did not know all the key figures in the Church's history personally, he had direct access to those who had living memory of all of them, such as Rev Lawrie. He would also have known William Leiper and his associate, Hunter McNab. His research on the Church built on the Rev Lawrie's notes and a fuller range of written records than has so far been possible to trace today. The Rev Matthew Baird, who was brought up under Dr Dickie's ministry

at Dowanhill remembered him as the greatest evangelist of the beauty of Dowanhill Church:

> *How proud he was of this Church, never weary of pointing out the beauty of its architecture and decoration. He was lovingly jealous of its well-being and permitted nothing that was mean or unworthy to enter into it, and you know only too well how in these latter years it was still his joy and crown.*[13]

### Rev William J Baxter

The induction of the Rev Baxter as colleague of Dr Dickie took place in September 1923, witnessed by a large audience including representatives from Presbytery, neighbouring congregations, and members from his previous charge in Willesden. The report in the Church's newsletter emphasised a strong and immediate bond between congregation and minister, describing the 'home-coming' as 'a happy affair', in which a 'tense, subdued spirit of thankfulness seemed to be present'. In his address to 'my people', the Rev Baxter looked forward to 'being co-workers with you for the extension of God's Kingdom in this place.' Afterwards, 'the new minister gave the right hand of fellowship to his new people'.[14] He led the tributes for Rev Dickie's ministerial jubilee in 1927 and at his funeral in 1935. In 1937, he worked with the Redecoration Committee and special advisors including the artist Sir DY Cameron in the decisions on the new scheme of painted decoration in the Church. His ministry continued during the Second World War, when the Dowanhill Manse was damaged by a bomb. After the war, one of his roles was to work to reunite returning servicemen within the Church. He retired from the ministry of Dowanhill in 1961 but remained a member of the congregation.

### Rev Henry Chisholm

The Rev Henry Chisholm accepted the call to Dowanhill in 1962. He was 'preached in' by his uncle, the Very Rev FP Copland Simmons, of St Andrew's Church, Frognal, London, a former Moderator of the Presbyterian Church of England, and was welcomed by the congregation for his youth and vigour.[15] The Church was redecorated during his ministry in 1963. He left Dowanhill for North America in 1967.

### Rev Robert Currie

The Rev Robert Currie (fig 51) accepted the call to Dowanhill in 1969. He moved from Clydebank, where he and his congregation had been closely involved in regeneration projects following the bombing during World War II. As a member of the Iona Community, founded in 1938, he brought a spirit of ecumenism to Dowanhill Church. Although the painted decoration had been completely covered over by the time he arrived, the Rev Currie was very appreciative of the beauty of the architecture and fought hard to ensure that the building would be saved when it ceased to function as a church in 1984.

**Fig 51** The Reverend Robert Currie, Minister at Dowanhill Church from 1969-1984. Courtesy of Robert Currie.

### Preaching the Word

Following the Reformation in Scotland, the role of the minister in preaching sermons which expounded on particular texts from the Bible acquired increased significance within the services of the Presbyterian churches. Ritual was minimised in order to focus on praise, prayer and sermon (all through the instrument of the human voice) as the essential elements of services. The design of post-Reformation churches responded to the new emphasis on preaching by replacing the altar with the raised pulpit as the focal point. From the end of the sixteenth century, radical designs, such as that of Burntisland Parish Church, began to substitute the traditional plan based on the Latin cross with an aisleless 'preaching box' which maximised the visibility and audibility of the preacher.

Although the ritual of the Mass had gone, Holy Communion, commemorating the Last Supper of Christ and his disciples, was still celebrated, albeit much less frequently. Under the ministry of the Rev Skinner, at Partick Secession Church, it was initially celebrated four times a year, but later with less frequency.[16] The challenge of introducing the Gothic Revival style in the design of Dowanhill Church without compromising Presbyterian principles is discussed above in Chapter 3. The spectacle of Roman Catholic ritual could nevertheless be said to have been replaced by a new form of drama, through the focus on preaching and the pulpit. This was often highlighted to great effect through the architecture and decoration of United Presbyterian churches, as in the case of Dowanhill. The parallel with secular theatre was further emphasised by the fact that each place or sitting within each pew was let to members of the congregation

according to a scale of prices (fig 52). Sittings were let annually, rather like season tickets for the theatre, though provision was also made for visitors. Seats at the back of the Church tended to command higher prices, no doubt partly because of the discretion they permitted in times of arrival and leaving.

The descriptions of the respective ministers of Partick Secession and Dowanhill frequently mentioned their talents as preachers. The Rev John Skinner was still remembered in Dickie's day by some of the older members of the congregation as having been of 'great eloquence in his pulpit ministrations'.[17] Likewise, Dickie recalled his own predecessor, Rev Lawrie, as having been 'an excellent preacher […] of remarkable distinction. He had a melodious voice, which he could use well, a good presence, and a virile and earnest utterance.[18] Dickie also recorded his own commitment to preaching: 'I had many interests in art and literature, but nothing was allowed to interfere with the great duty to which I felt called – the preaching of the Gospel.'[19] After Dickie's death, a 'protegé' of his, the Rev Matthew Urie Baird, minister of East and Belmont Church, Aberdeen, who had been brought up under Dickie's ministry at Dowanhill, paid the following tribute to his 'master': 'Under his care

**Fig 52** 'Church Sittings Area', *Dowanhill Church Reports – 1903-1912*, diagram used to define pew rentals in the ground floor area of the nave. Courtesy of Partick Trinity Church.

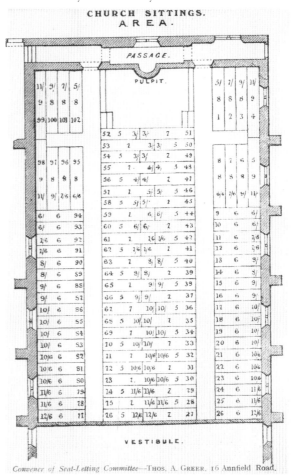

and fostered by the intellectual strength of his preaching, [Dowanhill] became one of the strategic centres of the religious life of the city of Glasgow.'[20] The tradition was continued by the Rev Baxter who, after his retiral, was remembered as 'a golden-tongued preacher with great power to move people and confirm them in the faith'.[21]

Gifted preachers were clearly much sought after, and there was often stiff competition amongst churches to secure their services. The first choice of minister for Partick Secession Church was Mr Ebenezer Halley of Kinross, who 'had the repute of being an eloquent preacher' but he accepted a call from St Andrews instead.[22] Similarly, after Rev Skinner's departure from Partick for the States, a call was made to Mr James Robertson 'a young preacher of great promise', the brother of Dr William Robertson of Irvine, a well-known poet and preacher. James Robertson, however, had calls from no less than four other congregations, of which he accepted Musselburgh. Later, he moved to Newington in Edinburgh, where he became 'one of the finest preachers to children in his day'.[23] After he accepted the call at Partick, the Rev Lawrie's gifts as a preacher were 'soon appreciated beyond the bounds of Partick'.[24] When he was sent to preside as Moderator at a vacant congregation in Belfast, the congregation there was so impressed that they twice issued a call to him to become their minister. He declined twice, much to the relief of his congregation in Glasgow.[25]

The level of interest in the performance of preachers and the content of their sermons may be difficult to imagine in today's largely secular age, but it continued to be high until well into the twentieth century. Sermons by noted preachers, or those celebrating special occasions were well attended, often by the wider public as well as the members of a particular congregation. Thus, at the time of the induction of the Rev Baxter as the new minister and colleague of the Rev Dickie at Dowanhill in 1923, the monthly newsletter reported large attendances of visitors as well as members. They awaited his first sermon with 'eager anticipation' and 'were not disappointed', as they 'listened to a sermon which in the highest, as well as the deepest sense, was a truly gospel one'.[26] One of the most highly charged moments of the induction ceremony was the Presentation of Pulpit Robes by the senior elder and two representatives of the Women's Guild, whilst the congregation sang 'The Lord bless thee and keep thee'. This symbolised the special bond between congregation and minister and, according to the monthly newsletter, it required only the Holy Spirit to seal it.

During the history of the Church, styles of preaching evidently changed. For example, though he never heard it himself, Dickie referred to the Rev Skinner's 'fine, dignified, ornate oratory, which is now quite out of date' and also considered Rev Lawrie's style of preaching to be 'somewhat ornate'.[27] By the time Rev Baxter arrived in 1923, Dickie's own style of preaching,

if not its content, may also have become a little out of date. In his first letter to his congregation in the monthly newsletter, Baxter sought to reassure them about his preaching: 'You know already that I bring no "new brooms" and no fancy gospel.' Nevertheless, as a 'child of this age', he went on, 'I necessarily think in its terms and express my message in its language, but my theme is the Cross, which has been the traditional teaching of your pulpit'.[28]

Amongst the constant qualities valued in the preaching skills of the ministers of Dowanhill were their innate sincerity and devotion. But preaching was also an art whose skills could be studied, as Dickie himself recognised: 'I devoted myself strenuously to preaching, which I regard as one of the highest of the arts.'[29] Not surprisingly, training in preaching traditionally formed part of the curriculum at universities and colleges for students who intended to enter the ministry. At Glasgow University in 1910, for example, Professor Henry Reid addressed students on *The Supreme Importance of Preaching* and *The Practical Training of Preachers*, while 'laymen's guides', such as *The Power of the Pulpit and Good Preaching*, published in Glasgow in 1887, were also popular.[30]

Interestingly, many of the stereotypes which continue to be associated with ministers and styles of preaching in the Presbyterian churches in Scotland were warned against by ministers and teachers alike. Dickie recorded his anxiousness to avoid the pitfall that 'preaching becomes lecturing or hectoring into self-righteousness'.[31] His success may presumably be measured by the assertion by his pupil, Rev Baird, that from the pulpit at Dowanhill, 'men were lovingly and skilfully taught the great truths of our faith'.[32] And much more than the ornate style, Dickie valued the Rev Lawrie's 'pawky humour' and 'jauntiness of manner', emphasising that he 'had no sepulchral airs which often pass for ministerial solemnity'.[33]

One of the greatest changes in preaching practice occurred during the period of the Rev Lawrie's ministry and around the time of the building of Dowanhill Church:

> At the beginning of his ministry, Mr. Lawrie used to preach for an hour and without notes. At that time [...] the manuscript was banned from the pulpit [...] The slavery of committing everything to memory broke the heart and often the health of many a young preacher. Once or twice Mr. Lawrie felt the burden so intolerable that he had serious thoughts of resigning his charge. But by and by [...] reasonably people began to find that the paper was likely to be a safeguard against prolixity and a guarantee of preparation.[34]

The move from memorising a whole sermon to the use of a written script of course tended to alter the character and style of delivery in preaching, as Alexander Melville Bell, father of Alexander Graham Bell, recognised in his book, *Sermon Reading and Memoriter Delivery*, published in Edinburgh in 1863. Bell lectured on elocution at Edinburgh University, before he moved to London and later Boston. He studied the external physiology of speech and developed a method of 'Visible Speech' or orthoepy for teaching deaf people. His book on sermons included discussion of the use of gesture in the delivery of read and memorised oratory.

The move to written sermons occasionally brought other anxieties, as Dickie recounted in an anecdote about the Rev Lawrie: 'Only once did I see Mr. Lawrie lose his self-possession.' He observed the Rev Lawrie looking anxious and flustered in the pulpit. Rev Dickie joined him and asked what was wrong. 'I've got the wrong sermon', complained Lawrie, or at least the Biblical text he proposed to interpret did not seem to match the sermon he had written. Fortunately, Rev Dickie had taken the precaution of always carrying a sermon in his pocket and was able to take over. In fact, the Rev Lawrie afterwards found that both text and sermon were fine, but 'the thought of having the wrong text or sermon had come into his mind, and [...] it became an obsession which he could not expel'. The Rev Dickie admitted: 'I had often had a similar experience in my Saturday night dreams.'[35]

## A Sermon on the House of God

To celebrate the jubilee of Dowanhill Church in 1916, the Rev Dickie preached a sermon 'In Praise of the House of God', based on Psalm 65, verses 1-4, 'Praise waiteth for Thee, O God, in Zion.' The published sermon gives an insight into his style of preaching and encapsulates the value he and his congregation attached to their church. The text is summarised and discussed below.

Dickie's sermon concerned the ways in which the church generally, and, in this instance, Dowanhill Church in particular fulfilled the function of the House of God for the congregation and the community: 'The opening verses of the Psalm set forth the place which the House of God should occupy in the affections and the life of His people; for it is in the House of God that God's people meet with God to see life in all its spiritual and essential bearings in the light of eternity.'[36]

He began, as does the Psalm, with emphasising the House of God as a House of Praise. Praise shows Christian worship at its brightest and most hopeful 'and for that reason is always associated with song'. 'Praise', he went on, 'is an integral part of public worship. Music is the natural expression and counterpart of the rhythmic movements of a soul that feels the thrill of joy in the presence of a Heavenly Father whose love overshadows it with care and kindness and redeeming grace.' Dickie declared that Praise was first of all an expression of joy, as Christianity 'strikes the lyric note in the human heart', lifting its believers' outlook on life both here and beyond. Secondly, he emphasised the role of Praise in

thanksgiving for gifts from God. Thirdly, he reminded the congregation that Praise 'not only expresses, but educates, the feeling of thankfulness for blessings received'. He concluded this point by noting that, for many of them, 'there is scarcely any other opportunity of telling out [their] gratitude to God in song except in God's House of Praise, when [they join] in worship along with [their] fellows [...] in Psalm and Hymn.'[37]

Rev Dickie then went on to consider the importance of the Church as a 'House of Self-Dedication', in accordance with the next part of the Psalm, which declares that 'unto Thee shall the vow be performed'. He recognised that, during the week, 'our spiritual life ebbs out', due to the stresses, sorrows and temptations of ordinary life. Going to church on a Sunday, however, offered the opportunity to return to contemplation of and rededication to Christian ideals. Dickie emphasised the dramatic impact which that experience could and should have: 'I believe that no man can worship in a living Church, in which there is a vital ministry, without passing judgment upon his conduct and his life'. Within the special environment of the Church, and prompted by the minister, those present should feel both 'rebuked and encouraged'. According to Dickie, this continuing process of renewal should lead to lasting change: 'if he has any earnestness of nature, he is impressed by the obligation to set himself right with God, so that the life he professes as a man in the world may be of a piece with the life he professes as a Christian in the Church.'[38]

Returning to the text of the Psalm, the Rev Dickie went on to examine the importance of the Church as a 'House of Prayer': 'O Thou that hearest prayer, unto Thee shall all flesh come.' He recognised the value of private prayer but stressed the powerful effect of 'public prayer in God's House' in confirming to believers that their experiences and needs were shared by their fellows: 'There they enter into the fellowship of prayer. They realise that their need is not singular, but common to all men; and that "all flesh" is subject to that weakness which makes us dependent upon God for [...] strength.'[39]

Finally, the Rev Dickie considered the role of the Church as a 'House of Pardon', as stated in the Psalm: 'Iniquities prevail against me; but as for transgressions Thou shalt purge them away.' He admitted that a sense of failure and sinfulness often prevented people from coming to Church: 'Many a man keeps away from the House of God because he knows his life will rebuke him when he comes into God's presence.'[40] But, argued Dickie, 'in reality, that is the reason for our coming into God's House. The Church is not a place of comfort for saints, but a place of refuge for sinners. Here broken men come to have their wounds bound up, their troubles smoothed out, their backslidings healed, their transgressions purged away. Here their ears catch the glad tidings of pardon and peace, which they cannot hear in the world.'[41]

Because the House of God fulfilled all these functions in a person's life, Dickie suggested, 'we can understand his love for it, his devotion to it, his sacrifices for it, his desire to beautify it as the home of the soul, his Father's House'.[42] In the rest of the sermon, he applied his analysis to the particular case of Dowanhill Church, whose congregation had come together fifty years previously to build a 'a beautiful house, without and within' which was recognised by 'every one who claims to have any knowledge of architecture to be one of the finest gems of Gothic art in the city or neighbourhood'. He admired the foresight, faith, devotion and generosity of those who had built 'this noble pile to the glory of God and leaving it as a gift for the use of new generations'. 'When we look upon these walls', he went on, 'we cannot but muse upon their spiritual significance'.[43] Here he was referring not only to the harmony underlying the colours, motifs and proportions but to the memory of all those who had contributed to this extraordinary creation, whose imprint also remained on the walls: 'They speak of sacrifices and offerings of rich and poor in beautifying this house of their spiritual affections.' And among such predecessors, there were, he acknowledged, 'families who emulated each other in their gifts', and who took 'a just pride in dedicating their wealth to God'.

Not only the walls but the pews too were 'consecrated by many memories', and the sense of the collective experience of worship over generations within a place of beauty clearly added to both the spiritual and the aesthetic value the Rev Dickie and his congregation attached to their church. As he stood in the pulpit, Dickie admitted that it often seemed to him that he 'gazed upon an audience of faces long lost but loved awhile:

> These old men and women [...] there praised God, there knelt in prayer, fortified themselves with Gospel hopes and promises, and passed the bread and wine in holy communion with God; and in God's time departed, as we too shall depart, to make room for others. Think you not that they perchance have memories of this House as well as we, as we for a brief space occupy the place which they left? Think of the stream of souls that has passed, and still is passing, and shall pass, through this Church during the years, each receiving refreshment and inspiration and cleansing on its way to eternity.[44]

Dickie's point about the building as a consecrated space which commemorated all who had worshipped within it would have had special poignancy during the dark days of the Great War. As he later recalled in his book on Dowanhill Church, 'the War monopolised, dominated, and absorbed all our thoughts and energies.'[45] By the end of the conflict, twenty-eight members of the congregation had died in service. Their names are engraved on the Church's War Memorial tablet (fig 53) which was designed by William Leiper's former associate, Hunter MacNab, and unveiled in 1920. Dickie himself

**Fig 53** Memorial Tablet, to the Members of Dowanhill Church who fell in the Great War of 1914–18, designed by WH McNab in 1920. Courtesy of Four Acres Charitable Trust.

also served as a chaplain and frequently preached to battalions which came to worship in the Church, and the pews were made free to soldiers who were billeted in the neighbourhood.[46]

Dickie's sermon also interpreted the Church as a work of art which commemorated those who had created it. In particular, he presented it as a memorial to its architect William Leiper, who had died some six months previously. He paid warm tribute to Leiper, as 'a son of the Congregation, his father having been long one of its most respected elders' (see below **The Role of the Kirk Session**). Dickie saw Leiper's achievement at Dowanhill as a reflection of his moral, as well as his artistic qualities, rather as the art critic John Ruskin might have done: 'It was the creation of a mind inspired by great devotion to, and youthful aspiration for, goodness and beauty.' And equally significantly, he claimed that Dowanhill Church had remained a special place for Leiper himself: 'Of all his works to be found in church and mansion and castle scattered over Scotland, his heart to the last always warmed especially to Dowanhill' (fig 54).[47]

**Fig 54** William Leiper, architect of Dowanhill Church, photographed in 1901. Courtesy of Michael Davies.

Dickie's tone in describing Cottier's ambition was rather more critical: 'In the interior decoration of the Church [Leiper] had a worthy collaborator in Mr. Cottier, then also a youth, greedy for name and fame.'[48] This harsh note was missing from the account of Cottier in Dickie's book on Dowanhill ten years later and especially from his highly appreciative article in the *Dowanhill Church Monthly Record* in 1930. Its inclusion in Dickie's 1916 sermon may have reflected his awareness of a sense of resentment or envy on the part of some of Cottier's former colleagues or surviving members of the congregation with regard to Cottier's success or a perception that he had abandoned the city that had made him. Nevertheless, Dickie's sermon went on to highlight Cottier's international importance and influence: 'Mr. Cottier became one of the greatest decorators and designers in London, Paris, and New York, and his scheme of decoration has not only been admired by lovers of art, but copied in many churches throughout the land.'[49]

Dickie went on to list other artists and artefacts associated with the Church, including the embroidered panel on the back of the pulpit sea, by Cottier's sister (see **Chapter 3**); the collecting box in the vestibule, designed by Leiper's associate, Hunter McNab, carved by John Crawford, and gifted by William Gibson; and of course the Willis organ (see **Chapter 9**), before returning to

and concluding with the broader theme of the Church as a constantly evolving entity, continuously defined and redefined by those that worship within its walls and their collective memory.

## The Congregation and the Kirk Session, 1855–1860

### The Role of the Kirk Session

The Minute book of the Kirk Session of Partick East United Presbyterian Church (later Dowanhill Church) reveals that the principal role of the Kirk Session in the nineteenth century was to look after the moral behaviour of the congregation, unlike that of the Board of Managers, which was to take care of the business and financial affairs of the Church, including maintenance of the building (see **Chapter 6**). The meetings of the Kirk Session were chaired by the minister, referred to as 'the Moderator'. Other members were the elected Elders of the Church. To be elected an Elder was considered an important honour and those invited to perform the role were expected to regard it as their Christian duty to accept it. Indeed, those who declined the honour were often written to by the Session and asked to reconsider their decision, unless satisfactory reasons such as ill health were offered. As part of its remit to guide the Christian behaviour of the congregation, one of the duties of the Kirk Session was to consider applications for membership of the Church and to instruct prospective members in their responsibilities. Before new members could be admitted, the Session had to be satisfied with their character and, where applicants had recently moved to the area, information on them was sought from their previous church. Another important responsibility of the Session concerned the liturgy of the Church.

During 1855 to 1859, William Leiper (1801-67), a schoolteacher and the father of the architect of Dowanhill Church, was Session Clerk, and kept clear, informative Minutes of the Session's meetings. Study of his period of office was chosen to begin the task of documenting the work of the Kirk Session, because of the detail and accuracy of his Minutes and because it offers a valuable insight into the profile of the congregation and the role of the Church within the local area in the years immediately preceding the decision to build the new church. Leiper clearly relished his involvement in the work of the Session and was frequently appointed to the many subcommittees which followed up cases brought before the Session.

The work and methods of the nineteenth-century Session with regard to the moral behaviour of the congregation is hard to understand from the perspective of today's much more secular society, with its emphasis on personal liberties. Likewise, the similarity of their procedures to those of a court of law, or to the Inquisition which formerly operated within the Roman Catholic church, would render them unacceptable in the modern Presbyterian church. Nevertheless, Rev Dickie, in his *History of Dowanhill Church* of 1926, referred to the continuing influence of the Session 'as a Court of the Church', although he acknowledged that society had already changed radically since the nineteenth century, when 'members were cut off from the fellowship of the Church for reasons which are now tolerated or ignored'.[50] The Session's Minutes of the mid-nineteenth century provide a vivid reminder of the power that churches generally still exercised over the lives of their congregations. Thus, although the attitudes and decisions of the Session may seem interfering, over-judgmental and draconian to modern minds, they would have been accepted as fair at the time, even by those who were disciplined by the Session. Likewise, the Elders who sat in judgment appear to have been respected for their fairness, diligence and sense of responsibility. William Leiper Sr appears to have been regarded as a model Elder, and the qualities which he brought to his work for the Kirk Session are likely to have been similar to those appreciated by his former school pupils, who erected his gravestone in Sighthill Cemetery, Glasgow as 'A tribute to the memory of William Leiper by his pupils' (fig 55). When Leiper resigned his office in February 1859 because he had 'removed to Glasgow', the Session, 'sensible of the valuable services which he rendered whilst among us, and of the loss which we sustain by his

leaving, resolved to record our regret at his departure, and that an extract of the Minute be sent to Mr Leiper.'[51]

Leiper's Minutes reveal how the Kirk Session dealt with cases reported to them. The Session generally met on a monthly basis in the Session Hall, a room on the upper floor of the buildings adjoining the Church and now part of Cottier's Restaurant (fig 56). Typically, transgressors were called before the Session and interrogated on their behaviour. They were expected to confess, show penitence and accept the punishment imposed by the Session, which was generally to suspend the offender 'from the privileges of the Church' until the Session was satisfied that the offender had reformed. The loss of privileges would have meant that offenders were not permitted to partake of communion, or of other sacraments, including baptism and marriage, which required membership of

**Fig 56** Entrance Turret and Stairway Leading to the Former Session House, Dowanhill Church, from a photograph illustrated in *Dowanhill Church Annual Reports,* early 20th century. Courtesy of Partick Trinity Church.

**Fig 55** 'A Tribute to the Memory of William Leiper by his Pupils', family gravestone in Sighthill Cemetery, Glasgow. Courtesy of Four Acres Charitable Trust, photograph Anne Clough.

the Church. Likewise, the offender would not have been able to call on the Church for character references for any purposes. In cases where an offender refused to appear before the Session, or otherwise rejected its authority, his or her name was deleted from the roll of membership.[52] It appears that the most frequent sin of which women were accused was that of 'fornication', whilst men were most often accused of 'intoxication'. In cases of 'pre-nuptial fornication', the man and woman were usually called to attend, and likewise in cases where a woman accused a man of being the father of her child. Thus, for example, Daniel McKenzie and Elizabeth Low were 'both repeatedly interrogated' about Low's charge that McKenzie was the father of her child.[53] The Session's sources of information are not revealed in the Minute book. Instead, the Minutes use impersonal forms such as 'It was reported that X has been guilty of the sin of Y' to record the alleged misdemeanours. It is not clear what steps, if any, were taken to verify the reliability of the sources of information. Once cases were reported, investigations seem to have focused mainly or exclusively on the alleged perpetrator of the misdemeanour, even though, as Dickie admitted, 'Dame Rumour' played an important role in bringing cases before the Session in the early days of the Church.[54]

One of the many women accused of fornication was Mary Ross, who was accused in February 1856.[55] Leiper was one of those appointed to follow up her case and he continued to report on her until 1858. In the meantime, Mary Ross appears to have left the congregation, but Leiper and a colleague nevertheless arranged to meet her in October 1857, and reported that 'they were so far satisfied with her expression of penitence'.[56] Another meeting with her was also arranged 'to examine the certificates which she may produce regarding her conduct since she left the bounds of the Congregation'. In January 1858, these were reported to be satisfactory and the case appears to have been closed.[57] The fact that this woman's case was pursued after she had left Dowanhill Church, as well as the reference to 'certificates' of conduct, reveals the extent of the Church's influence over the choices available to the individual. Satisfactory certificates of conduct from Dowanhill Church would have been required by Mary Ross before she could join another church and may also have been required as employment references.

Some of the cases heard by the Session reflected the Church's concern to influence and maintain Christian observance within the community generally. Thus, cases of 'profanation of the Sabbath' were investigated, particularly where the alleged profanation could also lead others to transgress. David Cowan, for example, was 'suspended from the fellowship of the church' in 1860, 'in consequence of keeping his shop open on the Lord's Day for the sale of vegetables, groceries and other commodities'.[58] Surprisingly, bankrupts, such as

Duncan McKenzie who was reported to the Session in April 1856, were also suspended from the fellowship of the Church, at least temporarily while their case was investigated.[59] As Rev Dickie explained, 'it was agreed that in the event of any member of the Church being reported bankrupt, he [was], in every case, required not to avail himself of his privileges until he satisfie[d] the Session of his integrity in the matter'.[60]

## The Kirk Session and the Socio-Economic Profile of the Congregation

Study of the Church Records and other sources offers ample evidence of the changing socio-economic aspirations of the Church, the most concrete of which was the decision to build a new church in the developing area of Dowanhill. In an article on the new church in the *Daily Mail* in 1866, the congregation was described as 'one of the most flourishing in that rapidly increasing locality', whilst in the same article, the minister of the Church, Rev Lawrie, described their Mission congregation, which was to occupy the old church building, as having been gathered 'mainly from among the poor and neglected classes'.[61] The Trustees of the Church elected in 1842 and 1863 were probably drawn from the upper range of the socio-economic spectrum represented by the Church's congregation. Those elected in 1842 were as follows:

*John Craig Sr, grocer; James Smith, slater; Thomas Baird, calico printer; Robert Fleming, surgeon; James McConnell, bleacher; James McAulay, merchant; Robert Brand, merchant; Alex Gunn, ferrier [sic]; James Carrick, Tacksman of Gartnavel Coalworks; William Taylor Jr, clerk, Clayslap Mills; John Hendry, Measurer; William Gibb, manager, Burnhouse Mills, Partick; James Watson, wright, Balshagray; and James Craig Jr, manager, factory, Partick.[62]*

Those elected in 1863 were:

*James Watson, wright, Balshagray; James Craig Jr, manager, factory, Partick; Capt. James Brown, shipowner; Alexander Honeyman, commission merchant; George Thomson, commission agent; John Fulton, farmer, Balshagray; Walter Hubbard, baker; Andrew Hosie, tailor & clothier; John McArthur, clerk & portioner; Thomas Brisbane Ewing, wright; James Craig Jr, accountant; Alexander Kay, merchant; Robert Kaye, merchant; and John Cairns, cotton broker.[63]*

The Minutes of the Kirk Session for the late 1850s appear to show that at least a proportion of the congregation still belonged to the 'poor and neglected classes' later associated more exclusively with the Mission congregation. Many of the cases heard by the Session concerned people from the poorer classes, though it would be too simplistic to suggest that the socio-economic polarisation between the Church and its Mission was paralleled in the relationship between

**Fig 57** Castlebank Street, Partick. © Glasgow Life (Museums).

the Elders of the Session and those whose cases they heard (see also **The Congregation and its Missions**). Indeed, Rev Dickie pointed out that 'the members of the Session themselves were on several occasions the subjects of discipline' and that at least three Elders had had to resign office in the nineteenth century.[64] Further study would also be required to assess which types of misdemeanour were associated with particular groups within the community. For example, accusations of non-attendance or irregular attendance at church appear to have been more frequently made against members from poorer classes. A frequent reason given for poor attendance was the lack of suitable clothes. In such cases, the Session generally advanced money to the accused to buy clothes, though there were cases where its charity was abused and the accused was later found to have spent the money on drink. The genuineness of Peter McIntyre's case remained in doubt. He was summoned before the Session for irregular attendance at Church on 27 April 1858, when 'it was reported that [he] was prevented at present from attending Church, owing to the want of suitable clothes.'[65] The Session agreed 'to advance him 20/- for the purpose of obtaining these – to be repaid when convenient'. However, the Session continued to be dissatisfied with his attendance at church, though it was reported on 7 December of that year that 'no facts could be proved in which a charge might be brought against him', as 'the said Peter McIntyre had died suddenly since last Meeting'.[66]

## The Drunken Precentor and the Session's Role in the Worship of the Church

The problems of drunkenness and alcoholism within the community later on in the nineteenth century are most clearly highlighted in the work of the Mission and its Temperance and Total Abstinence meetings (see below **The Congregation and its Missions**).[67] However, the frequency with which cases of 'intoxication' were dealt with by the Kirk Session shows that they were also prevalent within the Church congregation in the middle of the century. The most interesting and revealing case was that of the Precentor of the Church, Mr AD Thomson. The significance attached to his case by the Session also serves to underline the central importance of music within the worship of the Church, the special role of the Precentor, and the seriousness with which the Session regarded its own role in directing all aspects of worship. The case first appears in the Minutes of 27 July 1858, when 'it was stated that Mr AD Thomson, leader of the Psalmody, had been guilty on several occasions of the sin of intoxication'.[68] Thomson appeared before the Session on 3 August, when he 'confessed his sin' and was 'suspended from the fellowship of the Church and from his Office'.[69] On 7 September, 'it was reported that AD Thomson had again fallen into the sin of intemperance in a very aggravated form.' His suspension from 'the privileges of the Church' was therefore continued, but there was discussion of whether the Session had the power to deprive him of his office as Precentor 'while only in a state of suspension from fellowship', and it was decided to seek the advice of the Presbytery Clerk.[70] Thomson, however, resigned his office on 5 October, though the Session continued to monitor his case of suspension from the privileges of the Church.[71] On 21 October, John Fairlie and his wife were accused of having given 'intoxicating drink' to 'the late Precentor'.[72] They admitted their sin 'to a certain extent' and were in turn temporarily suspended from fellowship of the Church. John Fairlie appeared in front of the Session again on 2 November, when he 'admitted buying a Music Book from AD Thomson' but insisted 'that he did not sell him ardent spirits but ale'.[73] The Session decided there was insufficient proof against Fairlie and admonished him.

Thomson's case was re-examined on 9 May 1859, after he himself had 'expressed a desire that his case should be taken up by the Session with a view to his restoration'.[74] The subcommittee appointed to 'enquire into how he has been conducting himself since his suspension' reported on 24 May that they had interviewed Thomson's mother who declared that 'since the 8th of January last, he has not tasted spirituous liquors'.[75] However, they still wanted to interview Thomson himself 'to ascertain the state of his mind in regard to the sin for which he has been suspended'. Nothing more is mentioned about the case until 3 August 1860, when the Session received a letter from the Rev McInnes of the UP Church, Ayr, requesting them to take up the case of Thomson, who was still under suspension from the fellowship of Dowanhill Church. According to McInnes, Thomson had regularly attended his church since January last and his conduct had been 'in every way satisfactory'.[76] Unfortunately, no record of the outcome of this appeal has yet been found.

Meanwhile, the appointment of a new Precentor had raised questions about the respective roles of the Session and the Board of Managers, the latter of which dealt with the business side of appointments. The Session wrote to the Managers on the election of a new Precentor, and stressed that he should be 'fitted' by character to the office and that he should be a member of the congregation.[77] A row then ensued between the Session and the Managers, in which the Session insisted that they, and not the Managers, were charged with enquiring into the 'religious character' of prospective candidates.[78] Whatever the 'religious character' of Thomson's successor, John McLellan, there seems to have been some doubt about his competence as Precentor. On 2 July 1861, the Session expressed regret 'at the low state of the Psalmody of the Church and observing that a feeling of dissatisfaction prevails in the congregation on this account appointed Messrs. Hodgert & Mare to visit Mr McLellan the present Precentor and consult with him with the view of improving as much as possible this part of divine service in the Church'.[79] McLellan was replaced by James Reid in 1862.[80]

The tension between the Session and the Managers appears to have continued in matters concerning the role of music in the liturgy of the Church. In 1875, the important matter of whether the Church should have an organ was under consideration (see below, **Chapter 9**). Managers and Session met to decide on procedures in bringing 'the Organ Question before the Congregation'.[81] The Session, however, insisted that they alone could bring the matter before the congregation, 'the Session only having the control over the manner of Worship'. They therefore required the Managers (all male, of course) to retire to the Ladies Room whilst they deliberated the matter in the Session House and recalled the Managers only once they had made their decision.

## The Congregation and its Missions, 1849-1900

The relationship between the Dowanhill Church congregation and its Mission congregations in poorer areas of Partick (and for a time, Whiteinch) can be charted through the Dowanhill Church Records. The decision in 1864 by the congregation of Partick East United Presbyterian Church to build a new church for themselves in Dowanhill and to sell their existing one to their Mission congregation was typical of that of several UP congregations in nineteenth-century Glasgow who removed themselves from their less salubrious roots to re-establish themselves in areas of new developments affordable only by the wealthier classes.[82] Despite the greater physical distance from deprived areas, the efforts and funds expended by the congregation of the new Dowanhill Church on its 'Village Mission' in Partick were also increased, perhaps because the relationship between the two was now clearer; indeed, it became a good example of the polarisation identified by Drummond and Bulloch in their study of the nineteenth-century church in Scotland in general, and the UP church in particular: 'Church and Mission were associated but distinct; one gave charity and the other received it'.[83]

## History of the Partick and Whiteinch Missions

The work of the Mission was overseen by the Missionary Committee (later the Missionary Association) which was formed in 1849 and which also collected and allocated funds to other home and foreign missions.[84] The Mission work, including preaching at the Mission's services, was undertaken by a paid Missionary, later called a Mission Agent, appointed by the Missionary Committee and assisted by volunteers from the Church. Regular attenders at the Mission services formed themselves into a congregation of eleven in September 1863 and within a year their membership had swelled to 104.[85] Their petition to the Missionary Committee on 8 August 1864, for support in securing new premises for their church, prompted the discussions within Partick East Church which led to the decision to build a new church in Dowanhill for their own congregation and to sell their original building at a special price to the Mission congregation.[86] Although the Mission congregation's petition was the catalyst for the building of Dowanhill Church, the open letter to the members of Partick East from the Preses or chairman of the Board of Managers, George Thomson, explaining their decision to build a new church, also reveals that a new building had been an aspiration of at least some members of the congregation prior to the petition.[87]

The resolution of 15 November 1865 by the new Mission Church, ie. the new Partick East UP Church, to become self sufficient meant that there was now considerable overlap in the mission work of the two churches within the same area, and the Missionary Association of Dowanhill Church therefore decided in December 1869 to move their Mission to Whiteinch.[88] When their Missionary, Mr Cunningham resigned due to ill health in 1873, the Association could not reach agreement about the candidates who applied to succeed him but in the end Mr Williamson was appointed, despite the divisions.[89] It appears that Williamson never enjoyed the full support of the Association or of the Mission itself. He resigned in May 1874 but withdrew his resignation when differences were apparently resolved.[90] However, at a meeting of the Missionary Association on 26 January 1875, a motion was proposed by Mr Begbie and supported by George Thomson that 'the time had now arrived when an ordained Minister or Licenciate should be appointed for our Whiteinch Mission'.[91] The proposal was carried and the Association approached the Rev William Moffat of Alva to take up the post. Moffat declined, on grounds that Whiteinch was not constituted as a church and that he would lose his status as minister if he agreed to accept the post. A resolution was therefore hurriedly passed by the Missionary Association which allowed the Whiteinch Mission to be formed into a new congregation immediately.[92]

Williamson had also remained in post meantime, but the meetings and services of the new church directly competed with those of the Mission. He reported falling attendances by the end of 1875 and resigned in February 1876.[93] The new church in Whiteinch, like the previous Mission congregation in Partick, opted to become self sufficient of Dowanhill Church and also took over the mission work in Whiteinch. It was granted initially free use of the Mission premises and thereafter a low rent on them until 1880, when Dowanhill offered to sell the premises at 'an upset price of £350', an offer which was accepted by Whiteinch UP Church, after some haggling.[94] The main negotiators on behalf of Whiteinch Church were its Secretary, George Thomson, formerly Preses of Dowanhill Church, where he had played the key role in the building of the new church at Dowanhill, and John Craig, another former member of the Board of Managers at Dowanhill. The Whiteinch congregation also built their own new church designed by William Leiper. It was renamed Victoria Park United Presbyterian Church (figs 49 & 58). Sadly, it was demolished in 1967.

**Fig 58** Interior of Whiteinch United Presbyterian Church, later Victoria Park United Presbyterian Church, Glasgow. Glasgow Life / Libraries / Glasgow City Archives.

The decision by Whiteinch to form a separate congregation and become independent of Dowanhill appears to have upset some members of the parent church, including the minister, the Rev Lawrie who, at his jubilee soirée in 1890, allegedly let slip a comment that he had 'never missed' the men who had left Dowanhill to direct the setting up of the new church. The comment prompted an unsigned letter, apparently from George Thomson, in which he claimed that the decision to break away occurred only as a result of their efforts to secure the services of Rev Moffat.[95] For his part, Thomson complained of the uncharitable reception they had received from the Dowanhill congregation when they had sought support for their 'new cause'.

The creation of the new church at Whiteinch left Dowanhill Church once again without a local Mission. At the end of 1876, it was agreed to move Mission activities back to Partick, to premises in Kelvin St., although the boundaries of their new Mission area had to be negotiated with other churches in the vicinity, including their daughter congregation at Partick East and the Free Church.[96] Another difficulty was that the new Missionary, Mr Mabon 'seemed averse' to visiting much of the allotted district, as he claimed it was 'peopled by R.C.s [Roman Catholics]'.[97]

### The 'Biblewoman' and Voluntary Work by the Ladies of Dowanhill Congregation

Since the late 1860s, the Missionary had been assisted in his work by a 'Biblewoman', who offered Christian teaching and coordinated the Church's charity work to women and children in the Mission area. Her salary in the 1870s was around £40 per year, compared to that of £100 paid to the Missionary. At the same date, Rev Lawrie's stipend as Minister at Dowanhill was well in excess of £400 per year.[98] The Mission's first Biblewoman, Miss Lindsay, was followed by Miss Ellison, whose sudden death in 1882 was deeply lamented by the Missionary Association, who believed that many in Partick could 'trace to her influence the dawn of all that is best and brightest in their lives'.[99]

She was succeeded by Miss Burnside who continued to work in the Mission into the twentieth century. In the Annual Reports of Dowanhill Church, it is noticeable that whereas Miss Burnside's male counterpart, Mr Begg, the Mission Agent, who succeeded Mr Mabon in 1886, read his own reports at the Annual General Meetings, the Biblewoman's were read for her by a (male) member of the Missionary Association Committee.[100] Nevertheless, the Missionary Association was very aware of the important contribution women brought to the work of the Mission and, in 1885, began a sustained campaign to persuade many of the ladies of the Dowanhill congregation to volunteer to assist the Mission and the Biblewoman by 'carry[ing] on the work in the Meetings and connected with women'.[101] The plea was repeated in 1887, when the Directors of the Association 'earnestly recommend[ed] to the ladies of the congregation the necessity of coming forward to join in this labour of love', and again in 1890, when Rev Dickie urged, in his first pastoral letter to the Dowanhill congregation: 'We are anxious to see each close [tenement entrance] in the district visited regularly by some Christian lady of the congregation.[102] This concerted campaign led to the setting up of the Dowanhill Dorcas and Benevolent Society in 1893, which reformed and extended an earlier charitable association run by women of the Church. Its aims were to assist the Biblewoman in the work of the Mission and to carry out 'house-to-house visitation'.[103] The distinction between the 'ladies' of Dowanhill Church who gave their services to the Mission and the 'females' who received them is made very clear in the Biblewoman's report for 1885:

> Our Wednesday Evening Prayer Meeting for Females [...] having as its object to impress upon mothers the duty of praying with and for their children, is also well attended [...] Two of the females have been well married, and much interest was felt and taken in their marriages, three of the ladies having generously given marriage presents, which were gratefully received.[104]

### The Mission during Recession

During the 1880s, the major recession in trade made the charitable work of the Mission all the more important. It included a Poor Children's Dinner Table Society and a Blanket Society which made frequent appeals for blankets, without which 'many of the poor – old and young – [would perish] with cold'.[105] In her 1885 Report, Miss Burnside referred to 'the long continued and increased depression of trade, and consequent want of employment by the bread-winners', and she acknowledged 'the kind help given by a gentleman, who generously sent us a few loads of meal and a liberal quantity of milk'.[106] The Dowanhill congregation, on whom the work of the Mission depended, was not immune to the effects of the recession, as the Rev Lawrie made clear in his Pastoral Address in February 1887:

> The year through which we have passed, has been a trying one. Trade has been extremely depressed. The particular industry of this neighbourhood – Shipbuilding – has been almost at a stand-still. Not a few of those connected with the Congregation have been out of work for months. Their savings have been used up, and it has often been a wonder to me how they have got through a season of such deep and prolonged depression. Masters too, as well as men, have felt a pinch of the times.[107]

### The Mission and the Port

Glasgow's importance as a port also impacted on the character of the Mission in a different way, in that the meetings at the Mission were sometimes attended by transient sailors. In his 1887 report on the Mission, Mr Begg paid tribute to the lay work of Mr Spence, chief engineer of the steamship City of Lisbon, which had come to the Clyde to discharge cargo. Spence, 'an earnest and devoted Christian man', found his way to the meetings, where he 'at once in a quiet unobtrusive way laid hold of some anxious soul and in the gentlest way possible endeavoured to point him to the Saviour. Night after night he was engaged in this blessed work.' Mr Begg was in no doubt that 'many who attended these meetings will not soon forget Mr Spence. He has left behind him in Partick more than one who can call him their spiritual father.' At the meetings, Spence also succeeded in converting at least one of his fellow crewmen, who had 'avowed himself to be an infidel', prompting Mr Begg to observe: 'Who can tell the amount of good these sailors may be the means in God's hands of doing to others as they sail from port to port.'[108]

### The Mission and the Temperance and Abstinence Movements

The frequency with which cases of 'intoxication' were dealt with by the Kirk Session in the mid-nineteenth century suggests that drunkenness and alcoholism were already prevalent within the Church congregation and in the local community generally. By the end of the century, tackling these problems within the Mission area in Partick had become a major focus of the work of the Mission, which had also established strong links with the Temperance and Abstinence Movements (fig 59). In 1893, the Report on the Mission called for more support from the Church in its work in this field:

> All who visit in our Mission District are painfully conscious of the evil effects of strong drink. It is working deadly havoc amongst young and old, and if the Church would be faithful to its duty in this matter far more might be done [...] in bringing the Gospel to bear on this form of sin.[109]

Amongst the Mission's efforts to combat the evils of drink were the Gospel Temperance Meetings which were held on Saturday evenings, at which tea was served,

**Fig 59**  Temperance and Abstinence.

*A* Temperance Pledge Signed by William Wood, Motherwell. National Museums of Scotland. Licensor www.scran.ac.uk

*B* City of Glasgow Adult Total Abstinence Associations Certificate. © Glasgow Life (Museums).

and a gospel address and hymn-singing followed. A Total Abstinence Society was also formed by the Mission in 1894 .[110] Drink was a frequent problem amongst the men who lived at the Model Lodging House which opened in Douglas Street in 1893, with beds for 330 men. As the new Lodging House was within the Church's Mission area, it was decided to hold Sunday services there. Providing alternatives to the temptations of drink was also one of the motives behind the setting up of the Working Lads' Club in 1889.

## The Working Lads' Club

In his very first pastoral letter to the Dowanhill congregation, following his appointment as Associate Minister in 1889, the Rev Dickie dared to question the acceptability of the continuing separation of Church and Mission: 'We feel convinced that the real purpose of the Mission will not be served until those who have been brought in and established in the faith pass from the Mission into the Church'.[111] His remedies included a new venture, the Working Lads' Club, which, though it continued to reflect the polarisation between the two sectors of the community, nevertheless seems to have offered some real opportunities for change in the lives of its 'recipients'.

The Working Lads' Club was very much a personal project of Dickie's and was founded in his first year at Dowanhill.[112] Indeed, he seems to have presented it to the Missionary Association as a *fait accompli*, though fortunately, the Association were happy to add it to the Mission's range of activities. Its premises were in Castlebank Street (fig 57), in rooms which were 'tastefully decorated by the Kyrle Society, through the kindness of Mrs Adam Brand, and […] other friends', who donated 'pictures and illuminated Scripture texts'.[113] The Club's aims were set out in its first report:

*Those of you who are familiar with what the lower parts of Partick are, know something of the moral depravity and drunkenness which are too frequently to be met with, and the aim of this work is to get a hold of young working lads before they have had time to acquire or become confirmed in some of the evil habits to which they are in many cases exposed; and, in comfortable, well lighted, and cheerful rooms, to offer them the inducements of healthy recreation and useful instruction.*[114]

The report acknowledged that youths in the poorer areas of Partick had few recreational options:

*Their dwellings, as a rule, have little in themselves attractive, and it is not to be wondered at that these lads should seek their pleasure outside of them, if pleasure it can be called, their wont being to gather about the street corners and to indulge in talk little profitable, and too often, it is to be feared, demoralising in its tendency.*

By contrast, the Working Lads' Club, which was open every evening, offered 'several of the weekly illustrated papers and various magazines', as well as a range of 'healthy' pursuits, including draughts, dominoes, a football club and musical entertainment, the latter provided by ladies of the Church. There were also a number of evening classes: chemistry lectures and experiments on Mondays, drawing classes on Tuesdays, religious instruction on Wednesdays, wood carving and fretwork on Fridays and Bible Study on Sundays. Thursdays were reserved for elementary instruction, since 'although all these lads have gone through Board school, there are among them not a few who are, plainly speaking, practically ignorant'. The Club's Committee was proud of its enlightened policy on discipline:

*Considering the material we had to deal with, it was quite to be expected at the outset that we should have some trouble in maintaining good order and discipline, but in this there is now a pronounced change for the better […] brought about, not by the adoption of extreme or severe measures, but by the exercise of patient forbearance and moral suasion.*

Members of the Working Lads' Club paid a penny for weekly membership or three pence for monthly membership. Membership reached 90 in the first year, with average attendances of 33 per evening. The late hours which many had to work was one disincentive to attendance, as was lack of a change of clothing: 'many of them at their work being exposed to the weather their clothes get wet, and having no change they very wisely stay at home to dry them'. The Rev Dickie was a frequent visitor at the Club where, according to its first report, he permitted himself to behave more informally than might have been expected: 'you are not to suppose that he goes there with a very grave face solely to lecture and to admonish […] he never fails to leave behind him a kindly word of advice and encouragement, and on one occasion he has been even known to sing a song'.[115]

1 Dickie 1916 (2), 16..
2 Dickie 1926, 57-8.
3 Small 1904, II:116-9; Dickie 1916 (2), 11-16.
4 Small 1904, II:116.
5 Dickie 1926, 32-3.
6 Dickie 1926, 34.
7 Dickie 1926, 51.
8 Small 1904, 116.
9 Small 1904, 117.
10 Dickie 1926, 99; and 1916, 13.
11 Baxter 1935, 1.
12 Baxter 1935, 1.
13 Baird 1935, 16.
14 DCMR (Oct 1923).
15 *Evening Citizen* 1962; *Dowanhill Parish Church* 1966, [np].
16 Dickie 1926, 36.
17 Dickie 1926, 34.
18 Dickie 1916, 13.
19 Dickie 1926, 103.
20 Baird 1935, 12-13.
21 *Dowanhill Parish Church* 1966, [np].
22 Dickie 1926, 31.
23 Dickie 1926, 54.
24 Dickie 1926, 56.
25 Small, R 1904, 117.
26 DCMR (Oct 1923).
27 Dickie 1926, 51, 56.
28 DCMR (Oct 1923).
29 Dickie 1926, 103.
30 Reid 1910; *The Power of the Pulpit* 1887.
31 Dickie 1926, 103.
32 Baird 1935, 14.
33 Dickie 1916, 13; and 1926, 97.
34 Dickie 1916, 14.
35 Dickie 1926, 98.
36 Dickie 1916 (1), 5.
37 Dickie 1916 (1), 5.
38 Dickie 1916 (1), 6.
39 Dickie 1916 (1), 6.
40 Dickie 1916 (1), 6.
41 Dickie 1916 (1), 6-7.
42 Dickie 1916 (1), 7.
43 Dickie 1916 (1), 8.
44 Dickie 1916 (1), 10.
45 Dickie 1926, 132.
46 Dickie 1926, 132.
47 Dickie 1916 (1), 8.
48 Dickie 1916 (1), 8-9.
49 Dickie 1916 (1), 9.
50 Dickie 1926, 60.
51 Kirk Session, 8 Feb 1859, DCR CH3/1267/4.
52 See, for example, the case of Thomas Kerr, Kirk Session, 5 Oct 1858, DCR CH3/1267/4.
53 Kirk Session, 26 Feb 1856, DCR CH3/1267/4.
54 Dickie 1926, 42.
55 Kirk Session, 12 Feb 1856, DCR CH3/1267/4.
56 Kirk Session, 30 Oct 1857, DCR CH3/1267/4.
57 Kirk Session, 5 Jan 1858, DCR CH3/1267/4.
58 Kirk Session, 2 Apr 1860, DCR CH3/1267/4.
59 Kirk Session, 6 Apr 1856, DCR CH3/1267/4.
60 Dickie 1926, 61.
61 'New United Presbyterian Church at Partick', *Daily Mail*, 8 Aug 1865, a cutting of which is in Managers Minutes, DCR CH3/1267/7.
62 Congregational Meeting, 11 May 1863, Managers Minutes, DCR CH3/1267/7.
63 Congregational Meeting, 11 May 1863, Managers Minutes, DCR CH3/1267/7.
64 Dickie 1926, 60.
65 Kirk Session, 27 Apr 1858, DCR CH3/1267/4.
66 Kirk Session, 7 Dec 1858, DCR CH3/1267/4.
67 See, for example, Annual Report, 1893, DCR CH3/1267/10.
68 Kirk Session, 27 Jul 1858, DCR CH3/1267/4.
69 Kirk Session, 3 Aug 1858, DCR CH3/1267/4.
70 Kirk Session, 7 Sept 1858, DCR CH3/1267/4.
71 Kirk Session, 5 Oct 1858, DCR CH3/1267/4.
72 Kirk Session, 21 Oct 1858, DCR CH3/1267/4. The Fairlies' misdemeanour is also mentioned in Dickie 1926, 61.
73 Kirk Session, 2 Nov 1858, DCR CH3/1267/4.
74 Kirk Session, 9 May 1859, DCR CH3/1267/4.
75 Kirk Session, 24 May 1859, DCR CH3/1267/4.
76 Kirk Session, 3 Aug 1860, DCR CH3/1267/4.
77 Kirk Session, 2 Nov 1858, DCR CH3/1267/4.
78 Kirk Session, 28 Nov and 7 Dec 1858, DCR CH3/1267/4.
79 Kirk Session, 2 Jul 1861, DCR CH3/1267/4.
80 Dickie 1926, 68.
81 Meeting of Managers and Session, 30 Mar 1875, Managers Minutes, DCR CH3/1267/7.
82 Drummond and Bulloch 1975, 45-6.

[83] Drummond and Bulloch 1975, 50.

[84] Missionary Committee, 29 Jan 1849, DCR CH3/1267/43. See also Dickie 1926, 63 for this Committee's original title, 'The Association for Religious Purposes, in connection with the East United Presbyterian Church, Partick'.

[85] Undated MS document [1864?], DCR CH3/1267/98. For similar figures, see also Dickie 1926, 65.

[86] Missionary Committee, 8, 15 & 18 Aug 1864, DCR CH3/1267/43.

[87] George Thomson, Notice to Members of Partick East UP Church, 8 Oct 1864, DCR CH3/1267/102: 'Your Committee have reason to believe that some of the Members of our Congregation have for a considerable time been desirous of obtaining a new place of worship.'

[88] Missionary Committee, 15 Nov 1865, and Missionary Association, Dec 1869, DCR CH3/1267/43.

[89] Missionary Association, 20 Feb, 16 Apr, 27 Apr and 30 Apr 1873, DCR CH3/1267/43.

[90] Missionary Association, 31 May 1874, DCR CH3/1267/43.

[91] Missionary Association, 26 Jan 1875, DCR CH3/1267/43.

[92] Missionary Association, 3 Mar, 24 Mar and 8 Apr 1875, DCR CH3/1267/43.

[93] Missionary Association, 29 Dec 1875 and 1 Feb 1876, DCR CH3/1267/43.

[94] Missionary Association, 27 Nov 1876, 9 Jan 1878, 18 Feb, 5 Mar and 24 Mar 1880, DCR CH3/1267/43. George Thomson and John Craig, for Whiteinch, insisted that the price should include 'feu, furnishings and fittings'. Soon after, the managers of Whiteinch UP Church commissioned a new church by William Leiper. For the subsequent history of Whiteinch Church, later Victoria Park Church, see Herron 1984, no. 587.

[95] Unsigned letter, assumed to be from George Thomson, 14 Apr 1890, DCR CH3/1267/105.

[96] Missionary Association, 27 Nov 1876, DCR CH3/1267/43.

[97] Missionary Association, 8 Feb 1885, DCR CH3/1267/43.

[98] Mr Cunningham's salary as agreed by Missionary Association, 27 Dec 1871, DCR CH3/1267/43. Rev Lawrie's stipend, which was reviewed every year, was £400 in 1863, see Managers Minutes, 12 Oct 1863, DCR CH3/1267/7. The Biblewoman's salary was still just £40 per year in 1885, when a proposal to increase it to £52 was rejected.

[99] Missionary Association, 11 Jun 1882, DCR CH3/1267/43.

[100] See, for example, Annual Report, 1888, DCR CH3/1267/10.

[101] Missionary Association, 27 Oct 1885, DCR CH3/1267/43.

[102] Missionary Association, 18 Jan 1887, DCR CH3/1267/43; Pastoral Letter by Rev Dickie, in Annual Report, 1889, DCR CH3/1267/10.

[103] Annual Report, 1893, DCR CH3/1267/10.

[104] Annual Report, 1885, DCR CH3/1267/10.

[105] Mr Begg's Report, 1886, and Miss Burnside's Report, 1885, in Annual Reports, DCR CH3/1267/10.

[106] Miss Burnside's Report, in Annual Report, 1885, DCR CH3/1267/10.

[107] Pastoral Address by Rev Lawrie, in Annual Report, 1886, DCR CH3/1267/10.

[108] Mr Begg's Report, in Annual Report, 1887, DCR CH3/1267/10.

[109] Mr Begg's Report, in Annual Report, 1893, DCR CH3/1267/10.

[110] Mr Begg's Report, in Annual Report, 1894, DCR CH3/1267/10.

[111] Pastoral Letter by Rev Dickie, in Annual Report, 1889, DCR CH3/1267/10.

[112] See also Dickie's own account of this venture, in Dickie 1926, 106-9.

[113] Mr Begg's Report, in Annual Report, 1889, DCR CH3/1267/10.

[114] Annual Report, 1889, DCR CH3/1267/10.

[115] Annual Report, 1889, DCR CH3/1267/10.

# 6 DOCUMENTING THE BUILDING
## Hilary Macartney

**Plate XIX**

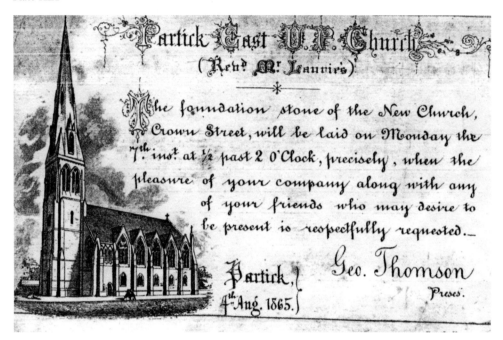

*A* Invitation to Attend the Ceremonial Laying of the Foundation Stone, *Dowanhill Church Records*, CH3/1267/7. Glasgow Life / Libraries / Glasgow City Archives.

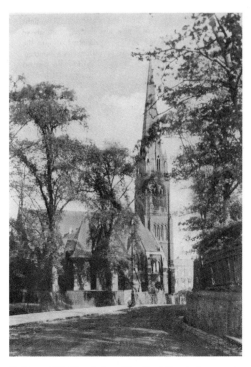

*B* Dowanhill Church from Hyndland Road, photograph from W Dickie, 1926, *History of Dowanhill Church 1823-1923*. Courtesy of Four Acres Charitable Trust.

*C* William Leiper FRIBA. Courtesy of *Dictionary of Scottish Architects.*

## Introduction

Study of Dowanhill Church Records is enabling a much fuller history of the building itself to begin to emerge. So far, this study has only been carried out in any detail for the period of 1864 to 1899 but it has already extended our knowledge of the building in several areas, including its architectural history and its relationship to the history of the development of Dowanhill generally. In addition, a number of details have emerged which are enabling a greater understanding of the fabric of the building, including how it was constructed, its upkeep and its problems. These are particularly relevant to the ongoing programme of restoration and are providing the architects currently involved in this project with valuable information which is unlikely otherwise to have come to light.

## The Site of Dowanhill Church

According to a notice of 8 October 1864 to the congregation of Partick East UP Church, 'some of the Members of the Congregation have for a considerable time been desirous of obtaining a new place of worship'.[1] The decision to build a new church, however, was prompted by the petition by the Mission congregation to obtain their own place of worship.[2] As far as the choice of sites was concerned, the Minute book of the Board of Managers of makes it clear that, as soon as the decision was taken to sell the earlier church to the Mission congregation, the Managers began to consider possible sites for their new church.[3] Four sites were considered at a meeting on 29 August 1864, all further north than their existing church, in areas of new developments in Dowanhill and Partickhill.[4] Apart from the site which was eventually chosen, to be feued by Thomas L Paterson at an initial asking price of 9 shillings per square yard, others were considered 'in front of Dowan Hill House @ 12/6 per sq yd'; 'on Partick Hill, Mr Aitken's property, 7/- per sq yd'; and 'another site, bounded on the north by a new street leading to Eldon Terrace, east of Hyndland Street & south by a new street, 8/- per sq yd'. The proprietors of the latter site were obviously keen to attract the new church building to their development, since they promised 'a subscription of £100 or thereby' towards its construction on their site, whilst Mr Aitken also made a similar offer regarding his site.[5] At a meeting at the end of October 1864, the Managers agreed that 'the preference be given to the site on Mr Paterson's property, should such site be obtainable at a fair price'.[6] At the same meeting, a subcommittee was appointed 'to call on Mr Paterson and ascertain the lowest price at which the site on Mr Paterson's grounds could be secured' and was given powers to make an offer on the site, subject to approval by the congregation. In early November, the subcommittee reported that Mr Paterson had 'agreed to accept 7/6d per sq yd for the site on his property'.[7] The site had also been measured by a surveyor, who reported its size to be 2224 sq yds (1859 sq m), although the size was given as 2212 sq yds (1849 sq m) in the feu contract.[8]

Doubts about the suitability of the site were, however, raised by the Preses (chairman) of the Board of Managers, George Thomson, who stated that, in the opinion of an (unnamed) architect friend of his, 'the angular nature of the ground' was 'not altogether adapted for the site of a modern church'.[9] The subcommittee's report of 18 November, which stated that Herbertson, the surveyor considered the site 'suitable with some slight alterations to the ground', was therefore welcomed by the Managers, who then formally recommended the purchase of the site.[10] The congregation was consulted on the Board's recommendations through a printed notice and an open letter from George Thomson, seeking their approval and requesting subscriptions for the new church. It was in this context that, in the second of these letters, on 26 November, Thomson defended their choice of a 'central and desirable' site for the new church: 'Some might have wished it further east, others further west, and others further south, but the aim has been to place the Church where it would best accommodate the existing Congregation, as well as with a view to its future prosperity'.[11]

Two of the Managers, Alexander Kay and Allan Arthur were appointed to visit Mr Paterson with the Church's solicitor, Mr Kidston to arrange the purchase.[12] They were also entrusted with negotiating and signing the feu contract on behalf of the congregation.[13] The missives of sale were signed on 24 January 1865, although an additional 7 ft (2.13 m) was acquired to the north of the site in May of that year, in order that a 'clear passage' could be made around the church and so that the whole property could be railed in.[14] The feu contract shows that Paterson inserted a number of conditions which would ensure that the new church was a high-quality building which would add prestige to his estate. These included the requirement 'to build erect and finish' the Church and adjoining buildings within two years of the date of the feu contract.[15] In addition, the building was to be constructed as follows:

> [...] in a substantial manner of stone and lime, and be covered with slates or metal, and the front and side walls thereof shall be of a smooth polished or droved stone ashlar of a white pile, and the north wall of square dressed ruble [sic] or droved or dressed courses combined with dressed work and of a white pile.

The plans were also to be submitted to Paterson for approval: 'before proceeding to build, the said second parties [the Church Trustees] [...] shall always be bound to submit the plans and elevations of their proposed buildings to the said first party [Paterson] [...] or their architect for his or their approval in writing'. In the event that Paterson did not approve the plans, the matter was to be decided by 'a neutral architect'. The precise dimensions of the 'building line' within which the new building was to be erected within the site were also stipulated in the contract, but any buttresses or tower were to be permitted to project beyond the building line by not more than 5 ft (1.52 m). For his part, Paterson was obliged to agree not to erect buildings of more than 18 ft (5.49 m) in height within 21 ft (6.4 m) of the north side and 60 ft (18.3 m) of the west side of the lane (fig 60).

### The Architecture Competition

Meanwhile, a subcommittee convened by George Thomson, and consisting of Alexander Kay and Allan Arthur, Robert Kaye, John Cairns, Alexander Honeyman, David More and Hugh Frazer was appointed to advise on obtaining plans for the new building and securing an architect.[16] At the end of November 1864, they 'unanimously agreed to advise a competition', and decided to invite six architects, or firms of architects to submit plans. These were John Honeyman (whose relationship, if any, to the Dowanhill Church Manager is not yet known), John Burnet, Messrs Melvin & Leiper, Messrs CH Wilson & J Thomson, Messrs Haig & Low, and Barclay (presumably Hugh).[17] It was also decided that prizes of £25, £15 and £10 would be awarded to three runners-up. A brief of instructions to the architects was prepared, with the help of Mr Herbertson, the surveyor.[18] The brief requested designs in the Gothic style, though it was made clear that additional designs in other styles would also be considered:

> It is desired that the Buildings be designed of the Gothic style of Architecture, substantial but without superfluous decoration, having a Spire or Tower with provision made for Bell and with or without space for clock [...] Should any of the Competitors think another order of Architecture more suitable to the site he is at liberty to furnish an additional design of such order or style.[19]

In accordance with the terms of the feu contract, the stone finishes were also stipulated: 'The East, South and West walls of Church are to be of hewn courses, and all other walls may be of square dressed ruble work'. The importance of submitting designs which would not exceed the budget of £5500 was also stressed in the brief. All fixtures and fittings, including heating and gas fittings, were to be included in this sum. The amount was also to include 'Glazier Work', though any 'stained

**Fig 60** The Dowanhill Estate, plan showing existing and proposed development, ca.1874. University of Glasgow Archive Services (GB0248 UGD092/81).

The then existing buildings including Dowanhill Church blocked in and proposed development in outline. Dowanhill Church stands at the apex of the triangle formed by Hyndland Road and Hyndland Street and the proposed buildings to the north accord with the building line stipulated in the feu contract.

or ornamental glass' was to be considered additional. No mention was made of painting, except of woodwork and ironwork (see **Chapter 7**). The importance of staying within the budget was again stressed at the Managers' meeting on 13 December, when they threatened to reject any over-budget plans.[20]

John Honeyman declined the invitation to submit plans, and was replaced by James Hamilton, whilst Burnet also announced he was unable to submit plans due to pressure of work.[21] The submitted plans were inspected at the Managers' Meeting of 24 January 1865, when a subcommittee of Messrs. Cairns, Arthur, A Honeyman, R Kaye, A Kay, Frazer and Captain Brown was appointed to examine them further and to report to the next meeting. The subcommittee was also given power to 'consult with Mr Burnet, if they think fit'.[22] Five of the submitted entries were also costed, presumably by Herbertson, and were perhaps considered the finalists. This document shows that all of these, except 'In Commendum No. 2', estimated at £5498, were expected to run over budget. The 'Veritas' scheme was estimated to cost £6370, 'Veritas B' £5970, 'Auditorium No. 2' £7073 and 'Diagram No. 1' £6550 (fig 61).[23]

**Fig 61** The Architecture Competition, Managers Minutes, 4 Feb 1865, Downhill Church Records, CH3/1267/7. Glasgow Life / Libraries / Glasgow City Archives.

On 4 February, the subcommittee 'unanimously recommend[ed]' the design 'Veritas' as the winner, with 'Veritas B' in second place, 'In Commendum' in third and 'Diagram' in fourth.[24] The plans were then displayed in the school room and a meeting of the congregation was arranged for 8 February. At the meeting, the Chairman, George Thomson, seconded by Alexander Kay, proposed that 'Veritas' be awarded the contract. The proposal was carried and 'The Chairman then opened the sealed envelopes when Messrs Melvin & Leiper were found to be the successful competitors'.[25] As 'Veritas B' was also discovered to be by Melvin & Leiper, it was agreed to award the second prize to Messrs CH Wilson & J Thomson. The third prize was awarded to Haig & Low and the fourth to James Hamilton. The Managers then appointed a Building Committee, comprising George Thomson as convenor, Alexander Kay, John Cairns, Allan Arthur, Hugh Frazer, Robert Kaye, David More, James Craig and Alexander Honeyman. Members of the Kirk Session, the Trustees and the Board of Managers were also appointed to the Committee as ex-officio members and invited to attend its meetings. The Committee began its work by arranging the return of competition entries.[26] However, the text descriptions of two entries, 'Auditorium Nos 1 & 2', by an unidentified competitor, remain in the Downhill Church Records, and give some insight into the form and range of the competition submissions. 'Auditorium No 1', for a Gothic design, proposed 'a compact parallelogram with slight projecting transepts', with 'a tower and spire occupy[ing] the south east angle and form[ing] one of the staircases to the galleries'.[27] The other staircase was to be 'a semi octagonal projection, forming a feature externally, being truncated by a hipped and crested roof and an arcade of pointed windows'. 'Auditorium No 2' proposed a design 'in the Italian style', which the competitors considered 'equally well suited for the site'. In particular, it stated that 'taking into consideration 'the two spires already erected in such close proximity with a third one half finished in the Free Church (Mr Anderson's) we are of the opinion that an Italian design with a bold campanile in front would form a new and striking feature in the architectural appearance of the locality'.[28] The interior was to have galleries 'supported on McGrind beams which require no supports underneath' and the architects drew attention to the fact that 'there are no pillars of any kind intervening betwixt preacher & hearers' and that 'the whole of the circular area [...] is free from obstructions of any kind'.

**Building the New Church**

On 2 March, Thomson reported that the Building Committee 'had suggested certain alterations in the details of the selected plans'.[29] Some of these are likely to have been cost-cutting suggestions, since Melvin & Leiper were requested to examine the plans 'with a view to reducing the cost of the building without impinging materially upon the appearance of the same'.[30] The

Committee met Leiper on 18 April, who reported that 'it could only be in matters of detail that some saving might be effected'. Once again, 'the necessity of keeping within the estimates as much as possible was then impressed upon the architect, and he was requested to hasten on the work as rapidly as could be done'.[31] Leiper agreed to the Minutes of this meeting on 1 May, when he was also invited to explain his plans to level the site.[32] From this date on, Leiper's name only is mentioned in the records of the project, rather than that of Melvin & Leiper, although at the laying of the memorial stone in August 1865, the latter firm was described as being the architects.[33]

The Minutes of the Managers' Meetings contain few details of the progress of the building or the work of the Building Committee once construction was underway. Leiper clearly heeded the instruction to 'hasten on the work as rapidly as could be done', for when a memorial stone was laid by George Thomson on 7 August 1865 (fig 62), its position in the northeast buttress of the tower, 15 ft (4.57 m) above the base of the tower, indicates the remarkable progress that had been made.[34] A report on the ceremony and the new building appeared in the *Daily Mail*:

> The site selected is on the rising ground at the northern extremity of Partick, where one or two new streets are springing up; and from its elevated position the edifice will be seen from a considerable distance […] The congregation is […] one of the most flourishing in that rapidly increasing locality […] [The place of worship] now in course of erection will form, when completed, one of the finest buildings in the place. The church, which is early Gothic in character, is a simple oblong in plan […] At the north end the pulpit platform will be placed, under an arched recess, the shafts and corbels, with their carved capitals, being of stone. The screen which is to form the front of the platform will also be of stone, having marble shafts and carved capitals. Access from the vestry will be provided by a stair leading to the platform. The church is to be spanned by a hammer-beam roof, and the spandrils [sic] are to be filled with pierced work. The roof will be plastered at the back of the curved ribs under principals, in order to prevent draughts and secure good acoustic properties.[35]

The Managers had clearly now accepted that the new building would cost even more than the initial estimate for the winning design, since the *Daily Mail* article reported that: 'The building is estimated to cost upwards of £6700, towards which about £3700 have already been raised by the congregation.' The paper also commented on the rapid progress of construction: 'The building was begun in May last, and has made such progress that about 30 feet of the walls, buttresses and tower have been erected.' According to George Thomson, who was quoted in the article, progress was

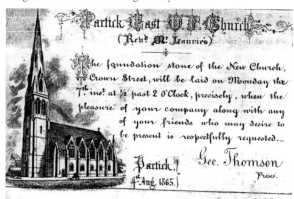

**Fig 62** Invitation to Attend the Ceremonial Laying of the Foundation Stone, Dowanhill Church Records, CH3/1267/7. Glasgow Life / Libraries / Glasgow City Archives.

such that the congregation 'could now judge somewhat for themselves of the appearance which the building would present when finished. It would be grand in its simplicity and massiveness, dependent for its beauty not on costly ornamentation, but rather on the harmony of its lines and proportions.'

The schedules of estimates for the various trades had been examined on 18 April 1865, in connection with the 'mason work, joiner work, slater work, plumber work, plaster work, smith & founder, and glazier'. Not surprisingly, it was agreed that the lowest estimates would be accepted in each case, unless there was 'good reason otherwise'.[36] The trades estimates accepted were as follows:

| | |
|---|---|
| Mason, Thomas McWalters | £4010 |
| Joiner, Alexander Marshall | £1854 |
| Slater, Thomas Black | £184 . 14 . 3 |
| Plumber, John Small | £198 |
| Plasterer, William Bremner | £117 |
| Smith, John Anderson | £175 . 18 . 0 |
| Glazier, J. Dale | £89 . 8 . 6 |
| Heating, Combe & Son | £115 |
| Gasfitting, Pennycook | £132 . 9 . 0 |
| Total | £6877 . 6 . 8[37] |

In fact, the final costs were higher in all cases, apart from those of the glazier, which was presumably reduced due to the decision to contract stained glass from Cottier. Final costs were as follows:

| | |
|---|---|
| Mason, Thomas McWalters | £4844 |
| Joiner, Alexander Marshall | £2638 . 9 . 8 |
| Slater, Thomas Black | £206 . 8 . 6 |
| Plumber, John Small | £213 . 10 . 0 |
| Plasterer, William Bremner | £143 . 5 . 6 |
| Smith, John Anderson | £258 |
| Glazier, J. Dale | £43 . 5 . 0 |
| Heating, Combe & Son | £159 . 12 . 0 |
| Gasfitting, Pennycook | £145 . 8 . 6 |
| Total | £8651 . 19 . 6[38] |

The Dowanhill Church Records also contain detailed surveys of the 'Carpenter and Joiner Work' and the 'Digging, Mason & Brick Work', including the materials and quantities used and their costs, though unfortunately the equivalent surveys for the work of the other trades do not appear to have survived.[39] These were compiled by Herbertson and signed as approved by Leiper. They provide an extremely rare and valuable reference resource which gives a remarkable insight into how the building was constructed. Some much briefer information on additional costs, including the painted decoration, which did not appear in the original costings, is given in an undated list of 'Mason's Extras' and a Statement of Extra Cost of Mason Work, both of which were presumably compiled after completion of all major work, in late 1866 or early 1867.[40] As a result of Herbertson's work, the costs of the carpenter and joiner work carried out by Alexander Marshall were in fact queried by the Building Committee, who considered them too high and the matter was taken to arbitration:

> Mr Thomson read [...] correspondence between Mr Marshall and the Preses of the Building Committee respecting the items of Mr Marshall's account (which were considered unusually high) and the conditions of arbitration for a settlement. Mr Marshall insisted that the accounts be referred to Tradesmen only, whilst the Committee were of the opinion that it was fair to offer that an Architect along with a Tradesman approved of by Mr Marshall be appointed referees. The Trustees and Managers coincided with the opinion of and action taken by the Building Committee and left the arrangement of the matter in their hands.[41]

A page of accounts attached to the list of Mason's Extras gives a breakdown of the total cost of the Church, and shows that the final figure was £11,106.12s.[42] Apart from the higher final costs for the various trades, there were also additional costs for carving, marble working, painting by Cottier ((fig 63)– see **Chapter 7**) and for umbrella stands, lightning conductor, weathervane and pulpit pendants. These brought the costs to £9349.2s.6d. A commission of 5% had been agreed as payment to Melvin & Leiper as architects. This percentage was originally calculated and paid out on the £5500 ceiling set by the Managers as the maximum cost of the Church. However, once costs had escalated to over £9000, the Managers agreed to pay Leiper 5% commission on the actual costs, rounded down to £9300. Thus, Leiper was paid an extra £190, bringing the total architect's fee to £465.[43] The Managers described the extra payment as 'a bonus', which may indicate that they were satisfied with Leiper's efforts to keep costs down. In the accounts, the architect's commission was included in the calculation of 'Preliminary Expenses' totalling £1118.0s.8d, which ranged from the cost of the plans, digging the foundations and scaffolding to legal fees, insurance and wages to the site watchman. These were additional to the £9349 for the work by tradesmen. Some other items were also still

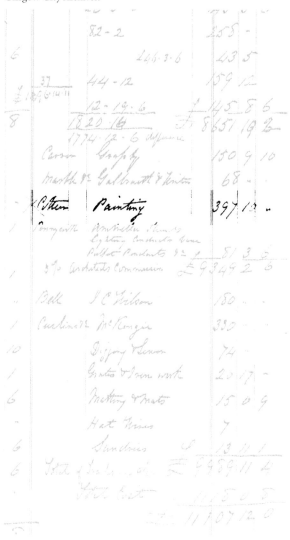

**Fig 63** Cottier's Payment Recorded in the Accounts, Dowanhill Church Records, CH3/1267/105. Glasgow Life / Libraries / Glasgow City Archives.

to be added, including £180 to JC Wilson for the bell and £74 for digging the sewer.

## Opening the New Church

The opening of the Church on Sunday 11 November 1866 was advertised in a printed leaflet and in a notice in the *Glasgow Herald*.[44] An admiring description was also given of the new church in an article on the 'Opening of Dowanhill U.P. Church' in the *Glasgow Herald* on Monday 12 November:

*Yesterday, the handsome church which has just been completed at Dowanhill, for the United Presbyterian congregation under the pastoral charge of the Rev. T.M. Lawrie, was opened for public worship. The building, which is situated on an angular piece of ground formed by the junction of Hyndland Road and Crown Street, is in plan a simple oblong, 79 feet long and 51 feet broad. At the south end a spacious corridor occupies the whole breadth of the church, at either end of which a wide stair leads to the gallery. The main entrance or porch is formed in the lower part of the tower, which is placed in front of the corridor.*

**Plate XX** The Bell, Dowanhill Church, J C Wilson manufacturers, photographed in 2001. Courtesy of Alan Ferdinand.

*At the north or opposite end is a great stone arch forming a recess, in which stands the pulpit platform, the front of which is of stone and marble. A light wooden screen surmounts the front of the platform. The roof is 51 feet in span, is constructed on the hammer beam principle, and is plastered at the back of the carved ribs under principals, forming one grand internal vault, and securing good ventilation. The church is lighted principally by the large traceried windows over the light gallery which runs round the sides. Accommodation is provided for 1000 sitters — 648 in the area, and 352 in the gallery. The whole church is painted throughout after the medieval manner, and, with the exception of Townhead Parish Church, is perhaps the only Presbyterian church in Scotland in which painted windows and mural decoration have been carried out as in the old times. The decorations and painted windows have been admirably executed by Mr Cottier, to whom praise is due for the manner in which he has carried out the views of the architect. The aim of the latter has been to build a Presbyterian church which might have some claim to be reckoned artistic. Externally the church is divided into six bays by massive buttresses. Simple two-light windows admit light below the gallery; and above these are large traceried windows carried up into the roof and gables. The tower and spire are above 200 feet in height. The former contains a fine toned bell, cast by Mr J.C. Wilson. Immediately adjoining the church is a large hall or classroom, 32 by 28 feet. The officer's house, vestry, session-house, and ladies' room, are above the*

*hall. The church has been built from the plans and under the superintendence of Mr Wm. Leiper, of the late firm of Melvin & Leiper, architects, on whose taste and judgment the work reflects no little credit. At the opening services yesterday, collections were made in aid of the building fund, amounting in all to £725.*[45]

Despite the impression given in the *Glasgow Herald* report that the building, including all decoration, was finished for the opening, a letter from George Thomson shows that the stained glass by Cottier and several other details were not finished until 1869-70:

> *I send you herewith […] Passbook containing list of subscribers to Choir window with receipts enclosed for £39.10/- paid Mr Cottier to a/c. In reference to this I may explain that as some alterations required to be made such as a <u>new</u> and <u>correct</u> inscription, a gutter for carrying off the water, two new heads of David & Miriam which I do not now think necessary, some alterations on the heads in the lower windows, and a little repair to the painting behind the last north hammerbeam above the gallery, I kept a portion of the subscriptions in hand, paying him £20 to a/c but in consequence of his own recent illness & the death of a child I thought it my duty to hand him the amount I had in hand viz £13.00/- the balance of £6.10/- being sufficient security that the work will be done.*[46]

As we have seen, the original brief to the architects allowed for the possibility of 'stained or ornamental glass', though there was no budget for it in the Managers' original estimate of the cost of the Church. This matter appears to have been debated by the Building Committee, as one of its members, Alexander Kay, offered a solution in a letter of 19 February 1866:

> *Seeing that the new church will cost more than the congregation was led to expect, I quite sympathise with the opinion entertained that by introducing stained glass into the windows the Committee might be held liable to blame. I am, however, of the opinion that it should be done, as being in accordance with the style of the building. And feeling assured that the beauty, and — allow me to add — the comfort of the Church would be so much enhanced, I am anxious to have this difficulty overcome; and for this purpose I am willing to subscribe £300 — say Three Hundred Pounds Stg. — to defray the extra expense, provided the Committee are agreed with me that such would be desired, and that all obstacles would be removed by my doing so.*[47]

It is possible that Kay's donation paid for all the stained glass, including the rose window but excepting the two-light window with full-length figures of David and Miriam, which was designed for the south gallery or choir.[48] The David and Miriam window was paid for by subscription of the Elders, Managers and Trustees, and according to Rev Dickie, cost 'about £40'.[49] A letter from Cottier, read at a meeting of the Managers on 24 November 1866, shows that its design was being planned. In it, Cottier stated that 'in the course of a fortnight, he expected to be able to show a drawing for, and give an estimate of the cost of window in Choir-room'.[50] The drawing referred to may have been the design for 'the south window' admired at the Managers' meeting of 13 May 1867, unless earlier designs had also been submitted.[51] Its inscription was also discussed at the same meeting, during which Kay refused to have his name included in the inscription. Instead, the Managers' thanks for Kay's 'handsome donation' were recorded in the Minutes. The inscription on the window was finally agreed at the meeting of 30 September of the same year: 'Mr Thomson read the inscription proposed to be placed on the South Window of the Church which was agreed to'.[52] Rev Dickie interpreted the matter of the inscription as follows:

*The Building Committee was anxious to indicate the sources from which the donations for these and the other windows of the Church came, but as Mr. Alexander Kay would not allow any reference to be made to his munificent gift (it should be noted that he subscribed also £500 to the Building Fund), no indication of the donors of any of the windows appears.*[53]

The inscription on the David window did, however, record the names of the Rev Lawrie, as minister of the new church and Leiper as its architect, whilst the Miriam window is signed 'Cottier 67' (fig 64). The full inscriptions are as follows: (on the David window) 'Praise ye the Lord. Dowanhill United Presbyterian Church. Erected under the pastorate of the Rev. T.M. Lawrie. William Leiper, Architect; 1866'; (on the Miriam window) 'Sing ye to the Lord. Congregation founded 1823. First Church 1824. This Church opened for worship 11 Nov. 1866' (fig 65).

**Fig 64** Cottier's Signature within the Miriam Window, Dowanhill Church, 1867. Courtesy of Tom Donald.

**Fig 65** Inscription below the Miriam Window, Dowanhill Church, 1867. Courtesy of Tom Donald.

At the first Managers' Meeting following the opening of the Church, some snagging details were raised, including complaints of draughts and 'the defective condition of the gas fittings'.[54] Nevertheless, the congregation appears to have been largely satisfied with their new building, and in particular with the efforts expended by the Preses, George Thomson in ensuring the satisfactory completion of the project: at their Annual General Meeting on 25 November, Alexander Kay proposed that 'a hearty vote of thanks be given to Mr Thomson for the great interest he had taken and the exertions he had made in the erection of the new church', a proposal that was 'cordially and unanimously agreed to'. They showed their appreciation of Leiper as architect by awarding him an extra bonus, as we have seen. In addition, the Managers agreed that 'a friendly dinner be given by the Managers and Session and friends to the architect and contractors for the new church'.[55]

## Praise and Appreciation of Leiper's Design

Leiper's success in winning the architectural competition for Dowanhill Church as his first major commission, and the gracefulness its Gothic design, were praised both at the time and by later commentators.[56] The design for Dowanhill Church was also selected for inclusion in the British architecture section of the Paris Universal Exhibition of 1867 where, like many of the architectural designs it was represented by a photograph.[57] Other exhibits selected included several schemes for the Albert Memorial in London by Charles Barry, Gilbert Scott and others, and designs by William Burges, GE Street, Owen Jones, Digby Wyatt and JL Pearson. Of the 77 architectural designs shown in the British Section, the only other exhibits of buildings in Scotland were a view of the interior of a church in Burntisland, Fife, by the London-based architect William Slater, a view of Kelvinside Church (now Oran Mòr) by Campbell Douglas and JJ Stevenson, and exterior and interior views of Townhead Parish Church by the same architects, the interior of which had been decorated by Cottier.[58]

The jurors for the British architecture section were James Fergusson, assisted by Lt-Col Scott. Fergusson was also vice-president of the international architecture committee for the exhibition. Its president was Félix Duban, one of the principal figures involved in the nineteenth-century restoration and interpretation of the Sainte-Chapelle in Paris, which may well have been one of Leiper's inspirations for the design of Dowanhill, and could have been visited by him on one of his trips to France.[59]

The longest and most admiring appreciation of Leiper's design for Dowanhill Church occurs, not surprisingly, in

**Plate XXI** Dowanhill Church from Hyndland Road, photograph from W Dickie, 1926, *History of Dowanhill Church 1823-1923*. Courtesy of Four Acres Charitable Trust.

**Plate XXII** Dowanhill Church, 1875. Scanned image courtesy of RCAHMS. Licensor www.rcahms.gov.uk

Dickie's book on the Church. Dickie began by noting Leiper's family connection with the Church and his precocious success in the commission, but his account laid greatest stress on the artistic and poetic qualities of both architect and building:

*Mr. Leiper was the son of one of our most respected elders. Dowanhill Church was his first commission, and for a youth of twenty-five it was a very notable achievement. But Mr. Leiper was essentially an artist, and a man of fine imagination, with a passion for beauty of form which made his devotion to architecture a calling rather than a profession. His sympathies were naturally with the Gothic style, though he frequently deviated into the Classic and sometimes into the Old Scots according as the nature and situation of the structure demanded. Mr. Leiper became in due time an R.S.A. [...]*
*The design of the Church is Early Gothic. The spire, rising to the height of 195 feet above the pavement, is one of the most graceful and proportionate in Glasgow, whilst the outbuildings on the west side of the Church are reckoned by experts as perfect in design and suitability [...] The dignity and massiveness of the spire are best seen when one approaches it on ascending the slope in Hyndland Street; the simplicity of the lines in church and spire when one views them from the Byres Road looking along Havelock Street; but the most charming view of the whole buildings is that obtained when approaching it from Hyndland Road, especially at that point at which the eye sees the church through the gothic tracery of the elms and birches (still happily with us), with the filigree spire of the University in the distance. From that point Dowanhill appeals to the artistic mind as a song or a poem.[60]*

## Maintenance and Repairs of the Church

After the building was finished, the Managers, through their building and repairs committees, made regular checks on the condition of the building and carried out maintenance and repairs. In August 1874, for example, the church doors were revarnished, the railings painted, and part of the stone coping was repointed.

Other 'minor repairs' were also carried out 'against the winter season'.[61] The story of the damage to Cottier's roundel of the head of David in the rose window, which was broken by a boy, is covered in Dickie's book on the Church.[62] It is also recorded in the Minutes of a meeting of the Managers in March 1875. Time and cost appear to have been major factors in the decision to employ a local firm, Keir's, rather than Cottier, to repair it:

*In reference to the stained glass broken in Rose window of north gable a note was read from Capt. Edwards intimating that the parents of the boy who broke it had agreed to pay the cost of having it replaced. Mr Thomson, who had been in communication with Mr Cottier on the subject, stated that the tracing of the head had been destroyed and that either what remained*

**Plate XXIII** Dowanhill Church, after 1898 with Dowanhill Park in the Foreground. Courtesy of Richard Stenlake.

*would require to be sent to London for a copy or a new design prepared. After some further conversation it was agreed to employ Messrs Keir of Glasgow to replace the broken part taking for their guidance what remained of the head and face.[63]*

The Minutes of the Managers' meetings also show that a number of problems with the building were recurring. The congregation continued to complain of draughts, and in January 1868, it was agreed 'to put a door at the entrance to the back lobby of the Church, Mr Ewing having offered one of the doors taken from the area of the Church for this purpose'.[64] In November 1869, members complained of draughts in the gallery of the Church, and the Repairs Committee was instructed 'to have the backs of the seats next the two doors raised 9 inches and doors placed at the entrance to the passages'.[65] At the same meeting, it was reported that 'water had been leaking through the Church building near one of the arches', and the Building Committee was instructed 'to consult with Mr Leiper and take steps to make the necessary repairs'.

Leiper continued to be consulted for advice on repairs and upkeep. In August 1874, it was reported that the lightning conductor was broken and Leiper advised on 'the best means of having it repaired'.[66] He reported that Mr Pennycook, who had originally erected it, had examined the conductor and 'thought it could be put right for £12, but offered to do it at cost price which might not be more than half this sum'. The repair was carried out and, at the same time, 'the spire [was] repointed, advantage being taken of the scaffolding being up to get this done and also to have the vane put in order'.[67] The spire, lightning conductor and weathervane are examples of several features of the building which continually caused problems, the history of which can be followed through the Church Records. In 1916, for example, soon after Leiper's death, his business partner, William Hunter McNab, claimed in a letter that he had 'recently superintended the repairs to the stonework & during these operations ascended to the apex of the

**Fig 66** William Leiper FRIBA. Courtesy of Dictionary of Scottish Architects.

spire to examine some disturbed stonework reported by the 'steeplejack'.[68] Further repairs to the spire and weathervane were required in 1939 and were carried out by John Cumming & Co, at a cost of £80:

*The Weather Cock does not turn round completely only half and causes a heavy strain on the Masonry by giving resistance to the Gales. Requires to be taken off and new Ball-race fitted, and treated with Gold leaf. The Finale is good also supports of finale, but very badly corroded. Body of Spire: the joints of Masonry is [sic] very open from finale down 90 ft, also the first stone below crown stone is off its bed, and is turned, half ways round.[69]*

Some of the recurring problems experienced with the spire, as with other areas of the building, may have been due, at least in part, to hasty construction and poor workmanship. This was the implication at a meeting of the Managers in 1879, when a report was read on repairs to the drains:

*A stoppage and stench led to a part being opened up; this was found to be so defective and ill constructed that it required to be followed out revealing as they progressed more defects, the result being that the whole drainage of the Church had to be taken up and either altered or reconstructed and this at a cost of upwards of £50.[70]*

## 1899 Repairs

Study of the Dowanhill Church Records has revealed that the repairs carried out in 1899 were much more extensive than had previously been realised. On 6 January 1899, the Preses, Mr J Hubbard, announced that 'some very important repairs' would have to be undertaken that year.[71] One of the many problems to be examined was the ventilation, which was a recurring cause for complaint. The matters were referred to the Repairs Committee, who were instructed to make 'a careful inspection' of the Church, in the company of Mr Dansken, one of the Managers who perhaps had professional experience as a surveyor or architect. On the following Saturday, the Repairs Committee 'spent several hours' going round the building with Mr Dansken and made their report on 14 January. The main problems were believed to have been caused by dampness:

*The stone round the base of the pulpit structure was found in many places to be showing symptoms of decay and with all the appearance of getting rapidly worse. In seeking for a cause we discovered the presence of dry rot in some parts of the wood lining of the passage which runs across the back of the Church and in a small press immediately underneath the Pulpit. From what cause there should be any damp here we are unable to say having had no means of investigating beyond this point. What it may entail it is impossible to forecast but unless seen to at once the consequences may prove very serious.[72]*

The Committee also observed that 'the whole stone work of the pulpit and of the window behind it is much in need of cleaning'. The plaster was also discovered to have been damaged by water:

*The plaster on one entire side of the window in the west staircase has fallen away and looks like being caused by water from the outside. We think it would be well to have the pointing round all the windows examined and redone where found necessary.*

Cracks were also found in the same staircase and in the front lobby which the Committee advised would need further investigation. Damage to the painted decoration was also reported: 'In many parts of the Church, mostly at the sides of the windows and in one or two places of the roof and front vestibule, the Painting will have to be gone over & touched up', whilst 'the staircases will have to be redone almost entirely'. With regard to the complaints about the ventilation, the Committee were of the opinion that 'if anything is to be done it must only be after careful and mature consideration', though it also pointed out that 'there is only one ventilator in the roof which measures about 2 feet square'. They also observed that 'the heating apparatus will perhaps need some overhauling', although examination of the water pipes revealed that they were 'covered with a thick accumulation of dust which may in some measure account for the difficulty at times of properly heating the Church'. Double-glazing of the larger windows was suggested by Mr Dansken as a remedy for the problem of draughts and it was noted that this had recently been done in Hyndland Church with good results. It is worth noting that Dickie records that the west elevation of the Church (and perhaps other areas too) had ivy growing on it to such a height that it covered the carved heads.[73] This may have been a contributory factor to the deterioration in the condition of the building.

Given the extensive problems discovered in the building, the Committee advised that:

> It may be found necessary to refer to some of the original plans of the Church. In such case the services of Mr Leiper the architect of the Church, in whose possession they are still likely to be, would require to be called on. The Committee is of the opinion that in any case it would be well to have his advice before proceeding with anything of a serious nature.

Finally, the Committee considered it vital for the Managers to seek the congregation's permission to be given 'a free hand in respect of putting the Church in thorough repair at this time'. These powers were requested by the Managers at the AGM of the congregation on 18 January. Although no estimates for the repairs had yet been obtained, the Managers suggested that costs were likely to be around £500. They also stressed the need to act at once, 'as some of the repairs suggested were most pressing in view of the ravages of dry rot'.[74] However, as closure of the Church for repairs during the summer months had already been discussed, a member of the congregation, Mr James Sinclair proposed that 'there was no especial hurry' for the repairs to be carried out. Replying, Mr Dansken 'emphatically denied that there was no hurry and said the Church at present was in a very dangerous condition and quite unfit for use'. The Managers were granted the necessary powers to carry out the repairs, although in fact the work was not carried out until summer, when the Church was closed from the last Sunday in June until Sunday 20 August.[75]

At the end of January, the Managers instructed the Repairs Committee to seek 'such professional advice with regard to the condition of the Church as they may consider necessary'.[76] On 1 June, the Committee submitted 'an exhaustive report upon the Church buildings prepared [...] by Mr Leiper the architect along with Estimates for work recommended therein'.[77] Leiper's report

covered 'Heating and Ventilation; Decay in Stone and Woodwork; Platform; Damp; Tiling of Floor and Walls of Vestibule, Lobby and Back Passage; Stairs; Plasterwork; Painting & Decoration; Washhouse &c; Upper Rooms; Outside Work; Pointing; Boundary and Enclosure Walls; Ironwork; Doors & Windows; Pavement &c.'

The Managers rejected one of the estimates in Leiper's report: they considered the price of £174.8s. by Galbraith & Winton for repairs to the tiling too expensive, and this item was dropped from the schedule. As regards the problems of heating, ventilation and draughts, they concurred with Leiper that these were mainly due to lack of adequate maintenance:

> The opinion of the Architect and those of the Committee competent to judge is that any failure to act properly in the past and thereby causing Draughts has been due less to any defect in the Apparatus itself than to the accumulation of dust collected about the pipes and to the want of proper attention in the heating of the Church and to the opening and closing of the ventilator at the proper times.

The estimates for the other work were accepted. These totalled £464, including the redecoration (the most costly item – see **Chapter 7**) and the architect's fee of £25. An extract from the Church accounts for 1899 shows that the total cost of all repairs was £634.7s.8d, of which around £50 was for ordinary repairs.[78] The Managers resolved to pay off the debt as soon as possible, through a special collection at the services for the anniversary of the Church that year and by members' subscription. In connection with the appeal for funds, a printed statement was issued by the Managers, in which they expressed the hope that 'this special appeal will be promptly and liberally responded to, and that every member will consider it a duty and a privilege to contribute towards the preservation and beautifying of the House of God'.[79] Their hopes appear to have been realised, as in his Pastoral Letter in the Church's Annual Report, published in February 1900, Rev Dickie thanked the congregation for their 'hearty' response to the appeal for funds, and observed: 'It is only right that we should give God our best, and make His House beautiful'.[80]

The Managers' statement gave a detailed summary of the repairs carried out:

> The first thing dealt with was the damp in the north end of the church. A very deep trench was dug underneath the lane. This was carefully drained and filled up with stone slivers, and the walls and foundations coated with cement. It was also found necessary on account of the damp to renew the platform and several of the beams carrying the passages to the right and left of the pulpit. The wear over thirty years had seriously told upon the steps of the stairs leading to the galleries, vestry, &c. These have been repaired with a patent safety tread

*which looks well and is noiseless. A large amount of plaster work had to be undertaken, mostly in the staircases and the ceiling underneath parts of the gallery. The surface of the stone inside the edifice has been cleaned, that at base of pulpit redressed, and where destroyed by decay or fracture, replaced by the indenting of entirely new pieces. Several of the door steps have*

*also been renewed with Caithness slabs, and the tiles in vestibule and back passage levelled, and damaged ones replaced. The plumber work has also been overhauled. Iron gutters and gas fittings have been repaired, an earthenware tank has been placed in what is called 'the washing house' – used on occasion of our socials – and altogether the sanitary arrangements are now very complete. The heating appliances have had a thorough overhaul, and will now admit a fine steady flow of fresh heated air into the church. Improved ventilation has also been introduced into the vestry, session-house, and class-rooms.*[81]

Details were also given of the redecoration of the interior (see **Chapter 7**) and of the repainting of outer doors, windows and railings. In addition, 'the stonework round large windows and main door' had been 'double-coated outside with a patent composition to exclude damp'. The David and Miriam windows were also moved at this time and reinstalled as the central panels of the two large, three-light windows at the northern end of the east gallery: 'The two stained-glass windows representing 'David' and 'Miriam' in the front gable of the church (the gift of generous members of the church gone to their rest), were completely hidden by the organ, and it was thought desirable to remove them to the upper windows of the east wall of the church, where they can now be seen and admired.'[82] Finally, the upholstery work, including that of the pulpit was also renovated. The Managers concluded their statement by pointing out that 'the work has all been undertaken under the direction and supervision of Mr William Leiper, R.S.A., the architect who planned the church, and to whom they are indebted for his courtesy and attention'.

**Plate XXV** Grave Inscription of Daniel Cottier, family gravestone in Woodlawn Cemetery, The Bronx, New York. Courtesy of Ezra Shales.

[1] Notice to Members of Partick East UP Church, 8 Oct 1864, DCR CH3/1267/102.

[2] Missionary Committee, 8, 15 & 18 Aug 1864, DCR CH3/1267/43.

[3] Managers Minutes, 18 Aug 1864, DCR CH3/1267/7.

[4] Managers Minutes, 29 Aug 1864, DCR CH3/1267/7.

[5] Aitken's offer was read at the Managers' meeting on 18 Nov 1864, by which time the price had, however, increased to 7/6 per sq yd, Managers Minutes, 18 Nov 1864, DCR CH3/1267/7.

[6] Managers Minutes, 31 Oct 1864, DCR CH3/1267/7.

[7] Managers Minutes, 8 Nov 1864, DCR CH3/1267/7.

[8] Feu Contract between TL Paterson and James Watson and others, Trustees for Partick East UP Church, 9 May, 12 Jun & 30 Jun 1865, copy dated 1881, DCR CH3/1267/106.

[9] Managers Minutes, 8 Nov 1864, DCR CH3/1267/7.

[10] Managers Minutes, 18 Nov 1864, DCR CH3/1267/7.

[11] George Thomson, Notice to Members of Partick East UP Church, 8 Oct 1864, DCR CH3/1267/102; and Open Letter to Members of Partick East UP Church, 26 Nov 1864, DCR CH3/1267.

[12] Managers Minutes, 18 Nov 1864, DCR CH3/1267/7.

[13] Managers Minutes, 28 Nov 1864, DCR CH3/1267/7.

[14] Managers Minutes, 24 Jan 1865, DCR CH3/1267/7. The additional ground was negotiated with Paterson in April 1865 and the agreement reported at the Managers' Meeting on 1 May.

[15] Feu Contract, 1865 (1881), DCR CH3/1267/106.

[16] Managers Minutes, 18 Nov 1864, DCR CH3/1267/7.

[17] Managers Minutes, 28 Nov 1864, DCR CH3/1267/7. Haig & Low had recently completed a UP church in East Campbell St, Glasgow, see Williamson, Riches & Higgs 1990, 452.

[18] Managers Minutes, 28 Nov 1864, DCR CH3/1267/7.

[19] 'Instructions to Architects invited to furnish Designs for UP Church for Mr Lawrie's Congregation, Partick', 2 Dec 1864, DCR CH3/1267/105.

[20] John Honeyman's decision was reported at the Managers' Meeting of 13 Dec 1864; and Burnet's on 24 Jan 1865, Managers Minutes, DCR CH3/1267/7.

[21] Managers Minutes, 24 Jan 1865, DCR CH3/1267/7.

[22] 'Estimate of Probable Cost of Sundry Designs for Partick East UP Church', DCR CH3/1267/105.

[23] Managers Minutes, 4 Feb 1865, DCR CH3/1267/7.

[24] Managers Minutes, 4 Feb 1865, DCR CH3/1267/7.

[25] Congregational Meeting, 8 Feb 1865, Managers Minutes, DCR CH3/1267/7.

[26] Managers Minutes, 8 Feb 1865, DCR CH3/1267/7.

[27] 'Auditorium Nos 1 & 2', Competition Entries for the Design of Dowanhill Church, DCR CH3/1267/104.

[28] The three spires referred to may have been those of Kelvinside Free Church, Great Western Road, designed by JJ Stevenson in 1862; Lansdowne UP Church, designed by John Honeyman, 1862-3; and Trinity Church (now Henry Wood Hall), also by Honeyman, 1864. Alternatively, they may have been referring to Park Church, by JT Rochead, 1856-8.

[29] Managers Minutes, 2 Mar 1865, DCR CH3/1267/7.

[30] Report of Building Committee Meeting, 17 Mar 1865, in Managers Minutes, 18 Mar 1865, DCR CH3/1267/7.

[31] Managers Minutes, 18 Apr 1865, DCR CH3/1267/7.

[32] Managers Minutes, 1 May 1865, DCR CH3/1267/7.

[33] 'New United Presbyterian Church at Partick', Daily Mail, 8 Aug 1865, see cutting in DCR CH3/1267/7.

[34] Report on the laying of the Memorial Stone, Managers Minutes, DCR CH3/1267/7.

[35] 'New United Presbyterian Church at Partick', Daily Mail, 8 Aug 1865.

[36] Managers Minutes, 18 Apr 1865, DCR CH3/1267/7.

[37] Managers Minutes, 18 Apr 1865, DCR CH3/1267/7. See also the list of 'Estimated and Finished Costs', attached to the document of 'Mason's Extras, Dowanhill Church', DCR CH3/1267/105; and Dickie 1926, 79.

[38] List of 'Estimated and Finished Costs', in 'Mason's Extras', DCR CH3/1267/105; and Dickie 1926, 79.

[39] 'Measurement of Carpenter and Joiner Work of Dowanhill UP Church', 3 Dec 1866, DCR CH3/1267/103; 'Measurement of the Digging, Mason & Brick Work of Dowanhill UP Church', 13 Nov 1866, DCR CH3/1267/103.

[40] 'Mason's Extras'; and 'Abstract and Statement of Extra Cost of Mason Work', DCR CH3/1267/105.

[41] Meeting of Session, Trustees and Managers, 13 May 1867, DCR CH3/1267/7.

[42] 'Mason's Extras', DCR CH3/1267/105. See also Dickie 1926, 79-80.

[43] Managers Minutes, 25 Nov 1867, DCR CH3/1267/7; 'Mason's Extras', DCR CH3/1267/105.

[44] Printed leaflet on the opening of Dowanhill Church, 3 Nov 1866, DCR CH3/1267/105; Glasgow Herald, 10 Nov 1866.

[45] Glasgow Herald, 12 Nov 1866, 4.

[46] Letter from George Thomson to Board of Managers, 1 Dec 1869, DCR CH3/1267/102.

[47] Dickie 1926, 74.

[48] Dickie 1926, 75, supposed this to be the case, though there is as yet insufficient evidence of the cost of the windows on the east and west elevations and the rose window to confirm this.

[49] Dickie 1926, 75.

[50] Managers Minutes, 24 Nov 1866, DCR CH3/1267/7.

[51] Managers Minutes, 24 Nov 1866, DCR CH3/1267/7.

[52] Managers Minutes, 30 Sept 1867, DCR CH3/1267/7.

[53] Dickie 1926, 75.

[54] Managers Minutes, 24 Nov 1866, DCR CH3/1267/7.

[55] Congregational AGM, 25 Nov 1866; and Managers' Meeting, 2 Dec 1867, DCR CH3/1267/7.

[56] See especially the obituary by McNab 1916, 302-5.

[57] 'Paris Universal Exhibition 1867, British Section, Group I, Class IV, no. 67: 'Leiper, W., Glasgow/ Church Patrick [sic], Glasgow'. The inclusion of Leiper's design is noted in Worsdall 1966, 30.

[58] Paris Universal Exhibition 1867, British Section, Group I, Class IV, nos 40 and 63. No mention is made in the catalogue of the decoration of Townhead by Cottier.

[59] Work officially began on the Ste-Chapelle in 1841 and continued through to the 1860s, though the chapel was not officially opened till 1871. See Cohen 2005, Leniaud 2007, Cohen 2007.

[60] Dickie 1926, 71-2.

[61] Managers Minutes, 10 Aug 1874, DCR CH3/1267/7.

[62] Dickie 1926, 76.

[63] Managers Minutes, 4 Mar 1875, DCR CH3/1267/7.

[64] Managers Minutes, 20 Jan 1868, DCR CH3/1267/7.

[65] Managers Minutes, 30 Nov 1869, DCR CH3/1267/7.

[66] Managers Minutes, 10 Aug 1874, DCR CH3/1267/7.

[67] Managers Minutes, 21 Sept 1874, DCR CH3/1267/7.

[68] Letter from William Hunter McNab, 8 Nov 1916, DCR CH3/1267/110.

[69] Report by John Cumming & Co, 7 Apr 1939, DCR CH3/1267/84.

[70] Managers Minutes, 26 Nov 1879, DCR CH3/1267/7.

[71] Managers Minutes, 6 Jan 1899, DCR CH3/1267/7.

[72] Report of Repairs Committee, in Managers Minutes, 14 Jan 1899, DCR CH3/1267/7.

[73] Dickie 1926, 72.

[74] Congregational AGM, 18 Jan 1899, DCR CH3/1267/7.

[75] Managers Minutes, 1 Jun 1899, DCR CH3/1267/7.

[76] Managers Minutes, 25 Jan 1899, DCR CH3/1267/7.

[77] Managers Minutes, 1 Jun 1899, DCR CH3/1267/7.

[78] Extract from Dowanhill Church Accounts, 1891-99, DCR CH1267/104. See also the 'Statement of the Managers', *DCMR* Nov 1899, and copy in DCR CH3/1267/7.

[79] 'Statement of the Managers', *DCMR* (Nov 1899).

[80] Dickie, Pastoral letter, in Congregational Report for 1899, DCR CH3/1267/11.

[81] 'Statement of the Managers', *DCMR* (Nov 1899).

[82] Dickie 1926, 75.

# 7 DOCUMENTING THE PAINTED DECORATION
## Hilary Macartney and Alan Ferdinand

Plate XXVI

*A* Graphic Reconstruction of Decoration on the Upper Nave Wall, Ceiling Spandrels and Timber Tracery of Dowanhill Church, 2010. Courtesy of Groves-Raines Studio.

*C* Decorative Scheme, Dowanhill Church Nave, D Cottier, 1866, detail from a photograph taken before 1906 illustrated in W Dickie, 1926, *History of Dowanhill Church 1823-1923*. Courtesy of Four Acres Charitable Trust.

*B* Decorative Scheme on the Nave Ceiling, Dowanhill Church, Daniel Cottier, 1866, detail from photograph taken in 1930s. Courtesy of Four Acres Charitable Trust.

*D* Ceiling Decoration, Dowanhill Church, D Cottier, 1866. Courtesy of Groves-Raines Studio.

## Introduction

Surprisingly, there is almost no reference to Cottier's painted decoration scheme in the surviving records of Dowanhill Church. The earliest documents relating to the building and decoration of the Church, including the brief to the architects and the Minutes of the Board of Managers for that period, make no mention of it. For example, the instructions to the architects involved in the competition for the building contract allowed only for 'Painting or Staining and Varnishing all wood and iron work' in the budget for the project.[1] Likewise, there is no mention of Cottier or a contract for painting in the schedule of quotes from the various trades considered at a joint meeting of the Managers, Trustees and Kirk Session of the Church on 18 April 1865.[2] It is possible that the decision to incorporate a scheme of painted decoration was taken only once the construction of the building was nearing completion. At the laying of a memorial stone on 7 August 1865, during the building of the Church, George Thomson, Preses (chairman) of the Board of Managers, gave a statement to the *Daily Mail*, in which he mentioned that the ceiling would be plastered to prevent draughts and to improve acoustics but declared that the Church would be 'grand in its simplicity and massiveness, dependent for its beauty not on costly ornament, but rather on the harmony of its lines and proportions'.[3] However, his comments on the intended lack of ornament may have referred mainly to the architecture and to the exterior of the building.

## The Original Decoration

The only document found so far which refers to the painted decoration by Daniel Cottier is a List of Mason's Extras relating to the costs of the Church, in which a payment of £397.10/- to Cottier for 'Painting' is recorded. This document is undated but probably dates from 1866-7, since the dates on the main documents relating to the measurement of masonry and joinery work date from the end of 1866.[4] The painting was presumably completed, or mainly completed by the time the Church was opened

Fig 67 Interior, Dowanhill Church before 1906, photograph from W Dickie, 1926, *History of Dowanhill Church 1823-1923*. Courtesy of Four Acres Charitable Trust.

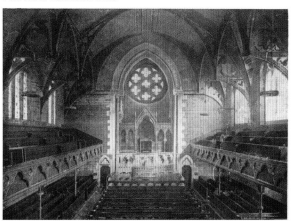

for worship on 11 November 1866, and both the painted decoration and the stained glass windows by Cottier were favourably mentioned in the *Glasgow Herald*'s report on the opening of the Church. The report also suggested that the harmony achieved between architecture and decoration in the scheme (figs 67 and 68) was due to the cooperative relationship between Cottier and the architect, William Leiper:

> The whole church is painted throughout after the medieval manner, and, with the exception of Townhead Parish Church, is perhaps the only Presbyterian church in Scotland in which painted windows and mural decoration have been carried out as in the old times. The decorations and painted windows have been admirably executed by Mr Cottier, to whom praise is due for the manner in which he has carried out the views of the architect. The aim of the latter has been to build a Presbyterian church which might have some claim to be reckoned artistic.[5]

The *Glasgow Herald*'s reference to Townhead Parish Church is significant, since this was Cottier's first major commission for a scheme of painted decoration and some stained glass in Glasgow in 1865. There, he is likely to have worked closely with the architect JJ Stevenson, within whose practice William Leiper also worked. Some idea of the boldness of this now disappeared decorative scheme, and an impression of the impact of its ground-breaking nature in a Scottish Presbyterian Church can be gained from an account by James Mavor, a prominent figure in literary circles in Glasgow:

Fig 68 Interior of Dowanhill Church after 1906, glass lantern slide. Courtesy of Four Acres Charitable Trust.

*Undoubtedly the decoration was striking enough. Great masses of positive colour, red and blue, with figures of dense black – the motif was Egyptian and the design might have found a fitting place in a great hall of the Pharaohs. In an ecclesiastical building it was inappropriate; in any building in Western Europe the effect would have been bizarre; the design was out of scale and wanting in the repose indispensable in church architecture. Nevertheless, the decoration was bold and in its way original. I felt at once, here at least is the work of a designer with brains and courage.*[6]

It is clear that the successful collaboration between Cottier and Leiper at Dowanhill was an important factor in the boldness and innovation of the scheme. The precise role of Leiper in its design is not known, but it is significant that in his obituary of the architect in 1916, William Hunter McNab, Leiper's principal pupil and architectural associate, stressed his master's painterly as well as his architectural qualities and qualifications, including his time spent studying as a painter at the Academie Julian, Paris, in the 1870s, and his election to the Royal Scottish Academy in 1896. In particular, McNab praised Leiper's sense of colour in his architectural and decorative schemes. He cited the touches of colour 'judiciously introduced' in the combination of mosaic, coloured glazed decoration and rich terracotta brick on the Venetian Gothic façade of Templeton's factory as the outstanding example in Leiper's architecture: 'The principal western front seen on a summer afternoon is rich and resplendent in brilliant and harmonious colour […] nothing finer, in the opinion of competent critics, is to be found outside of Italy.' Of decorative schemes, he mentioned Leiper's supervision of the scheme of coloured decoration for the Banqueting Hall in Glasgow City Chambers, the last series of decorative panels for which were completed just before his death. He also pointed to a specialism in decorative schemes for churches:

*Church decoration was one of Mr Leiper's strong points, his fine sense of colour giving him special powers in this direction. In addition to some of his own churches, where colour decoration came into play, he was called upon to design appropriate schemes for others affording less opportunity for satisfactory treatment. Amongst these may be mentioned Park Free Church and West Parish Church, Helensburgh, where, with very unpromising conditions, marked success was achieved in both.*[7]

No record has yet emerged of the reactions of the Dowanhill congregation and the Board of Managers themselves to their scheme of painted decoration and glass. However, an indication that some may have been taken aback – at least initially – by its boldness is suggested by a comment about the collecting plates by one of the Managers most closely involved in the

**Fig 69** Dowanhill Collection Stand, ca.1866, W Leiper & D Cottier. Courtesy of Four Acres Charitable Trust.

building of the new church, Alexander Kay (fig 69). At a meeting on 24 November 1866, Kay complained that the collecting plates 'were too highly decorated'.[8] The plate-stands closely match the colours and motifs used in the Church itself and are likely to have been executed at the same time as the main scheme or immediately after. Interestingly, however, Kay went on to commission Leiper to build his own house, Cornhill House, in which Cottier was involved in the interior decoration and stained glass. The interior was described as very brightly coloured (see **Catalogue** below). It may be, therefore, that Kay's tastes changed after completion of Dowanhill Church, or as a result of it. Or he may have considered bright colour more appropriate in a secular and domestic environment.

Reverend Dickie, who joined the Church as Associate Minister in 1889, records in his book on the history of the Church, published in 1926, that older members of the congregation remembered the scheme being arrived at through a process of 'rubbing in and washing out' over a period of weeks while Cottier adjusted the motifs and colour harmonies: 'At last, he was satisfied with his gold stars picked out in the deep blue of the roof, and his wonderful harmony of brick-red, brown, black and yellow covering the walls in parallelograms.'[9]

Modern examination of the paintwork shows that it appears to have a powdery surface, suggestive of a water-soluble pigment binder which has degraded through dampness over the years (fig 70). This seems to suggest that Cottier used a traditional distemper technique applied to damp plaster. Dickie, himself an accomplished artist, described the scheme as distemper, and this seems to be further borne out by the records of the 1937 scheme (see below) which claimed that the 'water colour' paint on the ceiling had to be sealed with a varnish in order to preserve it.

Modern examination of paint layers and paint samples reveals that the original scheme consisted of painted bands, imitating ashlar stone (fig 71), in Venetian red, burnt sienna and yellow ochre on the walls, with friezes of decorative motifs, including stylised flower roundels, quatrefoils and a complex pattern of pairs of semi-spirals with paddles and dots (fig 72).[10] Roundels were black on grey within the hammerbeams and grey on black on the walls (figs 73-75). In the recess of the pulpit wall, the perpends of the ashlar bands were finished with pairs of scrolls and dots. Radiating from the stone voussoirs around the arch surrounding the rose window on the same wall were patterned bands of roundels, flowers, scallop edging and dots (figs 76-77). The vaulting of the upper window arches between the hammerbeams in the nave (fig 78) were brightly painted in yellow ochre, rich brown and black, with sawtooth motifs, flowers, dots, curved wave lines and a bold, geometric pattern which frames a large, stylised leaf form. The ceiling was divided into six bays and was painted deep blue with star motifs and decorative borders of the sawtooth pattern, lunettes, dots and wave lines (fig 79). Star motifs typically consisted of gold stars (fig 80) and complex star shapes, made up of a red circle, surrounded by a green band, eight red dots and eight tendril-like points. There are also other variants of stars motifs on the lower vaulted areas. Some of the decoration on the ceiling and the springs of the arches appears to have been set out using stencils but executed freehand.

**Fig 70** Original Red Tempera Paint on Nave Ceiling, Dowanhill Church. Courtesy of Historic Scotland.

**Fig 71** Ashlar Banding Ground Floor Nave, Dowanhill Church. Courtesy of Historic Scotland.

**Fig 72** Nave 'Paddle' Design, Dowanhill Church. Courtesy of Historic Scotland.

**Fig 73** Nave Tracery Roundel, Dowanhill Church. Courtesy of Historic Scotland.

**Fig 74** Nave Roundel, Dowanhill Church. Courtesy of Historic Scotland.

**Fig 75** Nave String Course Roundel, Dowanhill Church. Courtesy of Historic Scotland.

**Fig 76** North East Nave Voussoir, Dowanhill Church. Courtesy of Historic Scotland.

**Fig 77** Nave Voussoir Ornament, Dowanhill Church. Courtesy of Historic Scotland.

**Fig 78** Decoration on Nave Clerestory Window Arch Spandrel, Dowanhill Church. Courtesy of Historic Scotland.

**Fig 79** Sawtooth Motif on Nave Ceiling, Dowanhill Church. Courtesy of Historic Scotland.

**Fig 80** Star Motif on Nave Ceiling, Dowanhill Church. Courtesy of Historic Scotland.

The hammerbeams, of yellow pine, were painted rich red with black bands and quatrefoils, with chamfers in red or green with black dots, and stop chamfers in red or green (fig 81). The hammerbeam edges were also ebonised. The inset designs on the wooden gallery fronts were picked out in gold, red and black. Wooden elements appear to have been finished with a coat of varnish, leaving the yellow pine to show through in unpainted areas. The cast-iron columns supporting the gallery were painted a deep Prussian blue, with bands of red and gold leaf. The wooden pulpit canopy was painted with curtain motifs, quatrefoils, lunettes, tongues of flame, dots and stars in green, gold leaf, red and black, with a painted red and black tile pattern on its roof (figs 82-85). The relief cinquefoils on the honey-coloured stone pulpit were picked out in red. Below it, a frieze of quatrefoils was painted in red with black dots on the sides and black with red dots on the central, projecting pulpit bay (fig 86).

**Fig 81** Nave Hammerbeam Arch Decoration, Dowanhill Church. Courtesy of Historic Scotland.

**Fig 82** Arcaded Pulpit Canopy, Dowanhill Church, W Leiper. D Cottier. Courtesy of Four Acres Charitable Trust.

**Fig 83** Pulpit Hood Underside, Dowanhill Church, revealing the original decoration beneath subsequent layers of purple paint. Courtesy of Historic Scotland.

**Fig 84** Pulpit Rear Panelling, Dowanhill Church. Courtesy of Historic Scotland.

**Fig 85** Pulpit Canopy Roof, Dowanhill Church. Courtesy of Historic Scotland.

**Fig 86** Pulpit Stone Balustrade and Base, Dowanhill Church. Courtesy of Historic Scotland.

**Plate XXVIII** Graphic Reconstruction of Decoration on the Upper Nave North Wall of Dowanhill Church, 2010. Courtesy of Groves-Raines Studio.

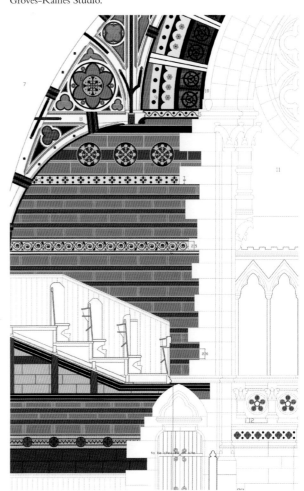

**Plate XXVII** Graphic Reconstruction of Decoration on the Upper Nave South Wall of Dowanhill Church, 2010. Courtesy of Groves-Raines Studio.

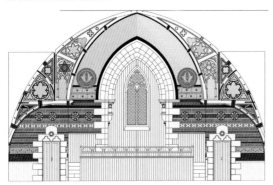

**Plate XXIX** Graphic Reconstruction of Decoration on the Nave Side Wall, Timber Gallery Front, Window Arch Spandrels and Timber Tracery of Dowanhill Church, 2010. Courtesy of Groves-Raines Studio.

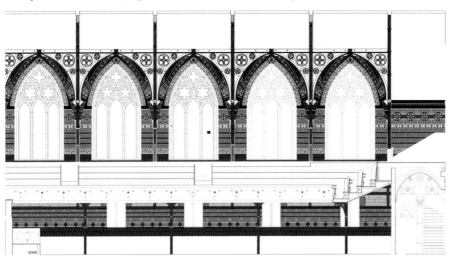

## Redecoration in 1899

The 1899 redecoration is well documented in the records of the Board of Managers of the Church. On 6 January 1899, the Preses, Mr J Hubbard, announced that 'some very important repairs' would have to be undertaken that year.[11] After a full inspection of the building, it was reported that the stone base of the pulpit was 'showing symptoms of decay' in many places, due to dry rot in the wood lining of the passage at the back of the pulpit and the cupboard below it.[12] It was also found that 'In many parts of the Church, mostly at the sides of the windows and in one or two places of the roof and

**Plate XXX** Graphic Reconstruction of Decorative Motifs and Banding from Dowanhill Church, 2010. Courtesy of Groves-Raines Studio.

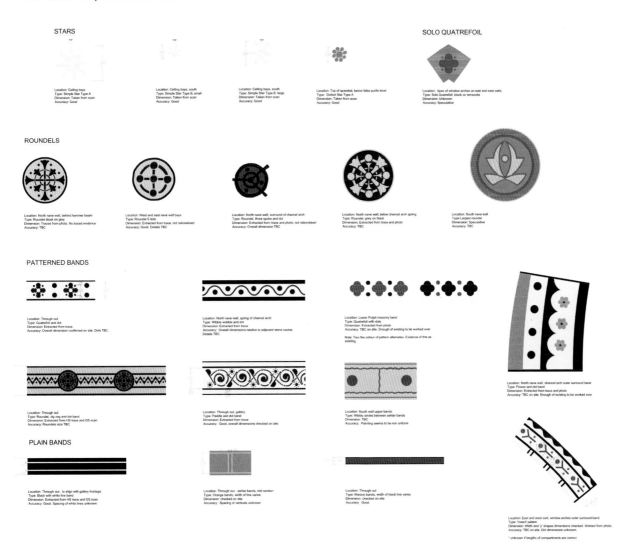

front vestibule, the Painting will have to be gone over & touched up', whilst 'the staircases will have to be redone almost entirely'. The fact that the West elevation of the Church (and perhaps other areas too) had ivy growing on it to such a height that it covered the carved heads may have been a contributory factor to the deterioration in the condition of the building.[13] The repairs required were so extensive that Mr Dansken, the Manager responsible for inspecting the Church on behalf of the Board of Managers, declared the Church to be 'in a very dangerous condition and quite unfit for use'.[14] It was considered advisable to consult the original plans of the building, if they still existed, and the architect, William Leiper was contacted. Leiper prepared 'an exhaustive report' on the state of the building, including the decay in the stonework and the state of 'Plasterwork, Painting & Decoration'.[15] The contract for repainting was awarded to Guthrie & Wells (which had been formed by two of Cottier's assistants), on the recommendation of Leiper. The cost was estimated at £272 out of a total estimated

cost of £464 for all the repairs. The Minutes of the Kirk Session show that the Church was closed to carry out the repairs and redecoration from 25 June to 20 August, 1899.[16] An extract from the Church accounts for 1899 contains an entry for 'Repainting the church' and shows that the total cost of all repairs was £634.7s.8d, of which around £50 were for 'ordinary' repairs.[17] In his Pastoral Letter in the Church's Annual Report for 1899, Rev Dickie thanked the congregation for their 'hearty' response to the appeal for funds for the redecoration, and observed: 'It is only right that we should give God our best, and make His House beautiful'.[18]

The most detailed record of the 1899 redecoration is a statement on the repairs and redecoration published by the Managers in November 1899. This shows that 'a large amount of plaster work had to be undertaken, mostly in the staircases and ceiling underneath parts of the gallery'. In addition, 'the surface of the stone inside the edifice has been cleaned, that at base of the pulpit redressed, and where destroyed by decay or fracture, replaced by the indenting of entirely new pieces.' The statement continues:

> The most important part of the work, however, has been the painting. The walls of the church were formerly painted in distemper, a medium which lends itself very well to mural decoration, but, unfortunately, is not lasting. The subject had the most thoughtful consideration of the Managers, and concurrent with the advice of the architect, it was resolved to repaint them in oil, which, although more costly, will no doubt be found cheaper in the end. No change has been made, however, in the original and beautiful scheme of colour and design, these, in almost every detail, having been faithfully reproduced. The walls, lobbies, staircases and ceiling under gallery received four coats oil paint, and the ten artistic gas pendants re-done with gold leaf. All the woodwork has been cleaned, and the decoration over the pulpit most carefully treated. The ornaments in front of the gallery have been filled in with fresh colour and regilded [...] In conclusion, the Managers have to say that the work has all been undertaken under the direction and supervision of Mr. William Leiper, R.S.A., the architect who planned the church, and to whom we are indebted for his courtesy and attention.[19]

In his book, Dickie claimed that in the 1899 repainting, it was 'principally [...] the re-decoration of the walls [that] required attention'. He also recalled his trepidation about the repainting:

> Some of us were apprehensive lest any proposal should be entertained to disturb Cottier's masterly scheme, which unfortunately had only been executed in distemper and lacked permanency. As it was, Mr. Leiper, the architect of the Church, having been called in for consultation, it was agreed that Cottier's scheme of colour and design should be adhered to, and reproduced as rigidly as possible in three coats of oil colour. It is to be hoped that in any future generations no Philistine will arise to propose any departure from Cottier's design which remains and should remain a charming work of art and a noble monument to his genius.[20]

In a copy of a letter from Andrew Wells to William Gibson in 1914, Wells states that Cottier 'was designer of the Glass Windows and interior of Dowanhill UF [United Free] Church with which I have long been associated myself'.[21] This statement probably indicates that Wells was personally involved in the 1899 repainting of the Church. It is also likely that he assisted Cottier in the original painting of it in 1866, as he is known to have been working as one of Cottier's assistants by that date.

Modern examination of the paint layers and paint samples appears to bear out Dickie's account that the 1899 redecoration consisted principally of repainting the walls. It also confirms that the medium was oil paint, several layers of which can be detected, though it

has not yet been possible to determine whether three coats (as Dickie claimed) or four coats (as the Managers stated) were applied. In addition, the repainting on this occasion does appear to have followed the original Cottier scheme, as both the Managers and Dickie reported. However, although it faithfully reproduced the motifs and decorative elements, these are slightly misaligned with the originals (fig 87). The original colours of the ashlar banding were also altered in this repainting, though the general principle of earth colours was adhered to. Such changes may explain the qualification in the Managers' Statement that the original scheme was faithfully reproduced 'in almost every detail'. The second coat of the three coats of varnish that can be detected by modern investigation on the woodwork may date from 1899. If so, the woodwork may not have been thoroughly washed down on this occasion, contrary to the Managers' Statement, as this layer of varnish contains soot which has darkened the original scheme, especially on the hammerbeams and the spandrels.

## The Rev Dickie and the Painted Decoration Scheme, 1930s

Another valuable document concerning the painted decoration in Dowanhill Church occurs in an article on Cottier which the Rev Dickie wrote for the church's newsletter for May-June 1930. His biographical information on Cottier appears to have been taken from obituaries of the designer. Most valuable, however, are Dickie's comments on the decorative scheme at Dowanhill Church, which convey his deeply felt reverence for the innovation and unity of Cottier's artistic vision:

> He had strong and decided opinions and very independent tastes, which led him often away from the conventions of his time. We have an example of his individuality in taste in the decorative scheme and colour of Dowanhill Church – the blue ceiling, picked out with gold stars, the bold parallelograms of brick-red, buff, yellow, and black of the walls, and the pulpit with the tongues of fire descending upon the preacher. This was something new in decoration, and at the time was considered rather bizarre, but it was not long till Cottier had his followers and imitators in decorative taste. You see also his love of colour and design in the windows of Dowanhill Church, which harmonise with the wall decorations. No matter how bleak and grey it may be outside, once you come inside its walls you feel that sunshine is streaming through the windows and the walls are always warm and comfortable, and you are at home, as you should be, in the House of God.[22]

Dickie concluded his article with a heartfelt plea for the preservation of Cottier's scheme at Dowanhill, which was only partly heeded in the redecoration of 1937: 'May his decorations in windows and on walls of Dowanhill be preserved for all time for their own sakes and in memory of a great Artist!'[23]

**Plate XXXI** Graphic Reconstruction of a Selection of Cottier's Colours, scanned image from colour swatches prepared by Jane Davies following analysis of original pigments. Courtesy of Four Acres Charitable Trust.

**Fig 87** Wells Decorative Scheme, Dowanhill Church. Courtesy of Historic Scotland.

**Plate XXXII** Ceiling Decoration, Dowanhill Church, D Cottier, 1866. Courtesy of Groves-Raines Studio.

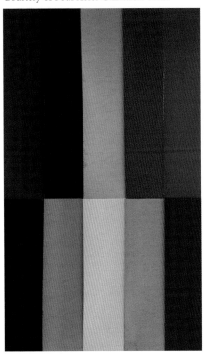

## Redecoration in 1937

The 1937 repainting of the Church, like that of 1899, is also well documented in archival sources. The condition of the painted decoration was again giving cause for concern in the 1930s, as was recorded at the Church's Annual General Meeting for 1933-4, when the Preses of the Board of Managers informed the congregation that 'the interior decoration of the Church was […] a matter which, in the near future, would call for very careful consideration.[24] Fundraising for the redecoration began in 1934 and included a sale of twenty-five watercolours and twenty-five pastels by the Rev Dickie on 11-13 December 1934, which raised nearly £200.[25] However, Dr Dickie died in 1935, before redecoration was carried out. In view of his warning against 'any departure from Cottier's design', and his belief in the importance of preserving it 'for all time', he might not have approved of the extent of the changes made to the original scheme in this redecoration. A joint appeal for funds for the redecoration and for a suitable memorial to the Church's 'beloved pastor' was officially launched in January 1937, when the congregation were reminded that 'we have had the privilege during many years to worship in a beautiful Church, and it is our duty to maintain the fabric worthily and in turn to hand it over to our children in a condition similar to that in which we have received it'.[26]

A committee was formed to advise the Board of Managers on the redecoration of the Church and the memorial to the Rev Dickie. They sought advice from Sir DY Cameron, who had been one of the pioneering group of artists known as the Glasgow Boys in the late nineteenth century.[27] Cameron, who had himself been baptised into the United Presbyterian Church, was responsible for the 'scheme of daring but harmonious decoration' which had transformed the hall in which the ceremony of reunification of the Church of Scotland and the United Free Church took place in Edinburgh in 1929. From 1934 until his death in 1945, he was Vice-Convenor of the Church of Scotland's Advisory Committee on Artistic Questions and advised on many programmes of redecoration of Scottish churches, in which he described his chief concern as being to achieve 'seemliness'.[28] After visiting Dowanhill Church, he wrote with his suggestions on 4 April 1937. This letter does not appear to have survived but in his reply of 8 April, the Session Clerk, Mr McAllister, thanked Cameron for his 'valuable suggestions' and for his 'very sympathetic consideration of our difficulties in the matter of the re-decoration of the interior', adding that 'we will be most grateful for the further help which you so kindly offer'.[29] The full extent of Cameron's input is not yet clear but he may have had a key role in suggesting the changes to and omission of some of the original motifs, such as the replacement of the flower at the apex of the pulpit canopy with the Church of Scotland's burning bush symbol or the replacement of the flower roundels within the hammerbeams on the north (pulpit) wall with Greek crosses. The precise role of another advisor, JD MacGregor, DA, HM Inspector of Schools for Art, who was co-opted to the Redecoration Committee, is likewise not known.[30]

The Rev Baxter also referred to the valued advisory role of DY Cameron, as well as that of the architect Thomas Taylor, of the firm of Hutton & Taylor, in the April issue of the Church newsletter, in which he urged everyone to contribute to the Redecoration Fund. According to Baxter, 'if the tributes of these experts regarding the beauty of our Church as a whole could be heard by all our members, there is not one, man, woman or child, but would be **eager to have some share** in the Re-decoration were it only by the humblest of gifts'.[31] Special fundraising events included a Grand Concert in the Church Hall, with choral and instrumental music, a 'distinguished Sketch Party', and 'a clever Conjurer'.[32]

Meanwhile, the architect Mr Taylor had been briefed on Cameron's suggestions and asked to supply estimates of the costs of the 'various schemes and alterations proposed' by 20 April.[33] The Board of Managers met the following day, when the options were considered of '1. Repainting Church with existing scheme including removal of all varnish and stain from all woodwork'; or '2. Washing, instead of painting, roof and walls'. The Redecoration Committee's recommendations were 'to wash and touch up roof & trusses; remove varnish & stain from all woodwork; repaint the walls in accordance with existing scheme omitting certain extraneous features', and these were unanimously adopted.[34] The final decision to go ahead with this scheme was taken at a meeting of the congregation on 4 July and the Church was closed from mid-July to September while work was carried out.[35]

The contract for redecoration was awarded to George W Sellars & Sons, 239 West George St., who submitted the lowest tender of £1250, though their final price was lowered to £771.13s.[36] One of the highest tenders, for £1347, was submitted by Guthrie & Wells Ltd, which had carried out the 1899 redecoration, and which had been formed with Cottier's former assistant Andrew Wells. As discussed above (**Redecoration in 1899**), the award of the contract to Guthrie & Wells in 1899 was made on the advice of Leiper himself. Significantly, the link with Cottier as the original designer of the entire decorative scheme at Dowanhill Church was thus broken with the contract for redecoration in 1937. This decision may in part have led to some of the difficulties encountered during the contract. According to the Report of the Redecoration Committee in the Church newsletter for September 1937, the work had at first proceeded steadily according to plan. However,

> It was then discovered that the roof was the original water colour paint done when the Church was built in 1866, and, in washing, had to be very carefully handled. It was then found necessary to varnish over in order to preserve it for the future. In addition, the plaster work was found defective in many places, and this has caused additional expense to be incurred. It is estimated £100 additional will be required to cover these items.[37]

A list of 'Principal Extras' in a statement of the costs of redecoration also includes entries for 'Cleaning down old stone', 'Plywood filling in at Canopy [of pulpit]' and 'Repairs to plaster Work after other Tradesmen and where rotted'.[38] 'Covering front of Gallery with Plywood' at an estimated cost of £50 was also listed as no. 12 in the Redecoration Committee's list of redecoration tasks for consideration at their meeting on 21 April.[39] The total cost of the repairs, including redecoration, alterations to the chancel and provision of elders' stalls, the memorial plaque to Rev Dickie and installation of new heating and lighting (which included new, overhead lighting cut into the ceiling bays), as well as slating and plumbing repairs, was £2608, towards which a special grant of £560 was obtained from the Trustees of the late James Baird of Auchmedden.[40]

The Managers and Kirk Session appear to have been pleased with the scheme of redecoration, and the Session Clerk reported in a letter of 5 October that, at the service of rededication, 'the Church was looking beautiful. The renovations have resulted in lightening the building'.[41]

Recent examination of paint layers and paint samples appears to bear out the archival evidence that the original scheme was broadly followed, though 'certain extraneous features' were indeed omitted or replaced. Overall, the decoration became less classical and more Celtic (compare pre-1906 and post-1937 scheme views, (fig 88). The roundels (fig 89) on the upper walls were replaced by gilded Celtic knots, the quatrefoils were replaced by intersecting circles and the pattern of dots and paddles was replaced by a Celtic intertwined rope design. On the lower walls, the frieze of roundels was dispensed with and painted over with ashlar bands. In the recess of the pulpit wall, the decorated ashlar bands of the original scheme were replaced by plain ashlar banding. Above this, on the same wall, the bands of decoration radiating from the stone voussoirs were rather gauchely replaced by horizontal ashlar bands which destroyed the harmony between architecture and decoration that was a key feature of Cottier's scheme. Otherwise, the original scheme of painted ashlar bands was generally repeated and the use of earth colours continued. The paint used was oil paint, though it seems to have been applied in very thin layers, particularly on the main areas of ashlar banding, with the result that it has proved difficult to reveal in recent tests. As stated in the church newsletter, the ceiling and the springs of the arches were not repainted but a coat of varnish was applied. The painted decoration on the inner surfaces of the pulpit canopy was covered over by plywood, as noted in the list of Principal Extras. The outer surfaces of the canopy, including its roof, was overpainted with woodgrain effect and the flower motif at the apex of the central bay was replaced by the burning bush symbol of the Church of Scotland (fig 90). The photographic evidence of the 1937 scheme appears to show that the painted frieze of quatrefoils on the pulpit stonework was modified to look less

**Fig 88** Celtic Decorative Scheme, photograph taken in the 1930s. Courtesy of Four Acres Charitable Trust.

**Fig 89** Celtic Ornament, Dowanhill Church. Courtesy of Historic Scotland.

**Fig 90** Pulpit Roundel, Dowanhill Church, before and after revealing the original decoration under the 1930s wood grain. Behind are remains of wallpaper from the 1960s decorative scheme. Courtesy of Historic Scotland.

*A* Pulpit Roundel, Dowanhill Church, showing original Cottier cinquefoil ornament containing a circular band with nine dots. Courtesy of Historic Scotland.

*B* Pulpit Roundel, Dowanhill Church, with Burning Bush motif from the 1930s Celtic decorative scheme. Courtesy of Historic Scotland.

prominent, although this has not so far been confirmed by modern examination of the paint layers. Likewise, it is not yet clear whether the tasks of 'remov[ing] varnish and stain from all woodwork' agreed by the Managers were actually carried out, or if the second, sooty layer of varnish was in fact applied at this date. The external faces of the wooden pulpit canopy show signs of having been washed and rubbed down before they were covered with oil paint with woodgrain effect.

**Redecoration in the 1960s**

The most radical departure from the original scheme of decoration occurred in the 1960s, when all remaining traces of the original Cottier scheme were painted over. The Dowanhill Church Archives at Glasgow City Archives contain few documents covering this period. The Minute Books of the Board of Managers and the Kirk Session have not been located to date, and further research on this period of the history of the Church and its fabric would be desirable. Fortunately however, copies of the church newsletter, the *Dowanhill Church Monthly Record* have been kept by Partick Trinity Church.[42] The

issue of the newsletter for November 1962 shows that there was concern about the condition of the interior decoration by this date and a desire to instigate an appeal for funds. A letter to the Editor made the case:

*Dear Sir*

*As members of this congregation we feel that our Church is badly in need of re-decoration. Realising that this is at the present day a costly business, requiring several thousands of pounds, we as a family have set ourselves a target, for session 1962-63, of endeavouring to raise at least £5 towards this project. We are certain that many other individual members, families and groups would be only too willing to raise something towards this project and we suggest that a target be set and a fund raised so that by our combined efforts, whether they be large or small, the goal may be reached and our Church made more beautiful. Enclosed is 10/- which is part of the proceeds from our first venture, the total of which we hope to forward within the next week or two.*

*Yours sincerely,*

*Church Members*[43]

The letter, the aim of making 'our Church more beautiful', and the initial donation were welcomed by the Editor as 'a worthwhile example of private enterprise'. A Redecoration Account was opened, and stood at £3 10s by the end of 1962.[44]

The letter proposing the redecoration project appeared in the same issue of the magazine as the first letter from the new minister, Rev Henry Chisholm, whose induction had taken place in September 1962, following the retiral of Dr Baxter at the end of 1961, and both Mr Chisholm's arrival and the repainting were seen as ways of revitalising the Church at the time. Further donations were acknowledged in the church newsletter in early 1962, and the appeal to raise funds for the redecoration was officially launched on 28 March 1963, at an Extraordinary General Meeting. A special committee was formed, consisting of three members appointed by the Kirk Session, three appointed by the Managers, one by the Women's Guild, three by the congregation, and a Convenor, Mr Norman S Miller. The appeal aimed to raise up to £5000, up to half of which would come from the Church's largest bequest, the Barbour Bequest, left by Dr William C Barbour in 1953. Promises of donations had to be made by the end of April, and the scheme was carried out between the end of June and the end of August that year, during which time services were held in the church hall.[45] Additional funds were raised by the Church's first garden fete, held in the Victory Ground (now Memorial Garden) behind the Church on 15 June, 'to contribute to the cost of painting and preserving the interior of the Church'.[46] In fact the total cost of the redecoration scheme was £3200, considerably lower than the £5000 budgeted for, which had included estimates for electrical work that was not in the end carried out.[47]

It is not clear exactly when the decision was made to paint over the painted decoration. In March 1963 a letter requesting donations was sent to members of the congregation by the Convenor of the Redecoration Committee. This contained a brief outline of the proposed work: 'We intend to repaint the walls and ceiling, clean and preserve the interior stonework and roof beams, overhaul and if thought desirable, alter the lighting, and refloor the porch and vestibule.'[48] Although an intention to 'repaint' the walls and ceiling was declared, this could have meant that the scheme visible at the time (the 1930s scheme) was intended to be preserved and reproduced. Significantly, the letter also gave the following assurance: 'We are of course, seeking the advice of the Assembly and Presbytery Committees on artistic questions and their recommendations will be given full consideration before we decide on the final scheme.' The publicity for the fete also referred to the aim of 'preserving the interior' and this may indicate that that the decision to cover over all visible painted decoration occurred at a late stage in the redecoration plans.

The lower costs incurred by simply painting over the decorative scheme, rather than trying to reproduce it (as had happened in 1899) or to simplify it (as occurred in 1937) must have made this an attractive option. It should be borne in mind too that at the time, the only decorative scheme visible would have been the 1937 Celtic scheme, except for the ceiling with its stars, which was the only area where the original Cottier scheme could still be seen. Whether the committee was aware of this, or whether they believed the Cottier scheme to be irrecoverable is difficult to determine. In any case, it is hard to imagine that the 1963 redecoration scheme would have been approved without considerable debate. Not surprisingly perhaps, the Rev Chisholm admitted in the church newsletter to feeling nervous the first time he mounted the pulpit to address the congregation again after the redecoration. The reopening was clearly regarded as a big event and was well attended by the congregation who came, wrote Rev Chisholm, 'to see the completed work with [their] own eyes and give thanks to God'.[49]

In the booklet published in 1966 to celebrate the centenary of the opening of the Church, a link was again made between the appointment of the new minister and the redecoration, as twin approaches in the programme of revitalisation of Dowanhill Church. It was felt that the Rev Chisholm and his Canadian wife had come 'with all the vigour and aspirations of youth to carry on a ministry in a world more beset by doubts than ever before [...] In token of a new start the church was re-decorated and the Cottier design changed into a more modern idiom. But a church is more than stone and lime. It is primarily a group of people [...]'.[50] The painted decoration, or at least the 1937 scheme, may therefore have come to be seen by modernisers as symbolic of old-fashioned attitudes within the Church. Others must have felt it to have been inextricably linked to the identity of Dowanhill Church, and it would surely have been one of the topics covered in Dr Baxter's sermon entitled 'A century of witness in stone and lime', preached at a special centenary service held in the Church on 13 November 1966.

Further information on how the 1963 redecoration scheme was decided on, and how it was received, would be of great value. One anecdotal account has already been collected by Alan Ferdinand. According to a former member of the congregation, the paint was obtained from Dulux, which ran a special promotion on paint for the redecoration of churches. The final choice of colour scheme was apparently made to match a blue Pringle sweater that was being worn at the time by a member of the Redecoration Committee.[51]

In the 1963 scheme at Dowanhill, the main wall areas were painted in pale blue emulsion, with a deep sky blue emulsion on the upper areas around the hammerbeams and on the ceiling (fig 80). The plywood on the inside surfaces of the pulpit canopy was painted in purple oil paint, picked out with bright magenta (fig 83). Some tufts of fabric which remain on the canopy appear to suggest that purple material was also pinned to parts of this structure. The pulpit stonework and its painted decoration, as well as all other dressed stonework in the interior of the building, was painted over with plain masonry paint generally and in some areas such as the vestibule with textured masonry paint. The recess of the pulpit wall was covered by William Morris wallpaper (fig 90), though the blue paint which was discovered below it suggests that there may have been more than one phase of this redecoration scheme. Some remnants of the wallpaper were also found on the interior of the pulpit canopy, suggesting that the wallpaper had covered parts of the plywood (and original decoration).

This scheme was the one that was in place when the Church was taken over by Four Acres Charitable Trust in 1984 (figs 91 and 92).

**Fig 91** 1960s Decorative Scheme, Pulpit View, Dowanhill Church, photograph taken in 1988 indicating the plain treatment of the 1960s. Courtesy of Historic Scotland.

**Fig 92** 1960s Decorative Scheme, Organ View, Dowanhill Church, photograph taken in 1988 indicating the plain treatment of the 1960s. Courtesy of Historic Scotland.

## An End and a New Beginning: Appraisal of the Painted Decoration, 1983

During 1983, negotiations were under way to merge the congregations of Dowanhill with Partick East and Partick Old to become Partick Trinity. The future of Dowanhill Church, as a building and as a monument of artistic and architectural importance, was very uncertain. A description and appraisal of the painted decoration was prepared by Michael Donnelly of the Peoples' Palace, Glasgow, as part of a Structural Report commissioned by Four Acres Charitable Trust from the congregation's architects Walter Underwood and Partners and completed in 1984. This described how elements of the decoration were rediscovered by 'scraping' the over-layers of paint on the walls and by removing boarding in the pulpit. The appraisal is an invaluable record of the state of knowledge about the painted decoration at the time, although as might be expected, many of its premises and conclusions have now been modified in the light of more recent research. It provided a key contribution to raising awareness of the importance of the decoration scheme at Dowanhill, and led to the gradual evolution of a plan for its conservation. Full conservation of this outstanding scheme of painted decoration has remained a prime objective of the project. It is intended that the story of the conservation of the building and its decoration will be recorded in the Conservation Report which will form the second volume of *Cottier's in Context*.

[1] Instructions to Architects, DCR CH3/1267/105.

[2] Managers Minutes, 1864-1866, DCR CH3/1267/7, including Minutes of the Joint Meeting of Managers, Trustees & Kirk Session, 18 Apr 1865, when quotes from masons, joiners, slaters, plumbers, plasterers, smiths and founders, and glaziers were considered.

[3] 'New United Presbyterian Church at Partick', *Daily Mail*, 8 Aug 1865, a cutting from which is in the Managers Minutes, DCR CH3/1267/7.

[4] 'Mason's Extras, Dowanhill Church', DCR CH3/1267/105; 'Measurement of Carpenter and Joiner Work of Dowanhill UP Church', 3 Dec 1866, DCR CH3/1267/103; 'Measurement of the Digging, Mason & Brick Work of Dowanhill UP Church', 13 Nov 1866, DCR CH3/1267/103.

[5] 'Opening of Dowanhill U.P. Church', *Glasgow Herald*, 12 Nov 1866. The opening of the Church was advertised in a printed leaflet of 3 Nov 1866, DCR CH3/1267/105; and in a notice in the *Glasgow Herald* of 10 Nov 1866. Although the *Herald* report shows that the stained glass was already in progress by the date the Church was opened, a letter from George Thomson shows that it was not completed until 1869, see DCR CH3/1267/102; and **Documenting the Building**.

[6] Mavor 1923, vol 1, 227-8.

[7] McNab 1916, 303-304.

[8] Managers Minutes, 24 Nov 1866. Alexander Kay was on the Building Committee and was one of the two Managers who negotiated the price of the feu for the site. He also paid for the stained glass windows (see **Documenting the Building**). The plate-stands are now in People's Palace, Glasgow.

[9] Dickie 1926, 73.

[10] Recent examination and analysis of the paint is reported in Allardyce, 1998; and Correia, 2007.

[11] Managers Minutes, 6 Jan 1899.

[12] Managers Minutes, 14 Jan 1899.

[13] Dickie 1926, 72.

[14] Report of AGM, Managers Minutes, 18 Jan 1899.

[15] Managers Minutes, 1 Jun 1899.

[16] Kirk Session, 13 Jun 1899, DCR CH3/1267/6.

[17] Extract from Dowanhill Church Accounts, 1891-99, DCR CH1267/104.

[18] Pastoral letter from Rev Dickie, in Congregational Report for 1899, DCR CH3/1267/11.

[19] 'Statement of the Managers', *DCMR* (Nov. 1890), a copy of which is in Managers Minutes, Nov 1899.

[20] Dickie 1926, 117-8.

[21] *Young's Glasgow Scraps*, ALS 4 (May 1914), vol 37, 70-71.

[22] Dickie 1930, 3.

[23] Dickie 1930, 4.

[24] *DCMR* (Feb 1934).

[25] *DCMR* (Dec 1934) and (Jan-Feb 1935).

[26] *DCMR* (Jan 1937), 6.

[27] We are grateful to a former Sunday School teacher at the Church, Mr Maxwell Thornton, for first alerting us to Cameron's involvement.

[28] Smith 1992, 102-3, 107, 110 & 126.

[29] Copy letter from Session Clerk to Sir David Y Cameron, 8 Apr 1937, DCR CH3/1267/82.

[30] Letter from JD MacGregor to Mr McAllister, 10 Mar 1937, DCR CH3/1267/81, in which MacGregor accepted the invitation to join the Redecoration Committtee: 'I shall be pleased to accept and shall give any service which lies within my power.'

[31] *DCMR* (Apr 1937), 2.

[32] *DCMR* (Apr 1937), 3.

[33] Copy letter from Session Clerk to Thomas L. Taylor, 7 Apr 1937, DCR CH3/1267/82.

[34] Managers Minutes, 21 Apr 1937, DCR CH3/1267/8.

[35] Copy letter from Session Clerk to Rev WH Harrowes, 23 Jun 1937, DCR CH3/1267/82.

[36] List of Tenderers opened 10/6/37, DCR CH3/1267/80; and letter from Hutton & Taylor, Architects, to A Reid Walker, 28 Jun 1937, DCR CH3/1267/80.

[37] DCMR (Sept 1937), DCR CH3/1267/21.

[38] Dowanhill Church Renovation and Re-Decoration Statement, DCR CH3/1267/80.

[39] Managers Minutes, 21 Apr 1937, DCR CH3/1267/8.

[40] *DCMR* (Mar 1938). For the application for a special grant from the Baird Trust, see Minutes of the Meeting of the Redecoration and Dr Dickie Memorial Joint Committee, 21 Apr 1937, DCR, CH3/1267/8.

[41] Copy letter from Session Clerk to Mr Taylor, 5 Oct 1937, DCR CH3/1267/82.

[42] We are most grateful to the Rev Stuart Smith, Minister of Partick Trinity Church, for providing access to these.

[43] *DCMR* (Nov 1962).

[44] Accounts 1962, *DCMR* (Feb 1963), 11.

[45] *DCMR* (Apr 1963), 6; and (Jun-Aug 1963), 2.

[46] See *DCMR* (May 1963), 4; and Accounts 1963, *DCMR* (Feb 1964), 9.

[47] *DCMR* (Feb 1964), 15-16.

[48] Undated letter [March 1963] from Norman S Miller to members of the congregation (copy in Cottier Archive).

[49] *DCMR* (Oct 1963), 2.

[50] *Dowanhill Centenary* 1966.

[51] Oral account given by a former member of the congregation to Alan Ferdinand at an open day at Cottier's.

# 8 DOWANHILL CHURCH AND NUMERIC PROPORTION

David Robertson

**Plate XXXIII**

*A* Cover Illustration, E–E Viollet-le-Duc, 1856, *Dictionnaire raisonné de l'architecture française du XIe au XVIe siècle.*

*B* Dowanhill Church, early woodblock engraving. Courtesy of Partick Trinity Church.

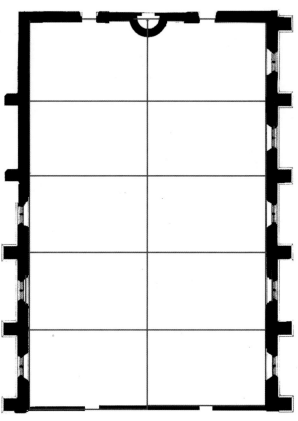

*C* Diagrammatic Plan of Dowanhill Church Nave. Courtesy of David Robertson.

**Introduction**

The aim of this chapter is to investigate what means of proportion, if any, was used in the design of the building and to do this in the context of those theories that were current at the time that it was constructed. The idea that there might be evidence of an underlying system of geometric proportion at work in the building was first proposed by the writer in reports to Historic Scotland in 1984 and these thoughts have been explored more fully in the intervening decades.[1]

There are philosophical and practical problems involved in trying to reconstruct the geometric basis of proportion in an architectural structure. The study of the measurements in particular of medieval buildings to establish what system of proportion was used in their design and construction, remains a legitimate and important analytical discipline in the history of art.[2] The study of the numerical properties of key measurements as a way of deciphering proportion in the design of a Victorian building is also a field of legitimate academic interest but one that is less researched.

The mid-Victorians were as inclined as any generation to carry out studies of pyramids, temples and cathedrals with a view to uncovering the methods of design that might have been employed and to apply such systems of proportion to their own constructions. This formed part of a search for a mathematical basis for aesthetic experience and a belief in the symbolic significance of numbers, ratios and geometric figures.

Nonetheless, without written evidence it is very difficult to establish from analysis of a building whether an architect used a system of proportion.

It can be deceptively easy to find apparent numeric and geometric relationships within the plans and elevations of historic buildings. The thicknesses of the walls vary and there are compound mouldings around windows and inner and outer edges to arches. This makes it difficult to establish the precise lines of reference that would have been used. Many illustrations of geometry superimposed on building plans look initially plausible but carry little weight on closer examination.

In order to try and understand the way that a Victorian architect of the later Gothic Revival might have set about proportioning a building it is first worth considering those theories that existed around that time about geometry and number as sources of both proportion and symbol.

Contemporary literature about Victorian buildings does not tend to dwell on theories of proportion. Nevertheless in the 1850s and 60s belief in laws that form the basis of aesthetic experience had survived the scepticism of writers and empirical philosophers of the previous century who argued otherwise and whose views have tended to prevail ever since.[3]

For example, interest in explaining the laws governing ancient buildings and their geometry remained a preoccupation of certain prominent Victorian writers on architecture, among them Eugène-Emmanuel Viollet-le-Duc in France and David Ramsay Hay in Scotland. In recent years there has been interest in the possibility that Alexander 'Greek' Thomson was advocating the use of specific classical systems of proportion when he expressed a belief that the laws of architecture were not invented by man but discovered by him.[4]

Before going on to set out the observations of this study, reference will therefore be made to Victorian theories of proportion that were current at the time when William Leiper, who was a younger contemporary of Thomson, developed his design for Dowanhill Church.

**Victorian Theories of Proportion**

Viollet-le-Duc was one of the most influential figures in the Gothic Revival and was an advocate of theories of proportion in historic structures as evidenced in his *Dictionnaire raisonné de l'architecture française du XIe au XVIe siècle, Tome 7, Proportion* (1854-68). In this account Viollet-le-Duc rejected any idea that immutable rules of proportion could be followed slavishly in architecture. He preferred to talk in terms of harmony of scale based on geometric principles that unified subordinate parts within the building in relation to the whole.

Viollet-le-Duc nonetheless believed that the medieval builders based their systems of proportion on the requirements of stability and made adjustments that were aesthetic, based on three triangles that he believed were used as guide to proportion – the isosceles based on a rectangle, a triangle he termed *égyptien* which was isosceles with the base of four units and height of two and a half (i.e. a ratio of 8 to 5), and the equilateral triangle.

He provided analyses of a number of medieval structures to demonstrate his theories of the geometric proportion underlying them: 'We have indicated how even in the minor details of architecture, lines inclined at 45° proportions, at 60° and at 30° have been used as generators for elevational drawings.'[5]

In Scotland, David Ramsay Hay was a proponent of a theory that aesthetic principles in architecture should be derived from systems of proportion, and wrote on the subject in the 1840s and '50s. As well as analysing historic buildings, he promoted the use of numerical ratios as a unifying theme in all fields of design, in particular, colour and decoration (fig 93). Like Viollet-le-Duc, Hay believed that the slavish use of geometry was wrong and that genius was also required to design an aesthetically satisfying structure that would be considered picturesque.

Hay appears to have influenced the architect Alexander 'Greek' Thomson in his classical designs. However, in his

**Fig 93** DR Hay, Table of Primary, Secondary and Tertiary Colours.

| Primary | | Equivalent proportion | Secondary | | Equivalent proportion | Tertiary | | Equivalent proportion |
|---|---|---|---|---|---|---|---|---|
| Yellow | | 3 | Purple (red + blue) | | 13 (5+8) | Citrine (orange + green) | | 19 (8+11) |
| Red | | 5 | Green (yellow + blue) | | 11 (3+8) | Russet (orange + purple) | | 21 (8+13) |
| Blue | | 8 | Orange (yellow + red) | | 8 (3+5) | Olive (green + purple) | | 24 (11+13) |

theorising about proportion, Hay did not stop at that most popular subject of study, the Parthenon, but was also concerned to demonstrate that Gothic architectural forms followed similar principles, providing a geometric analysis of the façade of Lincoln Cathedral to support his argument.[6] The properties of numbers and the ratios between them were at the core of Hay's theories of proportion.

In his *First Principles of Symmetrical Beauty*, Hay started from the fact that the circle is divided in 360 degrees and based his 'orders of symmetry' on the properties of the number 360 which is divisible by a great many whole numbers.[7]

Hay's influential aesthetic theories were primarily based on the unity of the arts, as he believed that there was a common mathematical basis for architectural, musical and colour harmony. Hay above all admired the Greeks as artists who excelled in the perfection of symmetrical beauty, and his theories were based on well-established classical and Renaissance traditions which he believed ultimately derived from the Egyptians, through Moses and Pythagoras.

It is perfectly plausible that Leiper's Dowanhill Church was conceived in this way, as a building within which the architectural forms, colour harmonies and acoustic properties followed definite ideas of proportion based on Victorian views of ancient traditions.

Whether the theories of Viollet-le-Duc and Hay had any merit in relation to those ancient Gothic buildings they chose to analyse (such as the Sainte-Chapelle in Paris and Lincoln Cathedral) is not the subject of this study. It is the influence these theories might have had on the then younger generation of architects and designers of the Victorian Gothic Revival that is of interest here, and Leiper's Dowanhill Church provides an opportunity to consider this possibility.

**Finding Key Measurements**

The drawings used in this study are illustrated in fig 94. Unfortunately the original drawings for Dowanhill Church have not survived.

**Fig 94** Dowanhill Church, survey drawings by Michael Burgoyne.

*A* South Elevation. Courtesy of Four Acres Charitable Trust.

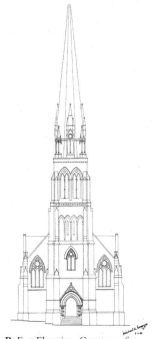

*B* East Elevation. Courtesy of Four Acres Charitable Trust.

An initial measured survey of good quality was undertaken in 1984 by Parvis Rezai an architectural student at the Mackintosh School of Architecture, Glasgow. Subsequent surveys of the Church were undertaken by Dr Michael Burgoyne in 1988, covering the plan and external elevations, and in 2002, a laser survey was carried out of the interior elevations which confirmed Dr Burgoyne's ground plan. All the measurements that are provided in this study are based on the 1988 and 2002 surveys which are considered to be very accurate.

By studying these drawings and the building itself the aim must be to establish those significant points and lines within the building that can be fixed as a sound basis for analysis, concentrating on those that can be determined by their nature as being in one and only one position relative to the building as a whole.

The centre-lines of the buttresses are important measurements because the width between them is repeated over five bays. The position of the centre-lines of these bays cannot be disputed, although there is some minor variation between the intervening buttresses and roof trusses as built, and an average width of bay must be presumed.

However, by contrast with the thicknesses of symmetrical walls and bays, the centre-lines of the perimeter walls cannot be determined by deduction. Unlike the bays, they do not repeat, the thickness varies according to the height of the wall and the wall construction itself steps out asymmetrically on the outer sides as the wall gets thicker. The architect may have used his own chosen 'centre-line' in a perimeter wall but we cannot know exactly which line he would have used.

The floor level and height to the apex of the ceiling are important measurements that can be known. Both the level at the surface of the floor and the inner surface of the ceiling at its apex are capable of precise determination, as are the inner surfaces of walls, although there are always risks in old buildings that

floors have subsided and ceilings, roofs or walls have settled.

The angles of triangles formed by external gables are precise indicators of proportion in a building because the angles of the gables are the same wherever they are measured. It is less straightforward to draw conclusions about the proportion found in the triangles and rectangles in the other parts of a plan and elevation because, as previously stated, the centre-lines of perimeter walls are not known, and with windows, the mouldings forming jambs, sills and lintels can be complex and varied. However the rectangles formed by the average centre-lines of buttresses and roof trusses and the inner surfaces of walls can be defined reasonably exactly and consistently.

The centre-points of circular features are important points that can be precisely determined. At Dowanhill there are three especially significant ones – the centre of the rose window, the centre of the pulpit medallion, and the centre of the porch medallion. These points naturally lie exactly along the central vertical and horizontal axes and have a precise height above the floor level. Fig 95 illustrates the three centre-points of the building.

In seeking out lines, angles and measurements in the building that might reveal an underlying system of proportion, used intentionally in the design, it makes sense to study, first and foremost, the relationships between these key points, centre-lines, angles and levels. Other shapes and forms that are important to the overall proportion and aesthetic of the building might appear to coincide with the relationships that are thus revealed and, to the extent that this is convincing, then it provides circumstantial support for the main findings but no more than that.

In addition, whether the builders set out the building, which was erected in a remarkably short period of time, accurately and in accordance with the intentions of the architect, cannot be established. If their work was significantly at odds with the architect's original drawings, then this would also create discrepancies that

**Fig 95** Dowanhill Church Circular Features on the Central Axis.

*A* Rose Window. Courtesy of Tom Donald.

*B* Pulpit Canopy Roundel. Courtesy of Historic Scotland.

*C* Tympanum Roundel. Courtesy of Four Acres Charitable Trust, photograph Michael Burgoyne.

make it harder rather than easier to prove any underlying relationships and proportions, given that the aim of finding the underlying system of proportion is that the evidence presented should be convincing and based on measured dimensions.

## Comparisons with Viollet-le-Duc

To provide an illustration of a possible parallel with theories of proportion that were being developed in the second half of the nineteenth century, I have taken the side elevation of the nave of Dowanhill, which bears some resemblance to the Sainte-Chapelle, and compared it with an analysis by Viollet-le-Duc of the latter.

Fig 96 shows that analysis: the French architect interprets the proportion of the bays of the side elevation of the Sainte-Chapelle in terms of the equilateral triangle, one of three triangles that he believed provided the basis of proportion and stability in ancient buildings. He suggests that the projection of the sides of the equilateral triangle at 60° gives rise to a series of lines that intersect with the different stages within the bays of the Sainte-Chapelle.

Applying these same principles to Leiper's elevation (fig 97), 60° lines can be projected down the copes of the gablets. They form equilateral triangles at clerestory level that coincide with the string course at the bases of the upper lancet windows. At lower lancet level equivalent triangles can be superimposed that have their apices at the apices of the buttresses and their bases at floor level interesecting with the centre lines of the adjacent buttresses.

The work of French restorers of the mid-nineteenth century made the Sainte-Chapelle a prominent case study for Victorian students of the Gothic Revival. There is something of the character of the Sainte-Chapelle in

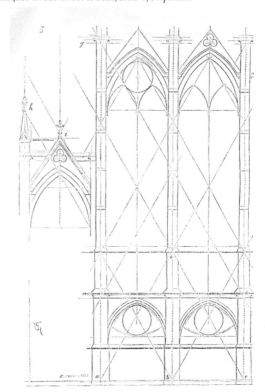

**Fig 96** 'The Sainte-Chapelle, Paris: Analysis of Two Bays', E-E Viollet-le-Duc, 1854-68, *Dictionnaire raisonné de l'architecture française du XIe au XVIe siècle, Tome 7, Proportion.*

**Fig 97** Dowanhill Church, Analysis of East Elevation. Courtesy of David Robertson.

the nave of Dowanhill and it is noteworthy that James Sellars' Hillhead Parish Church, which is a more direct interpretation of the Sainte-Chapelle, is generally believed to have been based on Leiper's competition entry for Hillhead.[9] The Sainte-Chapelle also involved recreations of medieval painted decoration, which have a parallel in the scheme at Dowanhill.[10]

## Comparison with DR Hay

For DR Hay, the rectangles and triangles in a building should be selected and composed so that the ratios that exist between the various angles can form an overall composition from which a harmony of proportion can be achieved. His theories of harmony in architecture, and harmony in colour, are theories of ratios, which are based on an analogy with music. They had widespread circulation and he read extracts of his published work to the Royal Institute of British Architects (RIBA) in London.[11]

According to Hay, just as there is a science of music then there must be a science of proportion. In music, consonance, or sympathy between vibrations occurs when certain notes are played together. The notes that play together with maximum consonance are those that occur by doubling or halving the number of vibrations. This is perceived as the same note only at a higher or lower pitch because it has full consonance. This fundamental ratio is therefore 1:2 or 2:1.

Recognising that musical harmony is essentially founded upon ratios, Hay developed his theory of proportion by deriving ratios from geometry and measurement, which form the basis of architecture. He asserted that an understanding and application of harmonious geometrical ratios have been behind all great periods of architecture, and he provided analyses of the Parthenon and Lincoln Cathedral in support of his claims (fig 98).

When ratios are applied to geometry, the subdivisions are in degrees and fractions of degrees, with 360 being the maximum number of degrees.[12] To apply the musical analogy, the ratios involved in a major chord which is made up of the notes bottom-doh, mi and sol and top-doh, are 1:1, 5:4, 3:2, and 2:1. By analogy, following Hay's theory, in architecture where geometric subdivisions of 90 degrees apply, these ratios could be expressed as: $90° : 90°, 90° : 72°, 90° : 60°, 90° : 45°$.

These relative angles could then form the basis of a simple system of proportion, for example, starting with the square, followed by a 72° diagonal rectangle, a 60° diagonal rectangle, and finishing with a double square rectangle. The relative ratios could also be expressed as triangular gables with 90°, 72°, 60° and 45° apices. These rectangular and triangular forms, when used to compose the building, would give rise to a sense of harmony in proportion.

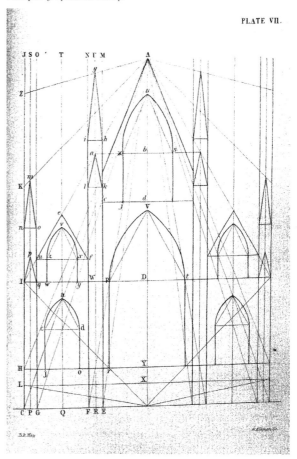

**Fig 98** 'Lincoln Cathedral: Analysis of Façade', DR Hay, 1846, *First Principles of Symmetric Beauty.*

The theories Hay developed are considerably more involved than is implied by the simple illustration given here which is provided in order to interpret the principal idea. Fundamental importance is given by Hay to the number 360. Hay observes that this number has particular significance because so many subdivisions by whole numbers are possible. Hay's approach is highly systematic, providing a vision of a building created by an architect who consciously exploits the ratios set up by the angles he chooses to employ, rather as a composer selects notes (which form interdependent ratios when played together or in sequence) to compose harmonies and modulations between chords.

If Leiper did apply Hay's theoretical approach to the design of Dowanhill, then it is first essential to establish if the angles used are subdivisions of 360. This will not in itself prove adherence to Hay's theories, since architects would have to use certain subdivisions such as 60°, simply to define an equilateral triangle. What is of interest is to establish whether a particular numerical relationship is at work that would point to the conscious use of a system of proportion in the form of a common element that relates the different parts.

Significant apices and pitches that characterise this building are the steeple, the main roof, the side gablets, the bell frame and the north-east pinnacle. The following angles are revealed (fig 99)

| 12° | Steeple apex |
| 24° | Pinnacle apex |
| 36° | Bell frame apex |
| 48° | Main roof pitch |
| 60° | Gablets pitch and apex |
| 72° | Bell frame pitch |
| 84° | Main roof apex. |

This suggests the conscious use of multiples of 12°.

Although significant features have been selected, there are others such as the gables over the porch and rose window, which are not multiples of 12 with the ratios that these imply. Nonetheless the correlation is interesting and provides a starting point in a search for underlying relationships.

For example, the ratio of the main roof apex to a gablet roof apex is 84°:60° or 7:5. The ratio of a gablet roof apex to the bell frame apex is 60°:36° or 5:3 and a gablet roof apex to the pinnacle apex is 60°:24° or 5:2. The four apices – the main roof, a gablet roof, the bell frame and the pinnacle stand in ratios 7:1, 5:1, 3:1 and 2:1 respectively to the steeple. This is what is intended by the idea of a harmony of scale based on geometric principles that unify subordinate parts within a building in relation to the whole.

**Fig 99** Dowanhill Church, Angles of the Main Roof, Gablet Roof, Bell Frame, Pinnacle and Steeple. Courtesy of David Robertson.

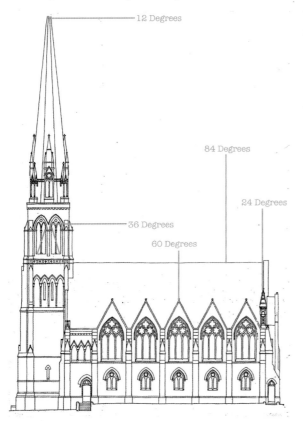

## The Metric System

At Dowanhill Church, the distance between the centre-lines of the bays is 4.8 metres on average, making five bays in all of exactly 24 metres, which is also the internal length of the nave. The bay length of 4.8 metres is just over 15 feet and the nave length of 24 metres is just under 79 feet. The length of the nave coincides with that given in the Reverend Dickie's book, *The History of Dowanhill Church* (1926).[13] At this point, it is interesting to examine the possibility that Leiper used the metric system to set up the proportion in the building, rather than the standard feet and inches that the builder would have used in its construction.

The imperial system which uses subdivisions of 12 inches would appear to be a basis for numerical proportion, given its relationship to that of degrees – 36 inches can be subdivided in the same way as 360 degrees. Unfortunately an inch is a very small unit to use, and most books that analyse ancient buildings see these as having been constructed in units that are closer in scale to a foot.[14]

The reason for suggesting that the metric system was used at Dowanhill to determine proportion is based on the recurrence of the series of multiples of twelve, when applied to measurements taken in decimetres rather than in feet and inches, together with the frequent occurrences of significant whole number, decimetre measurements. There were attempts to introduce the metric system into Britain in the second half of the nineteenth century, which coincide with the date of Dowanhill Church.[15] The metric system enables measurements to be scaled in one series of decimal units, rather than in combinations of feet and inches. This makes it easier to apply subdivisions of whole numbers and the properties of certain irrational numbers within a system of proportion.

Set into a hillside, the main Dowanhill Church building was designed as if on a plinth, with the only change in level taken up in the side hall. The main church is symmetrical in cross-section, and it makes sense to examine heights from the floor level, which is constant throughout the Church, and to consider heights from this level measured vertically along the centre-line.

Starting at the entrance to the building, the floor level and the centre of the medallion in the tympanum are known points. The distance from the floor level to the centre of the medallion is 48 decimetres, which is the same measurement as the width of the bays along the side elevation. From this it is reasonable to conclude that this is a significant measurement for a study of the proportions of the building. At the entrance to the building, under the steeple, is a porch, which is a perfect square with a length between the inner faces of the walls of 36 decimetres. In the vestibule beyond the porch, the distance from floor level to the apex of the ceiling is 48 decimetres.

Another important fixed point, the pulpit medallion, is 72 decimetres above floor level. The height to the apices of the gablet ceilings projecting from the nave at the hammerbeam posts is 120 decimetres. Within the nave itself, the height to the apex of the arched ceiling is 144 decimetres. As already established, the length of the nave is 240 decimetres.

In summary the following key measurements in decimetres have been observed in the building:

36    Sides of the porch
48    Height to the porch medallion
48    Height of the vestibule ceiling apex
48    Average width of the bays
72    Height to the pulpit medallion
120   Height of the apex of the ceilings in the side gablets
144   Height of the main ceiling apex
240   Length of the nave.

This suggests that the key measurements underlying the system of proportion could indeed be metric, since these are such significant dimensions within the building, and whole number ratios are possible due to their inter-divisibility by 12. In keeping with the use of a range of angles that can be subdivided by 12, this series of decimetre measurements can be subdivided by 12, and also sets up similar ratios for proportion. For example, the ratio of the length of the nave to the height is 240:144, which is 5:3, and the ratio of the height to the apex of the main ceiling to that of the projecting gablet ceilings is 144:120, which is 6:5.

The centre of the rose window does not fit into these twelve-fold subdivisions. However, it is precisely 100 decimetres above floor level. The relevant decimetre measurements are shown in fig 100. The 100 decimetres height of the centre point of the rose window adds weight to the observation that metric units might have been used.

**Fig 100** Dowanhill Church, decimetre heights from floor level. Courtesy of David Robertson.

## The Use of Golden Proportion

Rules of proportion in architecture, if they are used at all, are by no means universal or fixed. However, the use of the Golden Ratio (otherwise known as the Golden Section) as a basis for proportion in painting, sculpture, architecture and other arts and crafts has a good pedigree. The Golden Ratio was used and studied throughout the history of art and architecture as a way of giving lengths, shapes and architectural spaces a unique proportion.

The ratio expresses the division of a line at a given point so that the smaller portion of the line is in the same ratio to the larger portion as the larger portion is to the whole. This point of division into these rational but unequal portions is termed the Golden Section. The 'Golden Number' (to three decimal places), is the number 1.618. Multiply or divide any given number by the Golden Number and the ratio between the first number and the resulting number will always be equal to the ratio between the larger number and the two numbers added together. There are geometric procedures for arriving at Golden Proportion in architecture. Where a close approximation to the Golden Ratio is found between two strongly related measurements in a building such as the length and breadth of a room, this suggests that the architect is using Golden Proportion in the design.

The tradition in art and architecture is that the proportion existing between the two unequal lengths that result when a line is split at the Golden Section has aesthetic significance. Two unequal lengths that are in Golden Proportion can be used to form rectangles and triangles of varying sizes that always have a proportion in common and this produces an aesthetic effect. Golden Proportion has been applied in art since classical times and was prominent in Renaissance thinking. According to this principle, the artist or architect would use this ratio to create proportions that were perceived as possessing an underlying sense of harmony in the given work without recourse to pure symmetry. Other ratios could be used to the same end, giving a different underlying proportion, but proportion based on the Golden Ratio was considered to have a divine significance.[16]

It is interesting to study the features of Dowanhill that might indicate the use of the Golden Ratio, perhaps as a refinement within the ratios already set up by angles and measurements that are multiples of 12. Any proportional analysis based precisely on the Golden Ratio involves multiplying or dividing a whole number by the number 1.618. To study measurements in a building where whole numbers are in decimetres multiplied or divided by 1.618 requires accuracy in centimetres. The study of centimetre measurements at Dowanhill Church does provide some persuasive results. Figure 101 tabulates all the golden proportion measurements in centimetres that arise when multiples of the bay width of 48 decimetres and its double value of 96 decimetres are split into subdivisions at the Golden Section or multiplied by the Golden Number.

If significant inter-related dimensions occur along one of these rows then they are in Golden Proportion and related to a multiple of 12. The analysis below concerns the width of each bay (480 centimetres) and the proportions of the windows and hammerbeam roof trusses.

Within the nave the interplay of mass and void created by the clerestory windows reveals the Golden Ratio. The measurements are found consistently to be 183 centimetres of wall surface and 297 centimetres of window openings (fig 102) relative to the overall bay width of 480 centimetres.

Extending the theory that multiples of 12 decimetres were used in the interior of the nave, then it is the position of the inner wall surface, rather than the centre-lines, that would determine the space enclosed by the walls. For each bay-width of 48 decimetres, the half nave-width when multiplied by the Golden Number would calculate at 777 centimetres, giving rise to an inner wall surface to inner wall surface nave-width of twice this distance, which is 1553 centimetres and a five-bay length of 2400 centimetres. This closely accords with the actual dimensions given in Dickie's *History of Dowanhill Church* of a nave 51 feet by 79 feet (1554 centimetres by 2407 centimetres). The inner dimensions of the nave can therefore been reckoned by the scale of the inner wall surfaces to form ten mathematically quite precise Golden Proportion rectangles (fig 103).

## The Hammerbeam Roof and the Golden Ratio

The system of hammerbeam roof trusses and the vault they create is the outstanding architectural form within the building, and reads as a powerful architectural expression of its internal proportion. It is one of the building's most interesting features (fig 104).

**Fig 101** Table showing the numbers 48 and 96 subdivided and multiplied by the Golden Number.

| Multiples of 12 Decimetres | | Subdivided by Golden Number | | | Multiplied by Golden Number | |
|---|---|---|---|---|---|---|
| | | Shorter Section Centimetres | Longer Section Centimetres | | Shorter Section Centimetres | Longer Section Centimetres |
| 48 | | 183 | 297 | | 480 | 777 |
| 96 | | 367 | 593 | | 960 | 1553 |

**Fig 102** Dowanhill Church, Subdivision into Mass and Void in accordance with the Golden Ratio. Courtesy of David Robertson.

**Fig 103** Dowanhill Church, Nave Subdivided by 10 Golden Rectangles. Courtesy of David Robertson.

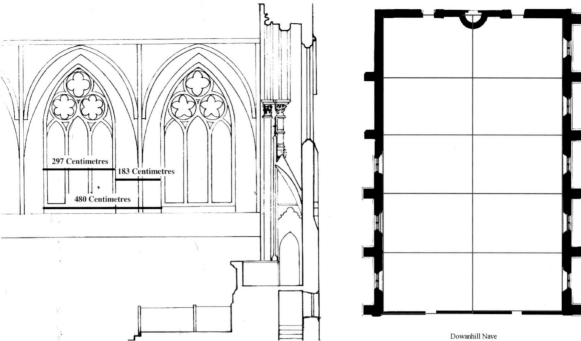

Dowanhill Nave

**Fig 104** Dowanhill Church: Hammerbeam Roof Trusses, inner surface dimensions in Golden Proportion. Courtesy of David Robertson.

A comparator building, which is likely to have inspired Leiper's choice of a hammerbeam roof, is to be found in Godwin's Northampton Town Hall, completed a year earlier in 1864. Godwin was convinced that his hammerbeam roof had fine acoustic properties and, writing in the third person, stated that:

> He [i.e. Godwin] had been complemented by prima donnas who had sung there. The reason he thought was because the entire wall on each side, above the head of the singer, was broken into a series of arcades recessed between the principals of the roof. The hammerbeams [...] were open iron work, offering slight but not, of course, solid resistance to sound; and there was a boarded ceiling at a tolerable height. There was a recess at one end, broken by an organ, and projecting balconies, and it was, he believed, to these breaks – not being very great, but being at regular intervals – and to the simple proportions of the hall, that its excellent acoustic properties were due. [17]

This description makes an interesting comparison with the interior at Dowanhill where Leiper appears to have provided an acoustic space using a system of hammerbeams designed in accordance with Golden Proportion.

Firstly, the inner face of the springing point of the principal arch is on the plane of the inner surface of the wall, and accordingly the distance between the span is the same, which is 1553 centimetres. Dividing this dimension by the Golden Number 1.618 gives a measurement of 960 centimetres (96 decimetres which is divisible by 12). This is the distance between the inner face of the downstand post that connects to the hammerbeam itself and which frames the tracery over the projecting side gablets. (fig 105). This tracery forms Golden Ratio rectangles between the principle arches because the downstand itself measures 297 centimetres, which is in Golden Proportion to 480 centimetres (ie. one bay-width).

**Fig 105** Dowanhill Church: Sketch of Hammerbeam Roof Structure Illustrating Golden Proportion. Courtesy of David Robertson.

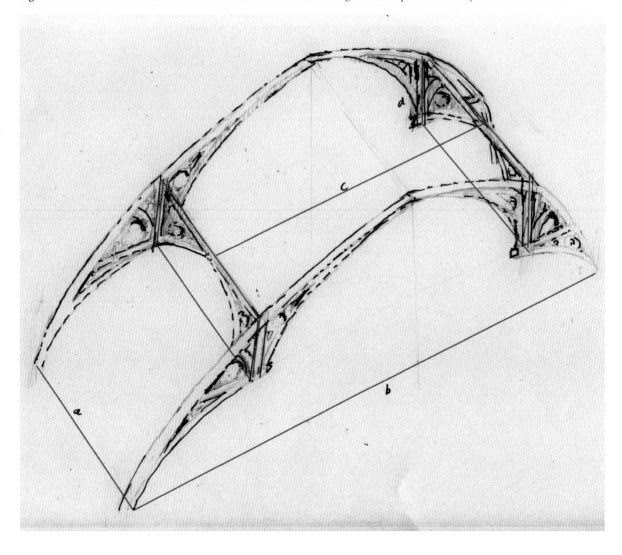

Similarly, on the long section, the average width of a bay is 480 centimetres, but the five bays are defined internally by the six hammerbeams, (which have been fitted into a 2400 centimetre length, so not all the hammerbeams are exactly 4800 apart).

The case is made that the hammerbeam truss arrangement is designed to accord with Golden Proportion within any reasonable tolerance given the scale of the building. It is analysed in Figure 105 as follows:

*a* is the width of a bay which is 480 centimetres;
*b* is the width between inner faces of main beams/wall surfaces which is 1553 centimetres;
*c* is the width between inner faces of downstand beams which is 960 centimetres;
*d* is the height of the downstands which is 297 centimetres.

The relationships are:

*b* is *c* times 1.618
*c* is two times *a*
*d* is *a* divided by 1.618.

## Conclusion

The analysis provided here of measurement and proportion opens up the question as to whether Leiper was using numerical properties principally as a way of achieving aesthetically pleasing proportion, or whether he was also using architecture as a means of expressing mathematical relationships.

Whatever numerical analysis is applied to inform an appreciation of this building there may be no better guide, aesthetically, than the end result – the proportions of the building itself. Dowanhill is powerful and full of the character and energy that comes with youthful work. Not everything seems as resolved as with the later churches by Leiper but here there are so many diverse aspects that are being forced together into one conception. Externally, the proportions of the building as a whole seem to be particularly powerful when viewed from the angle uphill or downhill, revealing all three dimensions, rather than straight on, as a more or less two-dimensional composition viewed on the level. This most satisfying result is essentially picturesque, with finely drawn silhouetted stone detailing which must be due to the artistry of the designer. This is what makes Dowanhill an especially fascinating subject to study. There is a tension between the symmetry across the north south axis of the Church, with its centrally placed spire, and the otherwise picturesque arrangement of the various elements of the Church and its adjoining hall.

The side hall on its own seems to be of an entirely different scale and proportion to the main church and yet the two buildings do work together remarkably well. The full effect clearly requires the reinstatement of the chimneys of the hall to their original heights and design. The gates and railings that surround the Church reinforce the triangular form of the site and its enclosure. They add another dimension in character, with their simple squares and circles which are quite nakedly geometric.

The interior provided a theatre for ritual and was fired by more than one imagination – William Leiper's and Daniel Cottier's certainly – who were themselves drawing on the imaginations of other leading architectural and aesthetic theorists of the age, and doubtless working with other artists in making a radical building. The spatial volume of the nave has a unity of form and the intended effect of the proportions internally cannot be fully appreciated without the missing dimension which is colour; Cottier's colour harmonies were created against the background of Victorian theories of proportion in the mixing of pigments as discussed earlier. Golden Proportion traditionally extended across the arts to encompass music, geometry, architecture and painting. Dowanhill Church thus offered a dramatic new aesthetic synthesis for nineteenth-century Presbyterian worship and praise. This wonderful synthesis will only be recovered with the reinstatement of Daniel Cottier's scheme of decoration.

[1] *Dowanhill Church: Structural Report* 1984.

[2] For recent studies in this field, see Wu 2002.

[3] David Hume, Edmund Burke and Archibald Alison being prominent British examples.

[4] Taylor 1999-2000, 25:5. The quotation is from Thomson's Haldane Lectures No. 2, see Thomson 1874.

[5] Viollet-le-Duc 1854-68, *Tome 7, Proportion.*

[6] Hay 1854, Plate VII.

[7] Hay 1846, 24.

[8] This is not to claim that the specific analysis of the Sainte-Chapelle provided by Viollet-le-Duc would necessarily have been known to Leiper but the concept of an underlying use of equilateral triangles in the proportion of Gothic architecture might well have been.

[9] Gomme and Walker 1987, 174.

[10] For nineteenth-century restoration and painted decoration schemes at the Ste-Chapelle, see Cohen 2005, 150, who notes that polychromy was planned for the upper chapel porch on the occasion of Queen Victoria's visit in 1855. See also Leniaud and Perrot 2007.

[11] Hay 1854

[12] Fractions of degrees are presented in minutes and seconds, e.g. 31°30'30".

[13] Dickie 1926, 71.

[14] A 'foot' was used to describe a range of similar but not identical measurements. The precise use appears to have varied according to most commentators, the Roman foot being a common one, measuring 29.57 centimetres.

[15] The Metric Weights and Measures Act 1864 made it legal to use the metric system in contracts in the UK.

[16] Livio 2002, is one of many accounts of the Golden Ratio.

[17] Quoted in Kinchin and Stirton 2005, 27-8. Similar comments have been attributed to Christina Dunwoody who sang with the Opera on a Shoestring company in Dowanhill Church following its incarnation as the Cottier Theatre.

# 9  MUSIC, HARMONY AND THE WILLIS ORGAN
## David Robertson, Kerr Jamieson and Hilary Macartney

**Plate XXXIV**   Measured Drawing of the Dowanhill Willis Organ Front before 1952. Courtesy of Four Acres Charitable Trust.

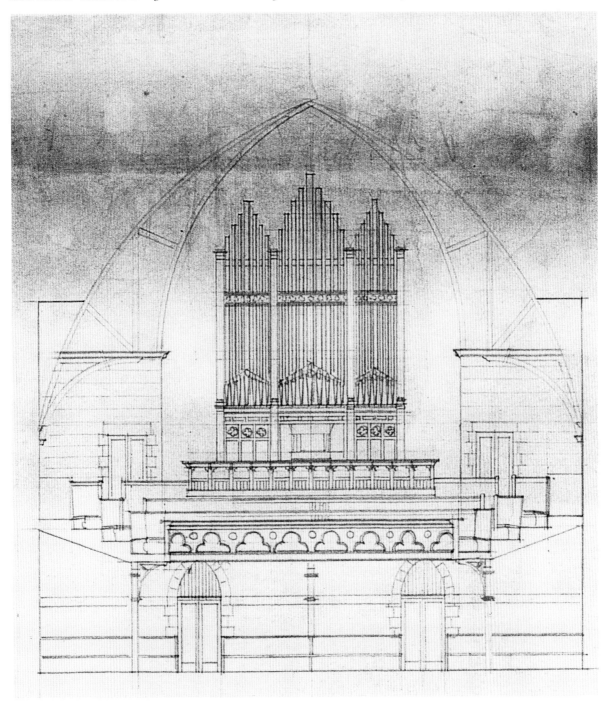

## Introduction: Music and Harmony at Dowanhill Church

The central role of music within the Church as reflected in its decoration, including the David and Miriam windows originally commissioned for the choir gallery (fig 106), and the concepts of colour harmony and harmonious proportion (fig 107) implicit in the painted decoration and the architecture are one of the themes of the present book (see also **Chapters 3** and **8** above). The significant place of music, not only in the formal services of worship in the Church, but also in the ancillary activities and entertainments organised by the Church committees is also clear from the records of Dowanhill UP Church, and the material presented by the Rev Dickie in his book on the Church. The details of the form of the music in the Church, and the maintenance of its high quality, were matters that were dealt with principally by the Church's Music Committee, although both the Kirk Session and the Board of Managers also discussed musical matters that were seen as having great relevance for the congregation and the Church as a whole, such as when the professional standards or moral character of the Precentor became an issue, as noted in **Chapter 5**.

All of this provides background to one particularly significant musical matter involving the whole church, its managing bodies and its architect Willaim Leiper. This concerned the commission of a church organ in 1875.

## The Dowanhill Organ: Decisions and Debates

The developments in organ-building and the increasing popularity of installing organs in churches was a matter of great contention within the Presbyterian churches in Scotland in the second half of the nineteenth century. For some, the move represented dynamism and progress, and a rejection of old-fashioned and excessively puritanical practices. For others, the coming of the 'Kist-o'-Whistles' was a departure from the purity of the Presbyterian tradition of praising the Lord directly and solely through the instrument of the human voice. The arrival of the organ also led to a number of other repercussions in the form of the music used in worship. The way in which the musical score of psalm tunes was written began to change with the introduction of the organ and the score itself often had to be compressed or adapted to suit the organ keyboard, a change bitterly resented by the old precentors, who complained that some of the finest

**Fig 106** The Choir Windows:

*A David with Harp*, Dowanhill Church, D Cottier 1867. Courtesy of Tom Donald.

*B Miriam with Tambourine*, Dowanhill Church, D Cottier 1867. Courtesy of Tom Donald.

Fig 107 'Example I', DR Hay, 1847, *The Laws of Harmonius Colouring*.

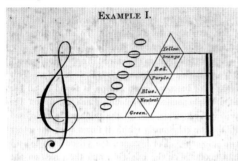

EXAMPLE I.

I cannot conclude this part of my subject, without noticing a striking coincidence between colour and sound, which has not been referred to in any work that I have consulted upon the subject. I have already mentioned the phenomenon discovered by Buffon, of the accidental colour which appears with any given colour, and that such accidental or compensating colour makes up the harmonious triad or concord. This, as I am informed by professors of music, is precisely the case when any given note is sounded on an instrument. It is always accompanied, or immediately succeeded, by those which form a chord, and are termed in music the harmonics. This phenomenon in acoustics, I believe, is most perceptible in the sound of a bell in succession, and in accompaniment on the string of the violoncello.

harmonies were thus sacrificed.[1] The process through which the momentous decision to commission an organ was taken by Dowanhill UP Church is documented in the records of the Church. The essential decision about installing an organ at all was the responsibility of the Kirk Session (see **Chapter 5**), and was taken in March 1875.[2] As the Rev Dickie explained in his book on the Church, the Kirk Session raised the issue with the congregation:

> Considering the thorniness of the subject, the Session resolved to 'gang warily'. It offered no opinion on the matter, but agreed to issue a circular to test the feeling of the congregation. The result was that 209 voted for the organ, 77 against, and 103 neutral.[3]

According to Dickie, however, the matter was still very sensitive, and despite the resounding majority in favour, the Kirk Session allowed a period of several months to elapse before proceeding any further, in order to determine whether those in opposition would decide to leave the Church.

Once the Kirk Session agreed to give their sanction to proceed with the organ, the matter was remitted to the Board of Managers, who then formed a committee and set about the business of obtaining prices. On 28 June 1875, the Organ Committee reported on initial estimates received: 'Offers were submitted from several makers at prices varying from £675 to £1133 complete.'[4] They also discussed the siting of the organ:

> Remarks were also made by some of the builders as to the most suitable site for the instrument, on this subject also a letter was read from Mr Leiper, the Church Architect; after considering the matter fully the managers decided that it would be impracticable to build a recess behind the Church or to remove the pulpit forward and that in the circumstances the back of the gallery was the most eligible site.

The selection of the choir gallery as the most suitable site within the Church also meant that the stained glass windows depicting David and Miriam, which had originally been installed in the south façade in 1867, and whose musical subject matter had clearly been chosen to reflect the function of the gallery, would be obscured by the new organ. These were relocated to the east façade in 1899 (see **6. Documenting the Building**).

On 28 July 1875, the Board of Managers noted that the Organ Committee had received fuller estimates from some of the organ builders 'which were gone into at some length'.[5] A further report is recorded in the Minutes of the Managers' meeting of 26 October 1875, where a Mr Miller, who appears to have been entrusted with much of the responsibility for obtaining prices, submitted a statement in the matter of the organ. Since the meeting of 28 July of that year, he had been in London. There, he had: 'waited upon two of the builders whose estimates had been entertained, from what he saw there, and from information acquired by careful enquiry elsewhere he formed the opinion that Messrs Willis were the likeliest parties to supply a really good instrument, their lowest quotation however was considerably above what had been previously named as a maximum price'.[6]

The interest generated by the quotation from the firm of Henry Willis, even though their lowest quote was well above the maximum the Dowanhill Organ Committee had resolved to commit to the project, needs to be understood in the light of the reputation which Willis enjoyed at this date. Henry Willis had first achieved fame as an organ builder of distinction at the time of the Great Exhibition in London of 1851. His firm, Henry Willis and Sons, went on to become the most famous in Britain. This rise to prominence took place over a period when organ manufacture in Britain was at a scale that outstripped that of the other leading organ-building countries of the Continent.[7]

Willis was born in London in 1821. Apprenticed to John Gray in 1835, he moved to Cheltenham in the early 1840s to join WE Evans, who specialised in reed harmoniums but also built organs. They produced a two-manual free-reed instrument, which was exhibited at Novello's in London. Willis's skill in voicing reed stops was due to this early experience. Willis then set up on his own at Gray's Inn Road, London, his first large job being to rebuild the Gloucester Cathedral organ in 1847. Willis visited

France in 1848 and 1849, meeting Cavaillé-Coll, whose instruments were notable for their harmonic stops, the dominance of reeds in full organ, the striking solo effects of loud reeds and the perfect cohesion of the whole.

The principal reason for Willis's remarkable success, however, stemmed from the efforts he made in the 1850s and 1860s to match or even surpass the achievements of his competitors, and to satisfy public demand for organs that were more powerful and better made. The most ambitious organ shown at the Great Exhibition in London in 1851 was built by Willis and possessed no fewer than seventy stops. Many commissions followed the success of Willis's Great Exhibition feat, including the large and impressive new organ for St George's Hall, Liverpool.

The main features of the Willis style of organ had become established by the late 1860s when, after years of struggle against more experienced competitors and several lean years in the turbulent economic climate following the banking crisis of 1866, Willis directed a number of spectacular projects that brought him considerable success and recognition. His organs for the Royal Albert Hall and Alexandra Palace in London played a vital part in establishing his pre-eminence. The former was completed in 1871 and was spectacular in size and complexity, a showpiece of Willis's technical skill. This and the Alexandra Palace organ, which was destroyed by fire in 1873 but replaced by Willis in 1875, established him in the secular arena and led to further commissions for concert organs. It was during this period too that Willis established himself as the pre-eminent church organ builder. He also patented his own pneumatic key action which provided the flexibility to divide organs.

At the same time that Dowanhill UP Church was considering the quotation from Willis and others, a neighbouring congregation, Hillhead Parish Church, whose minister was Dr David Strong, had set out on a similar project to acquire an organ. Mr Miller presented the Dowanhill Church Managers with a proposal for collaboration between the two churches which would, he believed, allow a cost-effective commission for organs for both churches to be negotiated:

> Mr Miller further stated that Mr Strong's Congregation had ordered an organ from Messrs Willis to cost about £1000 and that with Mr Begbie he had met Mr Willis, who with them visited the Church and suggested that an instrument somewhat similar to that ordered by Mr Strong's people would be suitable, and that were the two instruments ordered nearly alike and to be fitted up so close to each other a saving would be effected in which we would share the benefit, in the circumstances Mr Miller thought that we should place the order with Mr Willis.[8]

**Plate XXXV**  The Dowanhill Willis Organ. Courtesy of Historic Scotland.

At this point, however, 'a lengthy discussion ensued' and the meeting was adjourned without the disputed issues being resolved. Their nature was not recorded at this stage but the debates re-emerged at a later meeting.

In the meantime, a decision was made at the next meeting to seek professional advice. According to Rev Dickie, this was provided by AL Peace: 'the organ was built to the specification of Dr Peace, Organist of Glasgow University at the time when I was a student there.'[9] The introduction of the guiding hand of AL Peace is likewise noted in the Minute Book of the Board of Managers of Dowanhill Church, though his name is spelled 'Piece' or 'Peice' in the earlier references to his attendance.

> Mr Begbie suggested that before taking further steps in the matter of the organ, we should seek professional assistance and advice, that we might be guided as to the kind of instrument which would be most suitable, a specification drawn up accordingly, and that when ordered and being erected our adviser should see that the instrument was right in material and workmanship and also conformable to specification in extent and quality. Mr Peice was named as a suitable person to advise.[10]

Dr Peace was therefore invited to attend the next meeting of the Board of Managers on 4 November 1875:

> It was explained to him for what purpose he had been asked to be present, and having consented to advise and assist the managers in the procuring of an organ, the terms were arranged for which he gave his services, a specification was submitted by Dr Peice which was explained fully to the meeting and as it appeared to be for such an instrument as would suit the Church – Mr Begbie proposed and Mr Fowler seconded the motion that we adopt Dr Peice's specification for a two manual organ, small pipes to be of spotted metal, agreed to, and Mr Miller instructed to forward this specification to Messrs Willis asking their quotation for same.[11]

The response from Willis was reported at the following meeting on 10 November:

> Mr Miller submitted Mr Willis reply quoting price for Organ in terms of Dr Peice's specification which, with the addition of the Pneumatic Lever, which he thought, it should not in justice to the builder, want would cost £1,060 – he suggested some points where a saving might be effected, but urged very strongly that the Managers should reconsider their deliberation and in preference adopt an organ similar to that for Hillhead Church, that it would be a more complete instrument and that two being alike would enable him to give better value – after comparing relative prices it was agreed that we might sacrifice the extended compass and in lieu get the case and see if a rather lower offer would be accepted, in terms of this resolution Mr Fowler submitted the following motion seconded by Mr Curle – That Mr Miller be instructed to telegraph Messrs Willis an offer of

> £950 for an organ similar to that ordered for Hillhead Church, except that our compass is to extend from CC to G instead of to upper C as in theirs but that our offer includes cost of case and Pneumatic Lever.[12]

The continuing negotiations on price were reported at the meeting of 11 November 1875:

> Mr Miller reported having wired to Mr Willis as instructed, in reply to which he had a telegram, offering to split difference in price (say £975). As considering the instrument the price appeared moderate and as any further concession on Mr Willis part was unlikely Mr Aikman moved that we accept Mr Willis offer and authorize Mr Miller to complete the transaction. Seconded by Mr Curle and agreed to. Mr Aikman was approached to preside at the approaching annual meeting of the Congregation. Towards the close Dr Peace joined the meeting and concurred in the choice of the instrument expressing the opinion that a good bargain had been made.[13]

Arrangements for the installation of the organ were first discussed at the Managers' meeting of 22 November 1875:

> Mr Miller submitted Mr Willis signed Contract for the organ also a letter asking dimensions of place provided for it with a strong recommendation to have it placed as low as possible – The Managers instructed Mr Miller to communicate with Mr Leiper for the required information keeping in view the recommendation of Mr Willis – Mr Miller was also empowered to get an estimate from Mr Barr of Glasgow for Hydraulic Engine and all its fittings and fitting up.[14]

The dispute which had taken place at the earlier meeting of 26 October 1875 resurfaced during the meeting of 22 November, and it now becomes clear from the Minutes that this had concerned the issue of whether to press on with the contract before the money had first been subscribed, and indeed, whether such an expensive and elaborate organ was required at all. At the October meeting, a motion that no organ be ordered without the money having been first subscribed was carried by five votes to four. No record of this important motion appeared in the Minutes. At the November meeting, one of the Managers, Mr Sinclair, protested about this situation, arguing that 'such an expensive Organ as that of Messrs Willis' should therefore not have been ordered without all the money having been first subscribed. Mr Sinclair then raised his underlying complaint, that there was 'no necessity for such an elaborate instrument to conduct our Public Worship'.[15] Mr Sinclair's protest was recorded in the Minutes of the November meeting, but the Managers also appended a statement claiming that the voting on the motion at the October meeting had been informal, and that only if the vote had been formal, would the motion actually have been carried. It was then unanimously agreed that the vote on the issue should be declared null and void.[16] Thus it can be seen that the decision to acquire 'such an elaborate instrument' as a Willis organ was arrived at only after much consideration and not without some serious misgivings being raised within the Church and its governing bodies: even the Board of Managers was fairly evenly split on the matter.

Progress on the organ was reported at the start of 1876:

> Plans of the Organ by Mr Willis showing general arrangement and space taken up were submitted, and a note from Mr Leiper read stating that with Dr Peace he had examined the plans and that they both approved of them – the Secretary explained that Mr Miller was in London and that he intended to call upon Mr Willis after learning that the plans met with approval of the Managers.[17]

By the time of the Managers' meeting of 1 March 1876, manufacture of the organ was nearing completion:

> Mr Miller intimated that he had been in correspondence with Mr Willis regarding the progress being made with Organ from which he expected that it would be finished at the Works towards the end of this month – he had seen Barr repeatedly about engine but found that Messrs Willis and Barr could not quite agree as to what was needed and that Mr Willis has suggested that Organ should be blown by hand for a little and that the engine could easily be put in afterwards.[18]

A circular was also issued to subscribers that month, and the Dowanhill Church Repairs Committee was given powers to make the necessary alterations to the gallery. By 26 March, the organ was ready to be sent off, and 'Plans were shown prepared by Mr Leiper showing the alterations which would be necessary and the Repairs Committee was instructed to get them carried out'.[19] According to Rev Dickie, erection of the organ was also carried out 'on the advice of Mr Leiper', and its installation involved the removal of ten pews containing sixty-five places or 'sittings'.[20]

On 11 April, it was reported that the instrument was now in place and almost completed. Arrangements to celebrate its installation and inauguration were made by the Musical Committee, and consisted of 'an opening Recital and Concert in a Week evening' and 'us[e] in the Church Service the Sabbath following'.[21] Dr Peace, who had acted as advisor on the organ commission, also gave the inaugural recital.[22]

### The 'Brilliant' Characteristics of Willis Organs

The opening of the Dowanhill Willis organ was reported in the *Glasgow Herald*:

> On Friday evening, the Dowanhill U.P. Church organ was formally opened by Dr A. L. Peace, when the large building was completely filled. The instrument has been built by Mr. Willis of London from Dr Peace's specification.[23]

The article acknowledged that 'the Dowanhill U.P. congregation have good reason to be proud of their organ'. But in addition to this praise, it also criticised aspects of the instrument and the opening performance. The organist, it warned, should 'beware of the powers at his command'. According to the writer, churches should spend less money on their organs, as 'brilliant stops' were unnecessary. The *Herald's* comments reflect the controversies of the day, both in terms of the 'brilliance' of the Willis sound and the extravagance of congregations. As we have seen, the *Herald's* ambivalence was matched by the mixed views of the Dowanhill congregation and its Managers.

Today, the Willis organs that survive in unaltered or sympathetically restored state are valued for the unique and unprecedented power of their sound and effects. Thus, Stephen Bicknell observed, in *The Making of the Victorian Organ* (1996), that 'the mature Willis organ is an individual creation unlike any other'.[24] Willis's biographer, WL Sumner, was even more emphatic, believing that 'a Father Willis is part of our artistic heritage; it should be jealously preserved'.[25] Willis's organs were reliable and durable in their action and structure, but they were also arresting and inspiring in their tone qualities. In particular, new techniques of reed and flue voicing were incorporated in a tonal scheme of great originality and daring.

What does an unaltered Father Willis organ really sound like? Stephen Bicknell felt overwhelmed when he first saw – and heard – the organ in St Dominic's Priory, Haverstock Hill, in London. The location was close to Willis's home and Willis was known to have done the finishing personally in this instance. Bicknell felt confident that the voicing and regulation were as left by the man himself:

> The organ retains all its nineteenth century pipework without change [...] All the principal stops are voiced boldly and with a characteristic bright tone. The mixtures are, in their way, as uncompromisingly bright as some of the fiercest neo-baroque organs, but [with] a quite different kind of brightness [...] The organ is still at its original high pitch; only renovation work has ever been done on it.[26]

The qualities of boldness and brightness described here may well have been what attracted the Managers of Dowanhill Church to Willis's organs, and they may also have felt that these would resonate well with the qualities of the visual decoration of their church. The same qualities, in addition to the extravagance in monetary terms, are also likely to have been what others among the management and congregation of the Church and the wider public found distasteful, as the reference to 'brilliant stops' in the *Herald* review suggests, just as the collecting plates, and possibly other aspects of the painted decoration, had been complained of as too highly decorated (see above, **Chapter 7**).

In 1877, a year after the inauguration of the organ in Dowanhill Church, Willis completed his most acclaimed organ – that of Salisbury Cathedral. There, he even succeeded in winning over Sir Frederick Gore-Ouseley, who had been a major promoter of the German system of organ building. Sir Frederick wrote enthusiastically to the organist at Salisbury: 'I honestly believe you have the finest church organ in the world – certainly the best in England, and I heartily congratulate you on the same.'[27] Present-day assessments continue to support the nineteenth-century praise of this organ as virtually unrivalled in musical and historical terms, all the more so because it is believed that it sounds today much as it did in 1877. Before he died in 1901, Willis went on to build organs for many more cathedrals throughout Britain, including Glasgow. The organist at Glasgow Cathedral, Mr Walton, knew the Dowanhill Willis, and told Rev Dickie that the diapasons of the Dowanhill instrument – the stops which give the instrument its characteristic tone colour – had 'all the Willis quality and distinction, seldom equalled by any other builder'.[28]

### Cottier and the Decoration of Musical Instruments

The Dowanhill Willis was installed in the Church a decade after the building was completed and the decoration carried out by Cottier. No evidence has been found that Cottier or his assistant Andrew Wells were brought back to the church in order to decorate the instrument. By contrast, evidence uncovered in the course of the relocation of the 1860s Townhead Willis to St Margaret's Church, Knightswood has revealed coloured patterns (fig. 108) which provides a singular clue to the decoration from Cottier's famous scheme at Townhead, which, as has already been noted, was described by a contemporary commentator, James Mavor: 'great masses of positive colour, red and blue, with figures of dense black – the motif was Egyptian and the design might have found a fitting place in a great hall of the Pharaohs'.[29] As discussed above, it is likely that, to a Victorian sensibility, a Willis organ would have sounded overpowering. The combination of the Willis sound at Townhead emerging from a Cottier colour scheme would certainly have been calculated to shock. Interestingly, the twin sister of the Dowanhill Willis, the Hillhead Willis, before its considerable alteration, also had a scheme of decoration for the organ pipes which is likely to have been by Cottier & Co (Fig 109).

Archival research has also uncovered further evidence of designs for organ decoration by Cottier and his partners. A scheme of decoration was prepared but never implemented by Lyon and Cottier & Co in Australia.[30] In the course of restoration of the organ at St Paul's Anglican Cathedral, by Harrison and Harrison in 1989-90, Marc Nobel decorated the instrument in accordance with these designs (Fig 110).

**Fig 108** Decorated Pipework from the Willis Organ, Townhead Church, Glasgow, D Cottier, ca. 1865. Courtesy of Kerr Jamieson.

**Fig 109** Interior Hillhead Church, Glasgow, containing the Hillhead Willis Organ with its pipework decoration attributed to Cottier & Co. Courtesy of Kerr Jamieson.

**Fig 110** Organ in St Paul's Anglican Cathedral. Melbourne, recently decorated to a design by Lyon, Cottier & Co. Photograph by Brian Hatfield, Harison & Harrison.

Cottier's excursions into the field of decoration of musical instruments were not confined to organs. A number of pianos decorated by him are extant (fig 111), (see Catalogue in Appendix). The *New York Times* reported on October 28 1922 on a 'Cottier Piano to Be Sold':

*A Cottier piano is in next week's sale at the Silo Galleries. The materials of the case in themselves deserve a word of comment. Stained maple is the principal wood used, but the decorated panel above the keyboard and the interior parts are made of the beautiful comino wood, only one shipload of which ever was brought into this country. The wood had to be carried on muleback over the tops of the Andes to the coast, and even its rich colour and extraordinary grain could not justify further shipments. A little extremely fine furniture was made of it, however, and Cottier spared no pains to obtain artistic designs appropriate to it.*

## Restoration of the Dowanhill Willis

Very few Willis organs remain with the original fire and bravado undimmed by later alterations, and those built towards the end of Willis's life are considered neither as 'brilliant' nor as 'bright' as the most characteristic organs of the 1870s and 1880s, such as the one at Dowanhill. Later organists and builders have often tried to 'update' or 'improve' the Willis organs they inherited, with the result that the original conception is often completely obscured. The restoration of the Dowanhill Willis from 2004 was therefore a significant event. As in the case of the organ at St Dominic's, Haverstock Hill, Willis is believed to have carried out the voicing of the Dowanhill organ himself. Rev Dickie, recalled: 'Mr Willis's grandson,

who called on me some years ago, informed me that his grandfather had himself voiced the organ which was built for us.'[31] During the dismantling of the organ prior to restoration, a notebook, believed to be Willis's, was found, containing his notes on the voicing.

The Dowanhill Willis was dismantled in 2004 and taken to Durham for restoration by Harrison & Harrison Ltd. with a grant from the Heritage Lottery Fund. It will be reinstalled in its original site in the south gallery of the Church once the programme of building works and restoration of the painted decoration have been completed. A full record of its restoration will be included in the Conservation Report which will be published as the second volume on the Dowanhill Church Project.

**Fig 111** Detail from a Steinway Piano, decorated by Cottier & Co, New York. Photo: John Hammond.

[1] See Cameron 1936, Prefatory Note.
[2] Meeting of Managers and Session, 30 Mar 1875, DCR CH3/1267/7.
[3] Dickie 1926, 83.
[4] Managers Minutes, 28 Jun 1875, DCR CH3/1267/7.
[5] Managers Minutes, 28 Jul 1875, DCR CH3/1267/7.
[6] Managers Minutes, 26 Oct 1875, DCR CH3/1267/7.
[7] For Willis's biography and his importance, see especially Bicknell 1996.
[8] Managers Minutes, 26 Oct 1875, DCR CH3/1267/7.
[9] Dickie 1926, 84.
[10] Managers Minutes, 2 Nov 1875, DCR CH3/1267/7.
[11] Managers Minutes, 4 Nov 1875, DCR CH3/1267/7.
[12] Managers Minutes, 10 Nov 1875, DCR CH3/1267/7.
[13] Managers Minutes, 11 Nov 1875, DCR CH3/1267/7.
[14] Managers Minutes, 22 Nov 1875, DCR CH3/1267/7.
[15] Managers Minutes, 22 Nov 1875, DCR CH3/1267/7.
[16] Managers Minutes, 22 Nov 1875, DCR CH3/1267/7.
[17] Managers Minutes, 10 Jan 1876, DCR CH3/1267/7.
[18] Managers Minutes, 1 Mar 1876, DCR CH3/1267/7.
[19] Managers Minutes, 22 Mar 1876, DCR, CH3/1267/7.
[20] Dickie 1926, 84.
[21] Managers Minutes, 11 Apr 1876, DCR, CH3/1267/7.
[22] Dickie 1926, 84.
[23] *Glasgow Herald*, Apr 1876.
[24] Bicknell 1996, page no.26.
[25] Sumner 1955, page no.105.
[26] Bicknell 1996, page no.26.
[27] Mathews 1972, page no.18.
[28] Dickie 1926, 83-4.
[29] Mavor 1923, 1:227-8.
[30] For the restoration, see www.ohta.org.au/organs/organs/StPaulsMelb.html.
[31] Dickie 1926, 83-4.

# APPENDIX I: COTTIER'S:
# DOWANHILL PARISH CHURCH⋆
## Ranald MacInnes

The east window on the south side of the Church has the inscription: 'Dowanhill United Presbyterian Church. Erected under the Pastorate of the Revd T M Lawrie, William Leiper, Architect 1866'. This prosaic statement records the building of one of the greatest urban churches in the city, possibly in the whole country: a massive, yet elegant structure totally satisfying within itself but crucial in its setting; an essential pivot between the town houses and the tenements of Partick (ill. 1).

Illustration 1  Dowanhill Church, W Leiper, 1865. Courtesy of David Robertson.

⋆ Unpublished Guide, 1993

With his success in the competition for Dowanhill, William Leiper (1839-1916) launched his solo career and announced himself as the main rival to the brilliant and scholarly John Honeyman, Mackintosh's master and architect of the greatest of Glasgow Gothic Revival churches, Lansdowne (1862-3) (ill. 2). Leiper was a pupil of Boucher and Cousland (Casa d'Italia and St Mungo Club, both in Glasgow) who later worked for a short time in England, and then with Andrew Heiton in Perth for whom he built Findlater church in Dublin.

He then went, briefly, to work in the office of Campbell Douglas in Glasgow before setting up a relatively short-lived partnership with RG Melvin. For a time, in his later thirties, Leiper gave up architecture to study painting in Paris, but was tempted back to Glasgow to mastermind the fitting out of the circular Russian imperial yacht, *Livadia*, the first time an architect had been awarded such a commission. Leiper's late works were carried out in partnership with WH McNab.

Illustration 2  Lansdowne UP Church, Glasgow, J Honeyman, 1862. RCAHMS. Licensor www.rcahms.gov.uk

During his time in London, Leiper worked with William White and with JL Pearson, the celebrated Gothic Revivalist, from whom he would doubtless have drawn inspiration for archaeological correctitude, if not for urban composition, which is the hallmark of the urban church in Scotland, where a building's contribution to the city as a 'monument' is everything. Leiper's better known works in Glasgow include Templeton's Carpet Factory (1899), Partick Burgh Hall (1872), Hyndland Parish Church (1887) and the Sun Life Insurance building in West George Street (1892).

A Glaswegian by birth and by inclination, Leiper was a prolific designer, more famous, perhaps for his many large villas, mostly in Helensburgh where he was later to stay, but his two great church designs, Dowanhill and Camphill-Queen's Park are as important as any Gothic Revival churches in the country. The detailed sources for both designs are French (possibly also English, particularly the belfry stage of some Northamptonshire

churches): in particular, Normandy Gothic of the thirteenth century, and, in greater particular, the soaring, twin-towered St Stephen's at Caen, which was illustrated in the elder Pugin's volume on the subject (ill. 3). But the archaeological mania for 'correct' detailing which took root in England never got a foothold in Northern Europe nor, indeed, in Scotland, where the style was regarded by many as derivative: 'not national' as Alexander Thomson put it. From the earliest point of revival in Scotland, as with classical architecture, the scenic effort of a building was as important, if not more so, as its detailing. This is true of two Edinburgh churches, Gillespie Graham's Tolbooth St John's (1842-44) – whose details were drawn by AWN Pugin – and Pilkington's Barclay-Bruntsfield (1862), with which Dowanhill has compositional affinities. Dowanhill's spire, at 195 feet, is of course its most remarkable feature and as at Bruntsfield, set at the head of rising ground to the west of the street because of the imperative for uninterrupted straight lines (ills 4 and 5).

Illustration 3  Normandy Gothic.

*A*  Camphill UP Church, Glasgow, W Leiper, 1875. RCAHMS. Licensor www.rcahms.gov.uk

*B*  St Stephen's, Caen, illustrated in AWN Pugin, 1823, *Specimens of Gothic Architecture.* Courtesy of Robert Gibbs.

Illustration 4  Barclay Church, Bruntsfield, Edinburgh, FT Pilkington, 1862. Courtesy of Stewart Anderson.

Illustration 5  Dowanhill Church, W Leiper, 1865, viewed from Hyndland Street. Courtesy of David Robertson.

The unusual arrangement of gablets, in imitation of a succession of internal chapels, perhaps points to a continuing attempt, begun with Robert Adam's crow-stepped Barony Church in Glasgow, or his chapel at Yester (East Lothian), and ending with the ecclesiastical experiments of Lorimer and Burnet in the early twentieth century, to render Gothic 'national'. The gablet arrangement is, indeed, a national and European (mainly German) feature found at Elgin Cathedral (where each gable did express a chapel) and at St Giles in Edinburgh, which was, and is, of course, very much an ecclesiastical icon. The use of the feature in Glasgow became relatively common in the later nineteenth century after its use by JT Rochead at Park Church and later by Burnet (senior) at St Jude's (Woodlands Road) which is, externally at least, a squat version of Leiper's Dowanhill, but the tendency undoubtedly finds its fullest expression at James Sellars's Belmont and Hillhead Church (1875), which may have been based on a design by Leiper himself.

At Dowanhill we have an extremely fine church which tells us a great deal about our history and our culture.

### The Interior
The Presbyterian form of worship requires, quite simply, a great hall in which to preach. The contrived greatness of the space is achieved at Dowanhill through the relatively novel use of laminated timbers (ill. 6), which allowed a complete clear span where arcades, such as at Camphill-Queen's Park might have been expected. Many such single span churches were put up in the nineteenth century, by the Hays of Liverpool, for example, at Brechin, Bridge of Allan, and Greenock, but few have the impact of Dowanhill. Everything is, of course, focused on the preacher: this is neither a 'limitation' nor a 'failing', but a cultural fact; it does mean, however, that the Gothic, with its chapels, baptisteries, and transepts has little relevance in plan for Protestant worship. The ways round this problem for the revival of Gothic have been ingenious, for example at Rochead's Renfrew Old Parish Church, where the notional baptistery becomes an externally-expressed polygonal kirk session house. Equally, in Gothic architecture, no meeting room, vestry or hall was required, so these had to be architecturally incorporated. Leiper's interpretation of the Presbyterian requirement is, in its own terms, quite brilliant. The halls that Leiper designed at Dowanhill, their ingeniously-shaped roofs presaging the architect's domestic work, are incorporated into the whole without taking away from the monumentality of the church (ill. 7).

Illustration 6  Laminated Timbers in Downhill Church, W Leiper, 1865. Courtesy of Four Acres Charitable Trust.

Illustration 7  Dowanhill Church Halls, W Leiper, 1865. Courtesy of Historic Scotland.

As with many of our nineteenth-century institutions, such as the law and political administration, perhaps ironically for the Church's new use, there is a strong sense of theatre, both in the geography of the space and the way in which that space demands an unambiguous focal point, which, in Leiper's scheme is, of course the pulpit. But the pulpit is much more than a pedestal. At Dowanhill it is the architectural centrepiece of the (liturgical) east end; a huge stone balcony, almost at gallery height, which, as in most United Presbyterian churches, is reached by the minister, as if by magic, without passing

through the congregation. The pulpit itself – generously provided with space for demonstrative preaching – is the climax of a complex, almost unimaginably vivid, hand-painted colour scheme by a young Glaswegian, Daniel Cottier, a celebrated international designer. Cottier, who also provided the stained glass, crowned the whole 'Gesamtkunstwerk' with a vast painted sky of stars and planets on the hammerbeam roof. The painted decoration was later repainted by Cottier's associates, Guthrie and Wells.

### Daniel Cottier (1838-91)

Cottier was born in Glasgow and trained there as a stained glass artist with the firm of Kearney & Co before continuing his studies in Dunfermline, Leith and London, where he was exposed – if to no great effect – to the rantings of Ruskin and the Working Men's College. He was appointed manager of Field & Allen of Edinburgh in 1862, but set up on his own in Glasgow in 1865 to execute the Dowanhill decorative scheme. Cottier offered his clients the total aesthetic interior and to satisfy the demand he became a picture dealer and, in so doing, 'discovered' the Barbizon school along with earlier French masters such as Delacroix and Corot. As Cottier's memorialist put it, in the Durand-Ruel Catalogue in 1892:

> In England the parochial feeling was so strong [...] that even now the National Gallery contains no single specimen of the highest achievement of the century. But in Scotland, where the historical regard for France is yet a living sentiment, the case was far other. Scotland indeed abounds in examples of the art of the greater modern Frenchmen; and her good fortune is largely due to the insight, the activity, and the daring of Daniel Cottier.

But it is for his stained glass and decorative scheme that we celebrate Cottier at Dowanhill. The external promise of Dowanhill's gablets is kept in the stunning series of stained glass windows, framed in pseudo-aedicules and associated with one of the most arresting schemes of internal decoration ever attempted in Presbyterian worship. Heroic full-length portraits, Old Testament heads and geometric foliage are designed as an essential artistic whole with the stencilled wall decoration. In this way, the 'barn' problem – the problem of the huge single space – is brilliantly solved with Cottier's fantastic programme of decoration. This is the key to the success, as a work of art, of Dowanhill: the place of the building in the cityscape; its architectural detailing; its synthesis of architecture; and its unique interior decoration. In their patronage of Cottier in the 1860s, the congregation of Dowanhill was one step ahead of fashionable elites in America and Australia. On both continents he was to have a huge impact on progressive tastes in the fine as well as in the decorative arts. By 1873 he had established his own art furnishing firm, with showrooms in London,

New York, Sydney and Melbourne. It was in these centres that Cottier disseminated the artistic ideas of the Aesthetic Movement and introduced the art-buying public to the Barbizon Schools, examples of which already graced the walls of many Glasgow interiors. 'The great majority of people who are bent on being in the fashion and up to the times […] must be cared for, and the place for them is Cottier's', commented Scribner's, a New York magazine, in 1874: 'Let a few years pass and we are sure that the lesson that Messrs Cottier are teaching us will have been so learnt that they will be put upon their mettle to keep up with us. For in America […] we are all sick of tameness and copying and only ask to be shown the better way to walk in it with a will.'

As well as being an outstanding work of art in its own right, Dowanhill Church is a physical representation of the way in which the elite of Glasgow's West End thought about themselves: not simply as local or national leaders of taste, but in the vanguard of the Aesthetic Movement that was to influence the western world.

Ranald MacInnes
12 March 1993

# APPENDIX II:
## CATALOGUE RAISONNÉ OF THE PRINCIPAL WORKS OF DANIEL COTTIER; JOHN LAMB LYON; COTTIER & CO, LONDON AND NEW YORK; LYON, COTTIER & CO; AND LYON, WELLS, COTTIER & CO, SYDNEY AND MELBOURNE

David Robertson and Max Donnelly

### Introduction

This catalogue is based on the catalogue raisonné compiled by Max Donnelly for his MA dissertation on Cottier & Company (1998), and has been extended and updated with his permission for the present publication.

The current catalogue represents only the state of knowledge of the authors at the time of writing and cannot hope to be comprehensive, as much more research requires to be done. It is presented here in the hope it will stimulate further research.

The catalogue is organised in six sections reflecting the geographical distribution of Daniel Cottier's work and the different branches of his business. Within these sections works are identified by the original place they were commissioned for and listed by known date of manufacture. Works where the place of commission is unknown (which are taken to include works that may have appeared in exhibitions) are then listed by date, followed by works where the date is unknown, which are listed alphabetically by place. Works where neither place nor date is known are then listed alphabetically by their current location. Finally works that have been attributed mainly on stylistic grounds are listed, but placed at the end of the section and then ordered according to the same principles as the known works.

The main sections of this catalogue are:

1. Daniel Cottier in Scotland and North of England until 1869
2. Cottier in partnership and as Cottier & Co in UK and Ireland from 1869
3. Cottier & Co in USA from 1873
4. Lyon Cottier & Co in Australia from 1873
5. Lyon, Wells, Cottier & Co in Australia from 1887.

Each section represents the individual or firm responsible for the manufacture of the object or scheme. Within each of the sections, key designers are also noted. These are identified in the first instance as the relevant principals in the firms set up by Cottier – Daniel Cottier, John Lamb Lyon or Andrew Wells. If there are references available to

support a further attribution to specific designers either engaged by or collaborating with them then these names are also provided.

It is in the nature of many schemes where specialist decorators and designers are involved in building projects that the architect for the building will determine, guide or in some way influence the design of fittings and decoration. In some cases it has been possible to comment on this relationship but it should not be assumed that an architect would not have influenced the design where no such influence is referenced in the catalogue. Indeed it is more than likely where decoration or glass is executed at the time that a building is put up that the architect would have been the key determiner of the style and even the content of the design.

Coverage in England is confined mainly to the North of England due to lack of published information on Cottier & Co work in the South and Midlands. Coverage of Wales and Ireland is likewise limited for the same reason. The cataloguers have not always had direct access to the works covered and some of these works are only known from written sources. Due to the very varied nature and scale of the works included, the dimensions are not given and the amount of detail provided in the catalogue entries likewise varies. Where different commissions were executed at different dates within the same building they are distinguished from each other by Roman numerals.

The catalogue does not extend to cover the items of furniture, glass and other objects that have appeared in auction houses and salerooms and have been attributed to Cottier and his associates over recent years. The authors consider that a catalogue of movable items that have appeared in antique journals and salerooms would justify a separate if complex study. Only movable items that already form part of important collections or are associated with known places have been included here.

At the end of each catalogue entry, the key sources used to compile the entry are noted. A date in square brackets after a website address indicates the year in which the website was consulted.

# 1. DANIEL COTTIER WORKS IN SCOTLAND AND THE NORTH OF ENGLAND UNTIL 1869

## WORKS ASSOCIATED WITH PLACES OF KNOWN OR APPROXIMATE DATES

**1    Seaton Cottage, Extension, Stained Glass, Decoration and Furniture**

| | |
|---|---|
| Designer: | Daniel Cottier, possibly for Field and Allan |
| Date: | 1862-67 |
| Original Location: | Seaton Cottage, Bridge of Don |
| Patron: | Dr John Forbes White. |

**Description:**

Two-room extension to an existing cottage with hand painting and stencil work, stained glass, painted furniture, wallpaper, curtain fabric and other ornament. The stained glass in the dining room depicted ten artists: *Raphael, Crabbit, della Robbia, Titian, Velazquez, Palissy, Leonardo, Zeuxis, Rembrandt and Benvenuto [Cellini]*. The stained glass in the drawing room depicted eight women associated with poets: *Electra (?), Antigone, Cassandra, Emily, Miranda, Helen, Dido* and *Ophelia*.

Mary Harrower wrote in her biography of the patron John Forbes White:

> It was soon after this that he stayed in a friend's house which had just been decorated by the artistic genius Daniel Cottier. The harmonious work was a revelation to him, and he asked Cottier to redecorate his town house. A drawing-room and dining-room designed by Cottier were added to Seaton Cottage, and a stately drawing-room was built at Bridgefield, Bridge of Don, where his mother now lived. Up to its great bow-window over-looking the distant town of Aberdeen he rode daily to greet her on his way to business.

**Current position:**

Stained glass monograms survive from the front door although the whereabouts of the stained glass in the rooms is unknown. Items of furniture survive at the property and in family collections including an ebonised and stencilled wardrobe, a dressing table and a wash stand. The scheme of decoration was partially restored in 2005-06. The cottage is now known as Glenseaton Cottage.

**References:**

Gould 1969, 1-2; Harrower 1918, 31-32; Minto 1970, 11.

**2    Bridgefield, Drawing Room Extension and Decoration**

| | |
|---|---|
| Designer: | Daniel Cottier, possibly for Field and Allan |
| Date: | 1862-63 |
| Original Location: | Bridgefield, Bridge of Don |
| Patron: | Dr John Forbes White's mother. |

**Description:**

A drawing room built and decorated by Cottier at Bridgefield for John Forbes White's mother.

**Current position:**

Bridgefield and its drawing room still survive but the decoration by Cottier is painted over.

**References:**

Gould 1969, 1; Harrower 1918, 31-32.

**3    269 Union Street, Picture Gallery Decoration and Furniture**

| | |
|---|---|
| Designer: | Daniel Cottier, possibly for Field and Allan |
| Date: | c.1862 |
| Original Location: | 269 Union Street, Aberdeen |
| Patron: | Dr John Forbes White. |

**Description:**

According to Minto the furniture was 'elaborate [...] in the Flemish style'

**Condition:**

Not known

**References:**

Gould 1969, 2; Minto 1970, 11.

**4    By King's College Aberdeen, Stained Glass and Furniture**

| | |
|---|---|
| Designer: | Daniel Cottier, possibly for Field and Allan |
| Date: | c. 1863 |
| Original Location: | By Kings College, Aberdeen |
| Patron: | Professor Harrower. |

**Description:**

The stained glass depicted *Flora and Pomona*; the furniture was ebonised with painted and gilt panels of flowers and birds. Condition not known.

**Current Position:**

Not known.

**References:**

Gould 1969, 2.

**5    Pilrig Parish Church, Interior Decoration and Stained Glass**

| | |
|---|---|
| Designer: | Daniel Cottier, for Field and Allan |
| Date: | c.1863 |
| Original Location: | Leith, Edinburgh |
| Patron: | Not known. |

**Description:**

The nave contained a polychromatic scheme of decoration that was destroyed by fire in 1892 and a scheme of geometrical stained glass damaged in the fire and inscribed: 'F & A / EDIN/ LEITH' which survives.

**Current Position:**

The E gallery great rose survives, the west south and north having been replaced. The N and S galleries paired lancets survive. Now Pilrig and Dalmeny Church,

**References:**

Donnelly, Michael 1997, 28; Gifford, McWilliam and Walker 1984, 645.

## 6 St Machar's Cathedral (I), Stained Glass

Designer: Daniel Cottier, possibly for Field and Allan
Date: 1864–68
Original Location: Aberdeen
Patron: Dr John Forbes White.

**Description:**
S aisle, 1st from E, *SS John the Baptist and Peter*, in memory of White's brother Adam, a Christian missionary in India.

**Current position:**
*In situ.*

**References:**
Gould 1969, 1; Harrower 1918, 32; Munro 1909, 227.

## 7 Trinity Church Irvine, Stained Glass

Designer: Daniel Cottier, for Field and Allan
Date: 1864
Original Location: Trinity Church, Irvine, Ayrshire
Patron: Not known.

**Description:**
*The Pharisee and the Publican* and others.

**Current position:**
Around seven panels including the *Pharisee and the Publican* are now in the Stained Glass Museum at Ely Cathedral (76/9/5). Others are in the Glasgow Museums collection (PP 1981.3).

**References:**
Cowen 1985, 237.

## 8 The Elms Interior decoration, Stained Glass and Fireplace

Designer: Daniel Cottier
Date: 1864–66
Original Location: Cairnie Road, Arbroath, Angus
Patron: Provost D Corsar.

**Description:**
The extensive stencilled wall and ceiling decoration is typical of Cottier and compares closely with Seaton Cottage. Cottier was collaborating with Leiper on other houses at this time.

**Current position:**
The building is long neglected and becoming derelict.

**References:**
Kinchin, J 2009 Personal communication.

## 9 Townhead UP Church Interior Decoration, Stained Glass and Organ Pipe Work Decoration

Designer: Daniel Cottier
Date: 1865–66
Original Location: 176 Roystonhill, Glasgow
Patron: James Baird in memory of his brother Alexander Baird of Ury.

**Description:**
The architect was JJ Stevenson for Campbell Douglas and Stevenson. Cottier's first major scheme of church decoration in Glasgow, it was executed in distemper and included stencilled timberwork and decorated organ pipes. The decorated pipes have been relocated to St Margaret's Church Knightswood by organ builder James Mackenzie in the course of saving the organ. Stained glass by Cottier was located in the nave, N, S and W galleries and clerestory, fragments of which also survive also survive the demolition of the church. Of the building, only the tall steeple remains. The decorative scheme was described by James Mavor:

> Undoubtedly the decoration was striking enough. Great masses of positive colour, red, blue, with figures of dense black- the motif was Egyptian and the design might have found a fitting place in a great hall of the Pharaohs. In an ecclesiastical building it was inappropriate; in any building in Western Europe the effect would have been bizarre; the design was out of scale and wanting in the repose indispensable in church architecture. Nevertheless, the decoration was bold and in its way original. I felt at once, here at least is the work of a designer with brains and courage.

**Current position:**
Lost in its entirety apart from the decorated organ pipes and three fragments of glass, one in Glasgow Museums and two in private collections. The steeple of the church was saved.

**References:**
Donnelly, Michael 1997, 29; Mavor 1923, 227-8; Rush 1994, 184; Williamson, Riches and Higgs 1990, 421.

## 10 Dowanhill UP Church Interior Decoration, Stained Glass, Furniture Decoration

Designer: Daniel Cottier in collaboration with William Leiper, architect
Date: 1865–69
Original Location: 93/97 Hyndland Street, Glasgow
Patron: Alexander Kay, Board of Managers of Partick East UP Church.

**Description:**
Cottier's second major scheme of church decoration in Glasgow executed in distemper (walls) and oil paint. It included an elaborately painted pulpit, painted roof trusses, painted gallery fronts, stenciled pew ends, painted metal gallery columns, painted carved stonework, painted communion table and collection stands and a painted and crewelwork pulpit seat. The pulpit seat and two collection stands are now in the Glasgow Museums collection. The elaborate painted wall and ceiling decoration covered the nave and extended into the front vestibule and porch, The nave still contains a complete scheme of geometrical grisaille stained glass with figures comprising an E rose window with Moses, Jeremiah, Oded, David (replaced as Peter), Abraham and Jonathan, eight lower lancet windows with S Lydia, Dorcas, Esther, Abigail, Mary Magdalene, and N Ruth, Deborah and Mary. The ten clerestory upper lancets contain two figure windows of David and Miriam relocated in 1899 from the W tower above the choir from where a quinquefoil of vine leaves and grapes has been taken into store. Miriam is signed Cottier '67.

**Current position:**
The stained glass was repaired and conserved in 2005-6, the decoration is undergoing a programme of research with a view to conservation.

**References:**
Dickie 1926, 73-74; Donnelly, Michael 1997, 30; Green 2001, 40-2; Williamson, Riches and Higgs 1990, 356.

## 11   Kirktonhill, Stained Glass and Possible Interior Decoration

| | |
|---|---|
| Designer: | Daniel Cottier |
| Date: | 1866 |
| Original Location: | Dumbarton, Dunbartonshire |
| Patron: | William Denny. |

**Description:**
A French Gothic villa by William Leiper for which Cottier supplied glass.

**Current position:**
Demolished.

**References:**
*Dictionary of Scottish Architects* 2008, 'William Leiper'; Donnelly, Michael 1997, 30.

## 12   Woodside, Stained Glass

| | |
|---|---|
| Designer: | Daniel Cottier |
| Date: | c.1867 |
| Original Location: | Loch Goil, Argyll |
| Patron: | Donald MacVean. |

**Description:**
Now a five star hotel called The Lodge, this Victorian lochside retreat was modified by Leiper by the addition of a balcony. The glass originally part of a door consists of figure panels with decorated square quarries of antique glass varying in colour from pale green to light amber as a setting for monograms. The glass is full of playful zoomorphic imagery.

**Current position:**
Under restoration.

**References:**
Donnelly, Michael 1997, 29; Cannon L, personal communication 2010.

## 13   Westoe Hall (I), Stained Glass

| | |
|---|---|
| Designer: | Daniel Cottier |
| Date: | c.1867 |
| Original Location: | South Shields, Tees-side |
| Patron: | Not known. |

**Description:**
Stained glass for a private residence incorporating 40 German roundels from James Powell and Sons, Glass Manufacturers, London. Cottier's introduction to the Tees-side region was via the Stevensons of South Shields and Tynemouth, brothers of Cottier's friend, the architect JJ Stevenson.

**Current position:**
Extant.

**References:**
Donnelly, Max 1998, 103; Kinchin, J 2009 Personal communication; Powell Records (1867), 317.

## 14   Holmwood House, Interior Decoration

| | |
|---|---|
| Designer: | Daniel Cottier in collaboration with Alexander Thomson, architect |
| Date: | c.1867 |
| Original Location: | Cathcart, Glasgow |
| Patron: | James Couper. |

**Description:**
According to Thomson's grand-daughter, Mrs WL Stewart, who wrote a memoir in the 1950s: 'I think it was in the villa Alexander did at Cathcart that the drawing-room was paneled and into each panel was inserted a figure from the Legend of King Arthur and these were painted by Daniel Cottier. Somewhere there should be a letter from Cottier to Alexander saying that he is sorry Elaine wasn't dry.'

The extent of Cottier's involvement at Holmwood is not established and has been disputed. The paintings of the *Idylls of the King* for the upstairs drawing room at Holmwood do not appear to have survived or have not been traced. However according to *Villa and Cottage Architecture* they were executed by Hugh Cameron. Investigation of the wall surfaces and paint layers carried out by Alan Ferdinand for Historic Scotland when the property was first acquired by the National Trust for Scotland in the 1990s confirms that these were easel paintings or painted panels hung or attached to the walls to fit the spaces, as indicated by marks on the walls. If Mrs Stewart's memoir is accurate, it could provide intriguing evidence of Cottier commissioning works from other artists to incorporate into a decorative scheme.

The original scheme of painted decoration would have pre-dated Cottier's involvement as a collaborator of Thomson but research on the paint layers, including paint samples, carried out by Alan Ferdinand and Owen Davidson in the dining room, hall, cloakroom and downstairs parlour has provided evidence of a second scheme of decoration, and raises the probability that Cottier was involved in a repainting of the scheme at Holmwood which continued the use of familiar motifs favoured by Greek Thomson, such as dots and palmettes, but transformed by the distinctive palette associated with Cottier. Two signatures, now rather indistinct but perhaps of Cottier's assistants, as well as the date 1867 behind the headpiece in the dining room may offer further support for Cottier's involvement.

**Current position:**
Areas of decoration have been revealed at Holmwood.

**References:**
Donnelly, Michael 1981, 9; Ferdinand, A 2009 Personal communication; Stamp 1995 (2), 50-3. *Villa and Cottage Architecture* 1868, 96.

## 15  Millport West Church and Manse, Interior Decoration and Furniture Decoration

Designer:            Daniel Cottier
Date:                *c.*1867
Original Location:   Millport, Great Cumbrae
Patron:              Not known.

**Description:**
A full scheme of painted decoration including timber ceiling and walls.

**Current position:**
Church demolished 1999. Some fragments of the painted plaster and timber have been salvaged. Painted furniture also survives.

**References:**
Logan 1998.

**Plate XXXVI**  Millport West Church Interior, Great Cumbrae, Bute. Courtesy of Ian Begg.

## 16  Marleybank House, Stained Glass

Designer:            Daniel Cottier
Date:                *c.*1867
Original Location:   Dowanhill, Glasgow
Patron:              Not known.

**Description:**
*Summer, Autumn,* etc. for a private residence

**Current position:**
Extant.

**References:**
Donnelly, Max 1998, 105; Rickards 1995, 31-2.

## 17  Queen's Park UP Church, Interior Decoration and Stained Glass

Designer             Daniel Cottier in collaboration with Alexander Thomson, architect
Date:                1867–69
Original Location:   Langside Road, Glasgow
Patron:              Not known.

**Description:**
Cottier's third major scheme of church decoration in Glasgow executed in collaboration with Alexander 'Greek' Thomson in a Graeco-Egyptian style. The building was destroyed in an air raid, May 1942.

According to the congregation's Jubilee Book: 'Thomson cut the stencils with his own hands, and Cottier gave most valuable advice as to the colouring. Cottier afterwards went to New York to conduct the decoration of millionaires' mansions.'

Ford Madox Brown visited Glasgow in 1883. An interview with the *Evening Times* revealed his impressions:

> *His first questions were 'Why didn't Thomson come to London, and why did Cottier leave it for New York?' To the proposition: 'To what religion is the Church dedicated?' his companion tried in vain to explain the elastic comprehensiveness of the Presbyterian religion. 'Enough! enough!' he cried. 'I want nothing better than the religion that produced art like that. Here line and colouring are suggestive of paradise itself. I now know what has all along been wrong with my ceilings. Well done, Glasgow! I put the crypt of your Cathedral against anything I have seen in ancient Europe, as I do this Thomson-Cottier Church above everything I have seen in modern Europe.*
>
> *'The congregation may be likened to a man who purchases at an ordinary price what he thinks is an ordinary picture, and discovers he is the possessor of an old master.'*

**Current position:**
Building destroyed by an incendiary bomb in 1942.

**References:**
Donnelly, Michael 1981, 9; Rush 1994, 176-7 183-5, *Evening Times* 1893.

## 18  St Nicholas Church Cramlington (I), Stained Glass

Designer:            Daniel Cottier
Date:                1868
Original Location:   Cramlington, Northumbria
Patron:              Not known.

**Description:**
S aisle: *The Wise and Foolish Virgins*; Clerestory: *Jeremiah* (W) and *Memorial to W Striker Johnston* (E).

**Current position:**
Extant.

**References:**
Harrison 1980, 48; Hobler 1987, 6:23; Pevsner and Richmond 1982, 247.

**19    Prudhoe Hall, Stained Glass**

Designer:              Daniel Cottier
Date:                  1868–70
Original Location:     Prudhoe, Northumbria
Patron:                Not known.

**Description:**
Prudhoe Hall was designed by Archibald Dunn in 1868.
Stained glass includes monograms, birds and heraldic motifs.

**Current position:**
Windows are extant.

**References:**
Zielinski 2005.

## WORKS OF KNOWN OR APPROXIMATE DATE NOT ASSOCIATED WITH PLACES

**20    Stained Glass Including *Gentle Shepherd* Exhibited at South Kensington Museum**

Designer:              Daniel Cottier, for Field and Allan
Date:                  1864
Original Location:     South Kensington Museum (now
                       the Victoria and Albert Museum),
                       London
Patron:                South Kensington Museum.

**Description:**
From an exhibition in the South Kensington Museum in the
N and W cloisters. One or more panels by Cottier on W side,
illustrating Allan Ramsay's *The Gentle Shepherd*.

**Current position:**
Victoria and Albert Museum, London.

**References:**
Parry 1864, 7, no. 22; Harrison 1980, 48.

**21    Glazed Earthenware Panel *Day***

Designer:              Daniel Cottier
Date:                  *c.*1865–70
Original Location:     Not known
Patron:                Not known.

**Description:**
Female figure *Day*.

**Current position:**
Victoria and Albert Museum, London.

**References:**
V&A website: www.vam.ac.uk [2009].

**22    Armorial Window at the Paris Universal Exhibition**

Designer:              Daniel Cottier
Date:                  1867
Original Location:     British Gallery, Paris International
                       Exhibition
Patron:                Not known.

**Description:**
Armorial window.

**Current position:**
Not known.

**References:**
Donnelly Max 98, Ref

## WORKS ATTRIBUTED ON STYLISTIC AND OTHER GROUNDS

**23    Kelvinside Parish Church, Stained Glass and Gallery Front Decoration**

Designer:              Daniel Cottier
Date:                  1862–63
Original Location:     Byres Road, Glasgow
Patron:                Not known.

**Description:**
Attributed to Cottier on stylistic grounds by Max Donnelly.
Cottier was a friend of the architect of the church, JJ
Stevenson.

**Current location:**
The geometrical stained glass in the nave, galleries and
clerestory survives. The location of the gallery fronts is
unknown.

**References:**
Donnelly, Max 1998, 101.

**24    39 Partickhill Road, Door Panel Decoration**

Date:                  1865–70
Original Location:     39 Partickhill Road, Glasgow
Patron:                Not known.

**Description:**
Attributed to Cottier on stylistic grounds by Juliet Kinchin.

**Current location:**
The house was demolished in the 1980s.

**References:**
Kinchin 2009 Personal communication.

**25   4 Great Western Terrace, Interior
     Decoration, Stained Glass Quarries and
     Door Furniture**

| | |
|---|---|
| Designer: | Daniel Cottier and other designers |
| Date: | *c.*1867 |
| Original Location: | 4 Great Western Terrace, Glasgow |
| Patron: | James Macgregor. |

**Description:**
Aesthetic interior probably by Cottier and his associates, given the stylistic content and relationship with the architect of the Terrace, Alexander Thomson (see Holmwood House and Queen's Park UP Church above).

**Current Position:**
Extant, restored. Important door furniture was removed prior to restoration.

**References:**
Donnelly, Max 1998, 104; Macdonald 1987, 3 & 42; Rickards 1995, 16; Williamson, Riches and Higgs 1990, 313.

**Plate XXXVII** Door Furniture from 4 Great Western Terrace, Glasgow. © Glasgow Life (Museums).

# 2. DANIEL COTTIER IN PARTNERSHIP AND COTTIER & CO IN UK AND IRELAND FROM 1869

## WORKS ASSOCIATED WITH PLACES OF KNOWN OR APPROXIMATE DATES

### 26  Love Street Fountain Park Cast Iron Monumental Fountain Decoration

Designer:            Daniel Cottier
Date:                1869
Original Location:   Fountain Park, Love Street, Paisley
                     Patron:Coats family.

**Description:**
Elaborately painted decoration applied to zoomorphic fountain with life-like animals and figures.

**Current position:**
Fountain is extant but in need of restoration. The original Cottier colours have been researched by Historic Scotland.

**References:**
Pearce M, Historic Scotland unpublished report, 2008[Author, title and date for bibliog].

**Plate XXXVIII** Graphic Reconstruction of Decoration on Fountain Park Monumental Fountain, Paisley. Courtesy of Historic Scotland

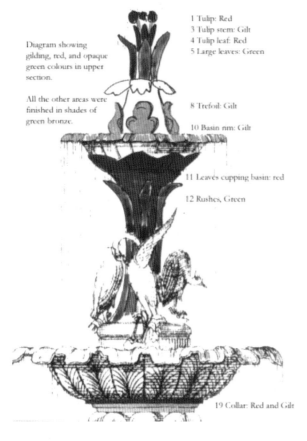

Diagram showing gilding, red, and opaque green colours in upper section.

All the other areas were finished in shades of green bronze.

1 Tulip: Red
3 Tulip stem: Gilt
4 Tulip leaf: Red
5 Large leaves: Green

8 Trefoil: Gilt

10 Basin rim: Gilt

11 Leaves cupping basin: red

12 Rushes, Green

19 Collar: Red and Gilt

### 27  The Retreat, Interior Decoration

Designer:            Daniel Cottier
Date:                c.1869
Original Location:   Kelmscott House, London
Patron:              George Macdonald.

**Description:**
Red walls stencilled with black fleur-de-lys and a dark blue ceiling with scattered stars in silver and gold and a silver crescent moon. The home of George Macdonald poet, writer and preacher, was decorated by Cottier, and subsequently leased by William Morris.

**Current position:**
Not known.

**References:**
Kinchin, J 2003 Personal communication.

### 28  St John the Divine Sale, Stained Glass

Designer:            Daniel Cottier
Date:                1869-91
Original Location:   Brooklands Road, Sale
Patron:              Samuel Brooks.

**Description:**
Brooks engaged Waterhouse as architect for his church. The glass may not be contemporaneous with the church.

**Current position:**
Stained glass is extant.

**References:**
http://www.achurchnearyou.com [2009]

### 29  Colearn House, Interior Decoration, Stained Glass and Fireplace

Designers:           Daniel Cottier and Bruce Talbert
Date:                1869-71
Location:            Auchterarder, Perthshire
Patron:              Alexander Stuart Mackintosh.

**Description:**
The hall contains three lights with monograms, sunflowers and a cat; in the dining room, portraits of the daughters of the patron Dorothy and Lucy, three birds, the *Four Seasons, Morning* and *Night*; on the stair landing *Pomona, Aphrodite* and *Ceres*. A fireplace in the drawing room is attributed to Bruce Talbert.

**Current position:**
Extant.

**References:**
Burke 1986, 415; Donnelly, Michael 1981, 11-12; Hobler 1987, 17.

## 30 Cornhill House, Interior Decoration, Stained Glass

Designer: Daniel Cottier
Date: 1869-73
Original Location: Biggar, Lanarkshire
Patron: Alexander Kay.

**Description:**

Stained glass roundels of four Renaissance figures, *Emperor Charles V, Contess de Horn, Geborn Pamgartin* and *Margaret de Austria.* Internally, the Leiper house was brilliantly decorated, with much of the paintwork done in white, bright blue, gold and brick red.

**Current position:**

Some stained glass extant including the above roundels, interior decoration removed or over-decorated by subsequent owners.

**References:**

Donnelly, Michael 1997, 30; Lambie, B 1998.

## 31 St Machar's Cathedral (II), Stained Glass

Designer: Daniel Cottier
Date: 1871
Location: St Machar's Cathedral, Aberdeen
Patron: Reid family.

**Description:**

E wall, N end, two lancets, *Magdalene and S James,* in memory of G. Walker; E wall, S end, two lancets, SS *Luke and John.*

**Current position:**

Extant.

**References:**

Munro 1909, 227.

## 32 Garthdee House, Stained Glass

Designer: Daniel Cottier
Date: 1872
Original Location: Garthdee Road, Aberdeen
Patron: Not known.

**Description:**

Glass by Cottier & Co.

**Current position:**

Not known.

**References:**

Brogden 1998, 169.

## 33 Advocates Library Aberdeen, Stained Glass

Designer: Daniel Cottier
Date: 1872
Original Location: Advocates Hall Aberdeen
Patron: Not known

**Description:**

Justice.

**Current position:**

Extant.

**References:**

Donnelly, Michael 1997, 30.

## 34 East Kirk of St Nicholas, Interior Decoration and Stained Glass

Designer: Daniel Cottier
Date: 1872
Location: East Kirk of St Nicholas, Aberdeen
Patron: Not known.

**Description:**

It was decorated throughout with a scheme of painted decoration and there was stained glass in an E central lancet in the nave.

**Current position:**

The scheme was destroyed by fire on 9 October 1874. Small elements remain of the decoration.

**References:**

Donnelly, Michael 1997.

## 35 Old West Kirk Greenock, Stained Glass

Designer: Daniel Cottier
Date: 1872
Original Location: Greenock, Renfrewshire
Patron: Daniel Cottier.

**Description:**

*Hope,* Daniel Cottier was the donor in memory of his grandfather, master mariner of Greenock Port (died 1847, aged 84).

**Current position:**

Extant.

**References:**

Harrison 1980, 47-8; Hobler 1987, 18-19.

## 36 Paisley Abbey (I), Stained Glass

Designer: Daniel Cottier
Date: 1872
Original Location: Paisley
Patron: Not known.

**Description:**

Nave S wall, 4th from E, two lancets, *S Enoch, Abraham and David,* in memory of Archibald A Speirs.

**Current position:**

Extant.

**References:**

Donnelly, Michael 1997, 28; Fisher [nd], 2-3.

## 37 St John's Church Birtley, Stained Glass

Designers: Daniel Cottier, possibly with Matthjis Maris (Harrison attr)
Date: 1872
Original Location: Birtley, Durham
Patron: Not known.

**Description:**

N nave, at least two windows: *Angels Plucking Virgins from the Earth.*

**Current position:** .

Extant.

**References:**

Harrison 1980, 57-8.

## 38 Cairndhu House, Interior Decoration and Stained Glass

Designers: Daniel Cottier with Bruce
Talbert, Charles Gow, *et al.*
Date: 1872-73
Original Location: Helensburgh, Dunbartonshire
Patron: Provost John G Ure.

### Description:
Anglo-Japanese style stencil work in the porch, hall ceiling, fireplace and drawing room and dining room ceilings; stained glass includes *Salve*, figures: *Adonis, Paris, Ulysses, Nestor, Beauty, Helen, Penelope, Knowledge, Good Cheer, Purity, Truth, Strength, Fortune, Love, Fame & Plenty; Veritas* and *Pulchritudo, Amor* and *Audentia, Notitia* and *Prudentia.*

### Current Position:
Extant.

### References:
Donnelly, Michael 1981, 12; Donnelly, Michael 1997, 23 & 47.

## 39 St Nicholas Church, Cramlington (II) Stained Glass

Designer: Daniel Cottier
Date: *c.*1872
Original Location: Cramlington, Northumbria
Patron: Not known.

### Description:
N aisle: *Christ in Glory,* flanked by *Psalms 116 and 103.*

### Current position:
Extant.

### References:
Harrison 1980, 21b & 48.

## 40 St Machar's Cathedral (III), Stained Glass

Designer: Daniel Cottier, possibly with
Matthjis Maris
Date: 1873
Original Location: Aberdeen
Patron: Not known.

### Description:
N aisle, 1st from E, two lancets, *Musician Angels*, in memory of Jacob Jamieson.

### Current position:
Extant.

### References:
Donnelly, Michael 1997, 31; Munro 1909, 227.

## 41 Crathie Church, Stained Glass

Designer: Daniel Cottier
Date: 1873
Original Location: Crathie, Aberdeenshire
Patron: Not known.

### Description:
*King David* and MacLeod memorial.

### Current position:
Now in store at the Burrell Collection, Glasgow.

### References:
Donnelly, Michael 1997, 29.

**Plate XXXIX** King David, stained glass window from Crathie Church, Aberdeenshire. © Glasgow Life (Museums).

## 42 Westoe Hall (II) Interior Decoration, Stained Glass

Designer: Daniel Cottier
Date: *c.*1873
Location: South Shields, Tees-side
Patron: Not known.

### Description:
Signed glass, including a *Baking Scene.*

### Current position:
Extant.

### References:
Donnelly Max 1998, 110.

## 43    St Cuthbert's Church Darlington, Stained Glass

| | |
|---|---|
| Designers: | Daniel Cottier, possibly with Matthjis Maris (Harrison attr) |
| Date: | 1874 |
| Original Location: | Darlington |
| Patron: | Not known. |

**Description:**
N aisle, W end, incorporating illustration of *A Greyhound*.

**Current position:**
Extant.

**References:**
Harrison 1980, 57.

## 44    Christ Church Felling, Stained Glass

| | |
|---|---|
| Designer: | Daniel Cottier |
| Date: | 1874 |
| Location: | Felling, Tyne and Wear |
| Patron: | WW Pattinson. |

**Description:**
N clerestory, E, two lancets: *Peter and Paul*.

**Current position:**
Extant.

**References:**
*Builder* 1874, 464; Gould 1969, 6.

## 45    Holy Trinity Church Darlington, Stained Glass

| | |
|---|---|
| Designer: | Daniel Cottier |
| Date: | 1874 |
| Location: | Darlington, Durham |
| Patron: | Marley *et al.* |

**Description:**
E end, central lancet: *New Testament Events*.

**Current position:**
Extant.

**References:**
Builder 1874, 424; Gould 1969, 7.

## 46    St Machar's Cathedral (IV), Stained Glass

| | |
|---|---|
| Designer: | Daniel Cottier |
| Date: | 1875 |
| Original Location: | Aberdeen |
| Patron: | Not known. |

**Description:**
S aisle, 2nd from E, three lancets: *Fides, Spes and Caritas*, in memory of local painters George Jameson, John Phillip RA and William Dyce RA.

**Current position:**
Extant.

**References:**
Hobler 1987, 9 & 22; Munro 1909, 227.

## 47    West Parish Church Aberdeen, Interior Decoration and Stained Glass

| | |
|---|---|
| Designer: | Daniel Cottier |
| Date: | 1875 |
| Original Location: | West Parish Church, Aberdeen |
| Patron: | Not known. |

**Description:**
Now West Kirk of St Nicholas, Aberdeen Nave and gallery vaults stencil work; nave ten arched lights.

**Current position:**
Decoration removed or painted over; glass extant.

**References:**
Donnelly, Max 1998, 111.

## 48    Camphill Queen's Park UP Church, Interior Decoration, Stained Glass, Painted Timber Pulpit, Hinge Brackets

| | |
|---|---|
| Designer: | Daniel Cottier |
| Date: | 1875-8 |
| Original Location: | 20 Balvicar Drive, Glasgow |
| Patron: | Not known. |

**Description:**
Nave ceiling and walls stencilled decoration, decorated pulpit, entrance door hinged brackets attributed to Cottier & Co. Stained glass: W window, three lancets: *Fides, Caritas and Spes*.

**Current position:**
Ceiling extant, walls decoration removed or overpainted, decorated pulpit removed at change of denomination, location unknown. Stained glass extant.

**References:**
Howell and Sutton 1989, 47; Pert 1995, 14-15; Williamson, Riches and Higgs 1990, 545.

## 49    Kepplestone Mansion, Interior Decoration

| | |
|---|---|
| Designer: | Daniel Cottier |
| Date: | 1875 |
| Original Location: | Aberdeen |
| Patron: | Alexander Macdonald. |

**Description:**
Home of Alexander Macdonald, art collector and quarryman, decorated by Cottier with elaborate floral designs and Japanese fans.

**Current position:**
Much altered and subject to residential conversion.

**References:**
Brogden 1998, 153; MacDonald, Melville 1998, 19.

## 50    Paisley Abbey (II), Stained Glass

| | |
|---|---|
| Designer: | Daniel Cottier |
| Date: | *c.*1875 |
| Original Location: | Paisley, Renfrewshire |
| Patrons: | Mary Whitehead, Thomas Coats of Ferguslie. |

**Description:**
N transept, E wall, S lancet, *The Resurrection* above *The Crucifixion*, in memory of Joseph Whitehead of Kilnside. Signed:'D Cottier & Co. / Regent St.' Transferred from E nave, 1907.

N transept, E wall, N lancet, *Confession of S Thomas* above *Christ's Baptism,* in memory of James Coats Sr.  Inscribed: 'D Cottier & Co. London & New York'. Transferred from E nave, 1907.

**Current position:**
Extant.

**References:**
Fisher [nd] 1 & 5.

## 51    Lord Tennyson's House, Stained Glass

| | |
|---|---|
| Designer: | Daniel Cottier |
| Date: | c. 1876 |
| Original Location: | Aldworth, West Sussex |
| Patron: | Alfred, Lord Tennyson. |

**Description:**
Stair landing: *Homer, Dante* and *Chaucer.*

**Current position:**
Not known.

**References:**
Cole 1879, 662; Hobler 1987, 29.

## 52    Dancing Girl Screen

| | |
|---|---|
| Designer: | Daniel Cottier with Matthjis Maris, painter |
| Date: | 1878 |
| Original Location: | Not known. |

**Description;**
Four panels of the same dancing girl in different poses. painted by Maris on Cottier's instruction.
Current Position: Now in the Rijksmuseum, Amsterdam.

**References:**
Rijksmuseum website: http://www.rijksmuseum.nl [2009].

## 53    Church of the Holy Rude Stirling, Stained Glass

| | |
|---|---|
| Designer: | Daniel Cottier |
| Date: | 1879 |
| Original Location: | Stirling |
| Patron: | Not known. |

**Description:**
E arm apse, choir aisle, E bay, 2nd from E: illustrations of *Hospitality.*

**Current position:**
Extant.

**References:**
Gifford and Walker 2002, 34.

## 54    Bothwell Parish Church, Stained Glass

| | |
|---|---|
| Designer: | Daniel Cottier |
| Date: | *c.*1879 |
| Original Location: | Bothwell, Lanarkshire |
| Patron: | Not known. |

**Description:**
*Parables,* after Millais (attributed to Lavers, Barraud and Westlake by Harrison).

**Current position:**
Extant.

**References:**
Donnelly, Michael 1997, 54.

## 55    Paisley Abbey (III), Stained Glass

| | |
|---|---|
| Designer: | Daniel Cottier |
| Date: | 1880 |
| Location: | Paisley, Renfrewshire |
| Patron: | Not known. |

**Description:**
Nave, 2nd from E, two lancets, two Parables and eight Virtues. Parables: *Labourers in the Vineyard, The Talents*; and virtues: *Caritas, Temperantia, Patientia, Modesta, Industria, Fortitudo, Veritas, Castitas.* Inscribed: 'Cottier & Co. Regent St. London'. In memory of Thomas Richardson.

**Current position:**
Extant.

**References:**
Fisher [nd], 1 & 4.

## 56    Ruthven Towers, Stained Glass

| | |
|---|---|
| Designer: | Daniel Cottier |
| Date: | 1882 |
| Original Location: | Auchterarder, Perthshire |
| Patron: | Not known. |

**Description:**
Front hall: *Music, Dancing, Art*; dining room and stair window: *Four Seasons*, three Portraits, a *Shepherd.*

**Current position:**
Extant.

**References:**
Cowen 1985, 299 & 238; Donnelly, Max 1998, 116.

## 57    Kirk Christ Lezayre, Stained Glass Window

| | |
|---|---|
| Designer: | Daniel Cottier |
| Date: | 1884 |
| Original Location: | Isle of Man |
| Patron: | Daniel Cottier. |

**Description:**
N side: the inscription states that it was erected by Daniel Cottier, Glass-painter, in 1884, in memory of his grandfather, Daniel Cottier, died 1803; and of his father, Daniel Cottier, died 1847. Two lancets, four panels in each, the panels represent – reading from top to bottom – on W: *Industria, Temperantia, Caritas, Veritas*; on E: *Modestia, Patientia, Fortitudo, Castitas.*

**Current position:**
Extant.

**References:**
Kermode 1954, 62.

---

## 58　St Giles' Cathedral (I), Stained Glass

| | |
|---|---|
| Designer: | Daniel Cottier |
| Date: | 1886 |
| Original Location: | Edinburgh |
| Patron: | Not known. |

**Description:**
Great W window: *The Prophets Isaiah, Jeremiah, David, Ezekiel, Daniel, Amos, Jonah, Elijah, Zechariah and Malachis*. In memory of Fanny, the wife of RT Hamilton Bruce.

**Current position:**
Replaced by L. Breidfjord's work in 1985; the Cottier window is now untraced.

**References:**
Donnelly, Max 1998, 119; Gifford and Walker 1984, 117; Harrower 1918, 32; Meikle 1883, 10 & 32.

---

## 59　Old Parish Church Peebles (I), Stained Glass

| | |
|---|---|
| Designer: | Daniel Cottier |
| Date: | 1887 |
| Original Location: | Peebles, Peeblesshire |
| Patron: | Not known. |

**Description:**
W window: *Scenes from the Life of Christ*.

**Current position:**
Extant.

**References:**
Cruft, Dunbar and Fawcett 2006, 616.

---

## 60　Christ Church Rathgar, Stained Glass

| | |
|---|---|
| Designer: | Daniel Cottier |
| Date: | 1888 |
| Original Location: | Rathgar, Dublin |
| Patron: | The congregation of Christ Church Rathgar. |

**Description:**
*Paul Taking Leave of the Elders of the Church of Ephesus*. In memory of the Very Rev Dr William Fleming.

**Current position:**
Extant.

**References:**
http://www.christchurchrathgar.org

---

## 61　Paisley Abbey (IV), Stained Glass

| | |
|---|---|
| Designer: | Daniel Cottier |
| Date: | 1888 |
| Original Location: | Paisley, Renfrewshire |
| Patrons: | The employees of James Arthur of Barshaw. |

**Description:**
Crown W window, five lancets: *Christ* and the *Four Evangelists*. In memory of James Arthur.

**Current position:**
Extant

**References:**
Fisher [nd] 2-3.

---

## 62　St Giles' Cathedral (II), Stained Glass

| | |
|---|---|
| Designer: | Daniel Cottier |
| Date: | 1890 |
| Original Location: | Edinburgh |
| Patron: | James Cameron Lees. |

**Description:**
N Nave, 2nd window, six lancets, etc.: *Six Christian Virtues*, The Virtues: *Faith, Hope, Charity*, above *Truth, Justice, Mercy*. Inscribed: 'Cottier & Co'. In memory of Rhoda Cameron Lees, wife of the donor.

**Current position:**
Extant.

**References:**
Meikle 1883, 32, Pollak 1998, 19.

---

## 63　Hillhead Parish Church (I), Stained Glass

| | |
|---|---|
| Designer: | It is not known whether Daniel Cottier was uncovered in their communication before his death in 1891 |
| Date: | 1893 |
| Original Location: | Now Kelvinside Hillhead Parish Church, Glasgow |
| Patron: | Not known. |

**Description:**
E apse, from N: *Jesus at Samaria, Lazarus' Grave, Cana*.

**Current position:**
Extant.

**References:**
Donnelly, Max 1998, 121.

---

## 64　Old Parish Church, Peebles (II), Stained Glass

| | |
|---|---|
| Designer: | It is not known whether Daniel Cottier was involved in the commission before his death in 1891 |
| Date: | 1893 |
| Original Location: | Peebles, Peebles-shire |
| Patron: | Not known. |

**Description:**
R window: *Cherubim*; S aisle: *Prophets, Saints, Virtues*; Galleries: *Apostles.*

**Current position:**
Extant.

**References:**
Cruft, Dunbar and Fawcett 2006, 616.

### 65 Tynron Parish Church, Stained Glass

| | |
|---|---|
| Designer: | It is not known whether Daniel Cottier was involved in the .commission before his death in 1891 |
| Date: | 1893 |
| Original Location: | Dumfries and Galloway |
| Patron: | Not known. |

**Description:**
Three light W window: *Truth, Justice* and *Mercy.*

**Current position:**
Not known – the church ceased to be a parish church in 1997 and was sold.

**References:**
Gifford 1996, 558.

### 66 25 Learmonth Terrace, Stained Glass

| | |
|---|---|
| Designer: | Possibly F Vincent Hart for Cottier & Co, W Scott Morton interior decorator |
| Date: | 1894 |
| Original Location: | Edinburgh |
| Patron: | Arthur Sanderson. |

**Description:**
Dining room: *The Seasons,* inscribed: 'C ★ Co [monogram] 1894.' Front door: floral panels, signature (?) unclear; attributed to F. Vincent Hart by Gifford; Entrance hall now window: *The Story of Theseus.*

**Current position:**
Extant.

**References:**
Gifford, McWilliam and Walker 1984, 339-400; *Twenty-Five Learmonth Terrace* [nd].

### 67 St Michael's Church Linlithgow, Stained Glass

| | |
|---|---|
| Designer: | It is not known whether Daniel Cottier was involved in the commission before his death in 1891 |
| Date: | 1895 |
| Original Location: | Linlithgow, West Lothian |
| Patron: | Not known. |

**Description:**
Chancel, S aisle, W window, three lancets: *The Women at the Sepulchre.* inscribed: 'Cottier & Co. London 1895.' In memory of Robert Riddoch Glenn.

**Current position:**
Extant.

**References:**
Cowen 1985, 234; McWilliam 1978, 289.

### 68 Hillhead Parish Church (II), Stained Glass

| | |
|---|---|
| Designer: | Possibly F Vincent Hart for Cottier & Co. |
| Date: | 1903 |
| Original Location: | Now Kelvinside-Hillhead Parish Church, Glasgow |
| Patron: | Not known. |

**Description:**
E apse, from N: *Jesus with the Rabbis; Woman of Samaria.* Inscribed: 'Cottier & Co. London 1903.'

**Current position:**
Extant.

**References:**
Donnelly, Max 1998, 122.

### 69 Old Parish Church Jedburgh, Stained Glass

| | |
|---|---|
| Designer: | Norman McLeod MacDougall for Cottier & Co |
| Date: | *c.*1905 |
| Original Location: | Jedburgh, Roxburghshire |
| Patron: | Not known. |

**Description:**
Apse upper: *Angels;* NE face lower: *Crucifixion*; SE lower: *Christ Blessing.*

**Current position:**
Not known.

**References:**
Donnelly, Michael 1997, 47, Cruft, Dunbar and Fawcett 2006, 419.

### 70 Scoonie Church, Stained Glass

| | |
|---|---|
| Designer: | Cottier & Co, individual designer not known |
| Date: | *c.*1910 |
| Original Location: | Leven, Fife |
| Patron: | Not known. |

**Description:**
N aisle, six E windows: *Evangelists, SS Dorcas and James.*

**Current position:**
Not known

**References:**
Gifford 1986, 312.

## WORKS OF KNOWN OR APPROXIMATE DATE, NOT ASSOCIATED WITH PLACES

### 71 Jacobean-Style Cabinet with Illustrations of *Seasons*

Designer: Daniel Cottier
Date: 1870–80
Original Location: Not known
Patron: Not known.

**Description:**
Ebonised and painted mahogany with figurative panels.

**Current position:**
Manchester City Art Galleries.

**References:**
Donnelly, Max 1999, 44.

### 72 Ebonised Cabinet with Inlaid Panel with Illustrations of *Amor, Mors, Fama* and *Fortuna*

Designer: Daniel Cottier
Date: 1870–80
Original Location: Not known
Patron: Not known.

**Description:**
Ebonised and penworked cabinet decorated with figures of *Amor, Mors, Fama* and *Fortuna*, Greek masks, and urns, designed by Daniel Cottier, London, 1870–80.

**Current position:**
Now in the National Museum of Scotland collection.

**References:**
http://www.scotlandsimages.com

### 73 Stained Glass and Furniture Exhibited at London International Exhibition

Designer: Daniel Cottier
Date: 1871
Original Location: South Kensington
Patron: London International Exhibition.

**Description:**
Cottier's contribution was awarded a prize.

**Current position:**
Not known.

**References:**
Cat nos 14, 25. Bibliog details

### 74 Stained Glass Portraits of a Middle-Aged Lady and her Daughter

Designer: Daniel Cottier
Date: 1876
Original location: Cottier Galleries, London
Patron: Not known.

**Description:**
Portrait of a middle-aged lady, inscribed: 'Thy will be done'; and portrait of the lady's daughter, inscribed: 'Faith is the substance of things hoped for, the evidence of things not seen'. Recorded by Vincent Van Gogh on a visit to London, October 1876.

**Current Position:**
Not known.

**References:**
Gould 1969, 3; Van Gogh 1958, vol I, 70.

### 75 Stained Glass Panel of *The Lady of Shalott*

Designer: Daniel Cottier, Matthjis Maris painter
Date: 1885
Original Location: Not known
Patron: Not known.

**Description:**
The *Lady of Shalott* is also the subject of a painting by Matthjis Maris belonging to Sir William Burrell and he acquired this glass panel produced by Cottier in part due to his admiration for the Maris's work.

**Current position:**
Burrell Collection, Glasgow Museums.

**References:**
Cannon 1991, 42.

## WORKS OF NO KNOWN DATE LISTED ALPHABETICALLY BY PLACE

### 76 Barony Church Glasgow, Stained Glass

Designer: Daniel Cottier
Date: Not known
Location: Glasgow
Patron: Not known.

**Description:**
Stained glass.

**Current position:**
Not known.

**References:**
Adam 1896, p?.

### 77 Devanha, Stained Glass

Designer: Daniel Cottier
Date: Not known
Original Location: Sherborne, Dorset
Patron: Not known.

**Description:**
Stained glass window by Cottier & Co in stairwell of private residence.

**Current position:**
Extant.

**References:**
Roxland Estates website:
http://www.fivepoundahouse.com/property-for-sale-England-Dorset-Shelborne-House-ref-3060.aspx [2009].

### 78 Dowanhill Convent, Stained Glass

Designer: Daniel Cottier
Date: Not known
Original Location: Glasgow
Patron: Not known.

**Description:**
Portrait panels.

**Current position:**
Not known.

**References:**
Cowen 1985, 235; McEwan 1988, 142.

### 79  Holy Saviour Tynemouth, Stained Glass

Designer:          Daniel Cottier
Date:              Not known
Original Location: Tynemouth, Northumberland
Patron:            Not known.

**Description:**
Stained glass

**Current position:**
Extant.

**References:**
Chesney, C 2009 Personal communication.

### 80  Links House, Stained Glass

Designer:          Daniel Cottier
Date:              Not known
Original Location: Links House, Mid Links,
                   Montrose
Patron:            Not known.

**Description:**
Stained glass on the main staircase, and possibly fireplace tiled surrounds by Cottier & Co.

**Current position:**
Extant, now the Links Hotel.

**References:**
Links Hotel website:
http://www.linkshotelmusic.com/images/links-leaflet.pdf [2009].

### 81  Park Church Stained Glass Window: *Scenes from the Life of Our Lord and Old and Types and Antitypes*

Designer:          Daniel Cottier
Date:              Not known
Original Location: Park Church, Glasgow
Patron:            Not known.

**Description:**
The subject is described on an extant cartoon as the Great Window in Chancel

**Current Position:**
Church demolished. A cartoon of the window signed by Cottier and Co survives in a private collection.

**References:**
Donnelly Max 2009, Personal communication.

**Plate XL** Original cartoon for stained glass window in Park Church, Glasgow. Courtesy of Max Donnelly.

### 82  St Oswald's Church Ravenstonedale, Stained Glass Window: *St Cecilia with Portative Organ*

Designer:          Daniel Cottier
Date:              Not known
Original Location: St Oswald's Church,
                   Ravenstonedale, Cumbria
Patron:            Not known.

**Description:**
The subject St Cecilia with Portative Organ, possibly after Burne Jones.

**Current position:**
Extant.

**References:**
Visit Cumbria website:
http://www.visitcumbria.com/pen/chp39.htm [2009].

## 83 St Mary's Cathedral Dundee, Stained Glass Window: *The Resurrection*

| | |
|---|---|
| Designer: | Daniel Cottier |
| Date: | Not known |
| Original Location: | St Mary's Cathedral, Dundee |
| Patron: | Not known. |

**Description:**
N side, nearest rear of church, below the gallery: *The Resurrection*. In memory of Thomas Smith.

**Current position:**
Extant.

**References:**
Dundee St Mary's website:
http://www.dundeestmarys.co.uk/tourwin.html [2009].

## 84 St Ternan's Arbuthnott, Stained Glass

| | |
|---|---|
| Designer: | Daniel Cottier |
| Date: | Not known |
| Original Location: | Arbuthnott, Aberdeenshire |
| Patron: | Not known. |

**Description:**
Stained glass by Cottier & Co that may be contemporaneous with the building's restoration in 1896.

**Current position:**
Extant.

**References:**
http://www.geo.ed.ac.uk/scotgaz/towns/townfirst4152.html [2009].

## WORKS OF UNKNOWN PLACE OR DATE LISTED ALPHABETICALLY BY CURRENT LOCATION

## 85 Stained Glass Panel: *Robert Burns*

| | |
|---|---|
| Designer: | Daniel Cottier |
| Date: | Not known |
| Original Location: | Not known |
| Patron: | Not known. |

**Description:**
Subject: *Robert Burns.*

**Current position:**
Housed within the Robert Burns National Heritage Park Alloway, Ayrshire. The park is currently under redevelopment by the National Trust for Scotland.

**References:**
*Scotland in Trust* (2008), cover; www.nts.org.uk/burns/ [2010].

## 86 Stained Glass: Scene from Sir Walter Scott

| | |
|---|---|
| Designer: | Daniel Cottier possibly with F. Vincent Hart |
| Date: | Not known |
| Original Location: | Not known |
| Patron: | Not known. |

**Description:**
Subject: Scene from Sir Walter Scott, inscribed: 'The Knight and Ladye fair are met/ and under the hawthorn boughs are set/ Scott'.

**Current position:**
In Glasgow Museums Collection.

**References:**
Donnelly, Max 1998, 119.

## 87 Stained Glass: *The Beguiling of Merlin*

| | |
|---|---|
| Designer: | Daniel Cottier, possibly with F. Vincent Hart |
| Date: | Not known |
| Original Location: | Not known |
| Patron: | Not known. |

**Description:**
Subject: *The Beguiling of Merlin.*

**Current position:**
In Glasgow Museums Collection.

**References:**
Donnelly, Max 1998, 119.

## 88 Stained Glass: *Jason and the Golden Fleece*

| | |
|---|---|
| Designer: | Daniel Cottier possibly with F. Vincent Hart |
| Date: | Not known |
| Original Location: | Not known |
| Patron: | Not known. |

**Description:**
Subject: *Jason and the Golden Fleece.*

**Current position:**
In Glasgow Museums Collection.

**References:**
Donnelly, Max 1998, 119.

## WORKS ATTRIBUTED ON STYLISTIC AND OTHER GROUNDS

## ATTRIBUTED WORKS ASSOCIATED WITH PLACES OF KNOWN OR APPROXIMATE DATES

## 89 Westbourne House Interior Decoration, Stained Glass

| | |
|---|---|
| Designer: | Daniel Cottier |
| Date: | *c.*1873 |
| Original Location: | 985 Great Western Road, 11 Hyndland Road, Glasgow |
| Patron: | Not known. |

**Description:**
Egyptian decoration in billiard room, quarried glass.

**Current position:**
Extant.

**References:**
Donnelly, Max 1998, 105.

## 90 17 South Audley Street, Interior Decoration, Stained Glass

| | |
|---|---|
| Designer: | Daniel Cottier |
| Date: | 1876–77 |
| Original Location: | Westminster, London |
| Patron: | Not known. |

**Description:**
Show rooms, some with friezes and covings, painted with birds and cherubs, stained glass, attributed to Daniel Cottier.

**Current position**
Not known.

**References:**
Pevsner 1968, 571.

---

### 91    Pendower Hall, Stained Glass

| | |
|---|---|
| Designer: | Daniel Cottier, but possibly GE Cook & Co |
| Date: | *c.*1885 |
| Original Location: | Benwell, Newcastle |
| Patron: | Not known. |

**Description:**
Glass within billiards room.

**Current position:**
Extant.

**References:**
Pevsner and Richmond 1992, 514.

---

### 92    Kinlochmoidart House, Interior Decoration

| | |
|---|---|
| Designer: | Daniel Cottier |
| Date: | *c.*1885 |
| Original Location: | Inverness-shire |
| Patron: | Not known. |

**Description:**
Eclectic decoration throughout.

**Current position:**
Not known.

**References:**
Donnelly, Max 1998, 118.

---

### 93    44 Athole Gardens, Stained Glass

| | |
|---|---|
| Designer: | Daniel Cottier |
| Date: | *c.*1890 |
| Original Location: | 44 Athole Gardens, Glasgow |
| Patron: | Not known. |

**Description:**
Subject: *Flowers.*

**Current position:**
Extant.

**References:**
Donnelly Max 1998, 120.

---

### 94    St Mary's Episcopal Church Newport-on-Tay, Stained Glass

| | |
|---|---|
| Designer: | Daniel Cottier, but signed F. Vincent Hart |
| Date: | *c.*1890 |
| Original Location: | Newport-on-Tay, Fife |
| Patron: | Not known. |

**Description:**
*Christ at the House of Bethany, Prophets (?), Calling of S Peter.* Central light signed by F. Vincent Hart.

**Current position:**
Extant.

**References:**
Gifford 1988, 335.

---

### 95    St Mary and St Cuthbert RC Prudhoe, Stained Glass

| | |
|---|---|
| Designer: | Daniel Cottier |
| Date: | 1891 |
| Original Location: | Prudhoe, Northumbria |
| Patron: | Not known. |

**Description:**
Geometric glass and Christian symbols, attributed to Cottier on stylistic grounds but more typical of an earlier period.

**Current position:**
Extant.

**References:**
Zielinski 2005.

---

### 96    Knockderry House, Stained Glass

| | |
|---|---|
| Designer: | W Leiper, JG Guthrie |
| Date: | *c.*1897 |
| Location: | Knockderry House Hotel, Cove, Argyll |
| Patron: | D Anderson. |

**Description:**
*The Four Seasons,* stylistic attribution to Cottier & Co.

**Current position:**
Extant.

**References:**
*Dictionary of Scottish Architects* 2008 'William Leiper'; Knockderry House Hotel website: www.knockderryhouse.co.uk/history.aspx [2009].

## ATTRIBUTED WORKS OF NO KNOWN DATE LISTED ALPHABETICALLY BY PLACE

---

### 97    Hillhead Parish Church (III), Interior Decoration, Furniture, Organ Pipe Decoration

| | |
|---|---|
| Designer: | Daniel Cottier, possibly F Vincent Hart for Cottier & Co after Daniel Cottier's death in 1891 |
| Date: | Not known |
| Original Location: | Now Hillhead Parish Church, Glasgow |
| Patron: | Not known. |

**Description:**
Nave decoration, table with harvest decoration, decorated organ pipework.

**Current position:**
Now Kelvinside Hillhead Church. Furniture extant, nave overpainted, organ pipework decoration removed or overpainted.

**References:**
Donnelly, Max 1998, 122.

## 98  Strathbungo Queens Park, Stained Glass, Interior Decoration

Designer:           Daniel Cottier
Date:               Not known
Original Location:  Strathbungo Queens Park, Glasgow
Patron:             Not known.

**Description:**
Painted wall decoration.

**Current position:**
Now Queens Park Parish Church. Some areas of decoration have been revealed.

**References:**
Small 2009, 156; Members of Queens Drive Baptist Church congregation 1997, personal communication.

# 3. COTTIER & CO (FROM 1873)
# WORKS IN USA

## WORKS ASSOCIATED WITH PLACES OF KNOWN OR APPROXIMATE DATES

## 99  Watts Sherman House, Stained Glass

Designer:           Daniel Cottier
Date:               c.1877
Original Location:  Newport, RI
Patron:             W Watts Sherman.

**Description:**
Main hall, three lights, depicting *Trellis of Morning Glory*; elsewhere, quarried glass.

**Current position:**
Only quarried glass remains. Now part of Salve Regina University.

**References:**
Burke 1986, 190, Hobler 1987, 40.

## 100  Trinity Church Boston, Interior Decoration and Stained Glass

Designer:           Daniel Cottier
Date:               1878
Original Location:  Boston, MA
Patron:             Not known.

**Description:**
S transept, lower S wall, windows from E: *Sower and Reaper,* in memory of Alexander Cochrane; *Five Wise Virgins,* in memory of Abby Matilda Loring, inscribed 'Cottier & Co'. New Testament Scene, *The Angel Troubling the Pool,* in memory of Charlotte Troup Winthrop; S transept, lower W wall: *The Storm on the Lake,* in memory of John Fenno. Responsibility for the interior decoration was a matter of some debate. It would appear that John La Farge was in overall control and Cottier's decorators were called in at some stage.

**Current Position:**
Extant.

**References:**
Burke 1986, 178; Hobler 1987, 28-33. See also *American Architect* 1878, 46.

## 101  New York Society Library, Interior Decoration and Stained Glass

Designer:           Daniel Cottier, with Leon Marcotte, decorator
Date;               1878
Original Location:  New York, NY
Patron:             Not known.

**Description:**
The decoration comprised of a green memorial alcove. The glass depicted *Knowledge, Prudence,* and four poets, *Homer, Virgil, Dante* and *Petrarch (Chaucer?)* in the corners.

**Current position:**
The decoration is lost and the stained glass, if not lost, is of unknown location.

**References:**
Burke 1986, 415; *Harper's Weekly* 1881, 118

## 102  Harvard University Memorial Hall (I), Stained Glass

Designer:           Daniel Cottier
Date:               1879
Original Location:  Harvard University, Boston, MA
Patron:             Class of 1857.

**Description:**
Two lights in the main hall, depicting *Sir Philip Sydney* and *Epaminondas,* supplied at a cost of 1780 USD. Other windows were by leading designers including John La Farge.

**Current position:**
Extant.

**References:**
Donnelly, Max 1998, 114; Hobler 1987, 33-4 & 36-7.

## 103  Calvary Episcopal Church, Stained Glass

Designer:           Daniel Cottier
Date:               1879
Original Location:  New York, NY
Patron:             Not known.

**Description:**
Three lancets depicting Biblical scenes and Parables: *Christ the Good Shepherd, The Good Samaritan, The Lost Sheep* and *The Leaven.* In memory of JA Robinson.

**Current position:**
Extant.

**References:**
Hobler 1987, 42 & 44-6.

## 104 St John's Canandaigua, Stained Glass

Designer:           Daniel Cottier
Date:               1879-83
Original Location:  Canandaigua, NY
Patron:             Not known.

**Description:**
Subjects: Parables, including *The Pearl of Great Price* and *The Lost Piece of Silver*, after JE Millais. In memory of Watts Sherman II.

**Current position:**
Not known.

**References:**
Hobler 1987, 39-41.

## 105 Union League Club House, Interior Decoration

Designers:          Daniel Cottier
Date:               1881
Original Location:  New York, NY
Patron:             Not known.

**Description:**
Elaborately decorated and furnished library alcove. Tiffany and La Farge were also involved in the decoration of this building.

**Current position**
Lost.

**References:**
Burke 1986, 415; Hobler 1987, 61 & 72-4.

## 106 Harvard University Memorial Hall (II), Stained Glass

Designer:           Daniel Cottier
Date:               1882
Location:           Harvard University, Boston, MA
Patron:             Class of 1858.

**Description:**
Two lights, N wall, *King of Sparta* and *Leonidas*, supplied at a cost of 1500 USD. Other windows were by leading designers including John La Farge.

**Current position:**
Extant.

**References:**
Donnelly, Max 1998, 117; Hobler 1987, 35-6 & 38.

## 107 State House Hartford, Granite Base for Statue of Governor Buckingham

Designer:           Daniel Cottier assisting Olin Levi
                    Warner, sculptor
Date:               1883-84
Original Location:  Hartford, CT
Patron:             Not known.

**Description:**
For a statue of Governor Buckingham by Olin Levi Warner. Hobler suggests that Cottier designed the base so that Warner could meet the commission.

**Current position**
Extant.

**References:**
Hobler 1987, 96.

## 108 Battell Chapel, Stained Glass

Designer:   Daniel Cottier
Date:       1883
Location:   Yale University, Newhaven, CT
Patron:     Not known.

**Description:**
Subjects: *The Lost Sheep* and *Charity, Fortitude, Patience, Truth*.

**Current position:**
Not known.

**References:**
Hobler 1987, 43 & 47.

## 109 Catherine Lorillard Wolfe's Cottage Furniture

Designer:           Daniel Cottier
Date:               1883-84
Original Location:  Newport, RI
Patron:             Catherine Lorillard Wolfe.

**Description:**
Piano case in canima wood, painted with figures and flowers, costing 3000 USD; and other pieces of furniture.

**Current position:**
Not known.

**References:**
*Artistic Country-Seats* 1886, vol II 186 check page no if poss; Hobler 1987, 66.

## 110 FW Steven's House, Interior Decoration and Fittings

Designer:           Daniel Cottier
Date:               1883-84
Original Location:  5th Avenue at 57th Street, New
                    York, NY
Patron:             FW Steven.

**Description:**
Patterned blue silk in reception room. Hand-painted mythological scene on one ceiling; chandelier made by Cottier after a Flemish original.

**Current position:**
Lost.

**References:**
*Artistic Houses* 1883-4, I (ii), *100-9*; Hobler 1987, 60.

**Plate XLI** Photograph of Interior of FW Steven's House, NY. Courtesy of Lewis, Turner & McQuillan, *The Opulent Interiors of the Gilded Age*, by Dover Publications, May 1987.

## 111 Joseph Decker's House, Interior Decoration and Furnishings

Designer:         Daniel Cottier
Date:             1883-84
Original Location: 18 W 49th Street, New York, NY
Patron:           Joseph Decker.

**Description:**
Throughout, rose-pink damask from wainscot to frieze; frieze and ceiling painted in shades of bronze. Mahogony cabinet with painted female figures, one of the many pieces of furniture supplied by Cottier & Co for this commission.

**Current position:**
Decoration lost, location of furniture unknown.

**References:**
Artistic Houses 1883-4, II (ii), 145-8.

## 112 Gilbertsville Presbyterian Church, Stained Glass

Designer:         Daniel Cottier
Date:             1884
Original Location: Gilbertsville, NY
Patron:           Not known.

**Description:**
Arched light: *S Cecilia*. Inscribed: 'Cottier & Co London & New York'.

**Current position:**
Extant.

**References:**
Donnelly, Max 1998, 108.

## 113 Church of the Incarnation, Stained Glass

Designer:         Daniel Cottier
Date:             *c.*1885
Original Location: New York City, NY
Patron:           Not known,

**Description:**
N transept, four lancets, three roses. Subjects included *The Discovery of Manna in the Wilderness* and *Christ's Compassion on the Crowd*.

**Current position:**
Not known.

**References:**
Hobler 1987, 44 & 48.

## 114 First Presbyterian Church (I), Stained Glass

Designer:         Daniel Cottier
Date:             1887
Original Location: 124 Henry Street, Brooklyn Heights, New York, NY
Patron:           Not known.

**Description:**
Subject: Gratitude.

**Current position:**
Extant.

**References:**
Hobler 1987, 44 & 49.

## 115 First Presbyterian Church (II), Stained Glass

Designer:         Daniel Cottier
Date:             1887
Original Location: 124 Henry Street, Brooklyn Heights, New York, NY
Patron:           Not known.

**Description:**
Subject: *Christ with Children*.

**Current Position:**
Extant.

**References:**
Hobler 1987, 44 & 49.

## 116 Grace Episcopal Church, Stained Glass

Designer:         Daniel Cottier
Date:             c. 1890
Location:         New York City, NY
Patron:           Not known.

**Description:**
Subjects: *Fides, Spes* and *Caritas*.

**Current position:**
Not known.
Hobler 1987, 44 & 50.

## 117 James Ross House Piano Decoration

Designer:         Daniel Cottier
Date:             1890
Original Location: Montreal
Patron:           James Ross.

**Description:**
James Ross, a well-known Montreal businessman, commissioned the piano as a wedding gift for his wife, Annie.

On August 28, 1890, Steinway shipped the piano - without legs, lyre or music-stand — to Cottier & Co's New York studio for completion of the cabinetwork. It took seven years to complete the case, which was ornamented using sixteen different exotic woods inlaid into Circassian curly walnut. Featured in intricate patterns are the names of many composers, in addition to beribboned fruit, musical instruments, and the words: 'Call in Sweet Music. I Have Heard Soft Airs Can Charm Our Senses and Expel Our Cares'.

**Current position:**
Now at Unitarian Church of Montreal, de Maisonneuve Boulevard, Montreal.

**References:**
Unitarian Church of Montreal website:
http://www.ucmtl.ca [2009].

## 118 Avery Architectural Library, Stained Glass

Designer:         Daniel Cottier
Date:             1891
Original Location: 49th Street, Manhattan, New York, NY Patron: D Cottier.

**Description:**
A memorial window presented by Cottier in memory of Henry Ogden Avery, the architect son of Samuel Avery, who had died at a young age in 1890. The *New York Times* recorded:

*The special room of the Avery books has an exquisite stained-glass window, the central design of which is the symbolical figure of architecture. The window records in a cartouche the initials, and under them the name and date of the birth and death of the young artist in whose memory it was presented, as a friendly offering by Daniel Cottier to the library.*

This offering was made in the year of Cottier's own death and the sketch of the window reproduced later in the 1895 library catalogue appears to be by his own hand.

**Current position:**
Demolished (the site is now occupied by the Rockefeller Centre). A copy of Cottier's original design is recorded in the 1895 library catalogue.

**References:**
*New York Times* 1892; *Avery Architectural Library* 1895.

## 119 Homewood, Interior Decoration and Stained Glass

Designer:         Not known, possibly James Inglis, Cottier's partner in New York
Date:             1903-04
Original Location: Pittsburgh, PA
Patron:           Henry Clay Frick.

**Description:**
Frick purchased Homewood in 1882, an Italianate house in Pittsburgh's East End. He remodelled it on more than one occasion. Cottier & Co redecorated the house in 1903-04 and installed an antique glass Cottier window, depicting *The Four Virgins.*

**Current Position:**
Not known.

**References:**
Pittsburgh History and Landmarks Foundation website:
http://www.phlf.org/2008/03/21/alfred-godwin-1850-1934 [2009].

# WORKS OF KNOWN OR APPROXIMATE DATE NOT ASSOCIATED WITH PLACES

## 120 Stained Glass: *Autumn* and *Winter*

Designer:         Daniel Cottier
Date:             1873-85
Original Location: Not known
Patron:           Not known.

**Description:**
Subjects: *Autumn* and *Winter.*

**Current position:**
Now in Columbia Museum of Art, SC.

**References:**
Columbia Museum of Art website:
http://www.columbiamuseum.org/art/collection [2009].

## 121 Stained Glass: *Spring*

Designer:         Daniel Cottier
Date:             1873-85
Original Location: Not known
Patron:           Not known.

**Description:**
This panel representing *Spring* was originally owned by a member of Cottier's family.

**Current position:**
Now in the Metropolitan Museum of Art, New York.

**References:**
Frelinghuysen 2007, 50.

## 122 Book Cover Design: *The House Beautiful*

Designer:         Daniel Cottier
Date:             1878
Location:         Not applicable
Patron:           Clarence Cook.

**Description:**
Cottier designed this book cover for Clarence Cook's *The House Beautiful.* Inscribed with entwined 'C's.

**Current position:**
Extant.

**References:**
Gere and Hoskins 2000, 90.

## 123 Decorated Frame for *The Culprit, Fay*

Designers:        Daniel Cottier, Stanford White, Albert Pinkham Ryder
Date:             1879
Original Location: Not known
Patron:           Charles de Kay.

**Description:**
Frame designed by Stanford White, made under the direction of Daniel Cottier, and painted by Albert Pinkham Ryder. The frame contains several vignettes illustrating the poem *The Culprit, Fay* by Joseph Rodman Drake who was de Kay's maternal grandfather.

**Current position:**
Now in Whitney Museum of American Art, New York, NY.

**References:**
Burke 1986, 310-11;
http://helenadekaygilder.org [2010].

---

### 124  Steinway Piano Decoration and Inlay

| | |
|---|---|
| Designer: | Daniel Cottier |
| Date: | *c.*1889 |
| Original Location: | Not known |
| Patron: | Not known. |

**Description:**
Grand piano case for a Steinway & Son piano, inlaid and painted with musical themes; tortoiseshell and mother of pearl inlay, panels depicting composers, revellers, etc.

**Current position:**
Not known.

**References:**
Donnelly, Max 1998, 120.

---

### 125  Steinway Piano, Decoration and Inlay

| | |
|---|---|
| Designer: | Not known for Cottier & Co |
| Date: | 1906 |
| Original Location: | Not known |
| Patron: | Lady Fairhaven. |

**Description:**
Piano case for a 1906 Steinway piano, ordered for Lady Fairhaven from Cottier & Co New York.

**Current position:**
Now at Anglesey Abbey, Cambridge, UK.

**References:**
Anglesey Abbey website:
http://www.nationaltrust.org.uk/main/ [2009].

## WORKS ATTRIBUTED ON STYLISTIC AND OTHER GROUNDS

### 126  Decorated leather: *Children Frightened by a Rabbit, Woman with a Deer, Children Playing with a Rabbit*

| | |
|---|---|
| Designer: | Daniel Cottier, Albert Pinkham Ryder, |
| Date: | *c.*1880 |
| Original Location: | Not known |
| Patron: | Not known. |

**Description:**
Ryder's oeuvre includes a number of decorative screens painted on leather, among them the tripartite one in the collection of the Smithsonian American Art Museum in Washington, DC. His work in this vein also includes A Stag Drinking and A Stag and Two Does, outdoor nature scenes which originally formed part of a three-panel screen. In all likelihood, these vignettes were done in the early 1880s for Cottier & Co., New York.

**Current Position:**
Extant

**References:**
Spanierman Gallery, New York, NY website:
http://www.spanierman.com/Albert-Pinkham-Ryder/A-Stag-and-Two-Does,-A-Stag-Drinking/ [2009].

### 127  Decorated leather *A Stag Drinking* and *A Stag and Two Does*

| | |
|---|---|
| Designer: | Daniel Cottier, Albert Pinkham Ryder, painter |
| Date: | *c.*1880 |
| Location: | Not known |
| Patron: | Not known. |

**Description:**
Ryder's oeuvre includes a number of decorative screens painted on leather. *A Stag Drinking* and *A Stag and Two Does*, outdoor nature scenes originally formed part of a three-panel screen. *Children Frightened by a Rabbit, Woman with a Deer, Children Playing with a Rabbit*, (No. 126) is in the collection of the Smithsonian American Art Museum in Washington, DC. His work in this vein was done in the early 1880s for Cottier & Co., New York.

**Current Position:**
Extant

**References:**
Spanierman Gallery, New York, NY website:
http://www.spanierman.com/Albert/Pinkham/Ryder/A-Stag-and-Two-Does,-A-Stag-Drinking/ [2009].

# 4. LYON, COTTIER & CO WORKS IN AUSTRALIA

## WORKS OF KNOWN OR APPROXIMATE DATES ASSOCIATED WITH PLACES

### 128 Cranbrook, Stained Glass and Interior Decoration

| | |
|---|---|
| Designers: | John Lamb Lyon |
| Date: | 1875 |
| Original Location: | Sydney, NSW |
| Patron: | James White. |

**Description:**

The stencilled and painted decoration was illustrated in early twentieth-century photographs. The central painted overdoor panel derives from a bird and fruit pattern produced by Daniel Cottier (Montana 2000, 129). The glass depicts *Captain Cook's Arrival at Botany Bay*. It was commissioned by a wealthy grazier and politician, James White, who had purchased a stately home in the exclusive Sydney suburb of Bellevue Hill in 1873.

All nine windows (each approximately 47 x 60 cm) are mounted together and are located above a staircase in the foyer of the main building. The windows portray various aspects of the *Endeavour's* voyage along the East Coast of Australia. Cook appears in several of the windows. The *Endeavour* appears on two windows.

**Current position:**

According to Montana, Lyon, Cottier & Co's mid 1870's stencil and painted decoration survives in the hall. The stained glass window is also extant.

**References:**

Montana 2000, 128-9; Sheahan 2004, 45.

### 129 St Saviour's Cathedral, Stained Glass

| | |
|---|---|
| Designer: | John Lamb Lyon |
| Date: | c.1875 |
| Original Location: | Goulburn, NSW |
| Patron: | Not known. |

**Description:**

Stained glass designed for architect Edmund Blacket.

**Current Position:**

Extant.

**References:**

http://en.wikipedia.org/Edmund_Blacket [2010].

### 130 St James Anglican Morpeth, Stained Glass

| | |
|---|---|
| Designer: | John Lamb Lyon |
| Date: | c.1875 |
| Original Location: | Morpeth, NSW |
| Patron: | Not known. |

**Description:**

Stained glass including geometric windows.

**Current position**

Extant.

**References:**

Organ Historical Trust of Australia website: http://www.ohta.org.au/confs/Sydney/STJAMESANGLICAN.html [2009].

### 131 Glenyarrah, Stained Glass and Decoration

| | |
|---|---|
| Designers: | John Lamb Lyon, Daniel Cottier |
| Date: | c.1876-7 |
| Original Location: | Double Bay, Sydney, NSW |
| Patron: | SD Gordon. |

**Description:**

Subjects: *Flora & Pomona, The Four Seasons*, Heraldry. The Seasons window bears the same design as the painted ceiling depicting the *Seasons* in Government House, Sydney (ref no.136). Adapted from designs supplied by Daniel Cottier and comparable with those at Cairndhu House, UK (ref no.38).

**Current position:**

Extant. Now Gladswood House and a residential conversion.

**References:**

Montana 2000, 133-4.

### 132 St Andrew's College Sydney, Stained Glass and Interior Decoration

| | |
|---|---|
| Designer: | John Lamb Lyon |
| Date: | 1876 |
| Original Location: | Sydney, NSW |
| Patron: | Not known. |

**Description:**

Library: depictions of *Dante, Homer* and *Chaucer,* and decorated ceiling.

**Current position:**

Not known.

**References:**

Ellsmore 1982, 7; Hobler 1987, 23-5 & 29; Montana 2000, 134.

### 133 All Saints Anglican Church, Condobolin, Stained Glass

| | |
|---|---|
| Designer: | John Lamb Lyon |
| Date: | c.1878 |
| Location: | Condobolin, NSW |
| Patron: | Not known. |

**Description:**

The church has a full set of windows made by Lyon and Cottier.

**Current position**

Extant.

**References:**

NSW Government press release: http://www.planning.nsw.gov.au/mediarelplan/fs20080318_686.html [2009].

### 134  Congregational Church Sydney, Interior Decoration

Designer:            John Lamb Lyon
Date:                1879
Original Location:   Pitt Street, Sydney, NSW
Patron:              Not known.

**Description:**
The decoration included antique script and a painted organ.

**Current position:**
Not known.

**References:**
Montana 2000, 171-2.

### 135  The Garden Palace, Decorations, Furnishings and Tinted Glass

Designer:            John Lamb Lyon
Date:                1879
Original Location:   Sydney International Exhibition, NSW
Patron:              Not known.

**Description:**
Decoration of the Garden Palace for the Sydney International Exhibition included wall frescoes, stained glass, gilding and a lantern light. Lyon Cottier & Co were responsible for the dome's decorations, the nave, the transept, the European section and part of the basement.

**Current position**
Not known.

**References:**
Montana 2000, 135-40.

### 136  General Post Office Sydney, Interior Decoration

Designer:            John Lamb Lyon
Date:                c.1879
Original Location:   Sydney, NSW
Patron:              Not known.

**Description:**
Interior decoration of the principal rooms.

**Current position:**
Not known.

**References:**
Ellsmore 1982, 5.

### 137  Government House, Interior Decoration, Fabric and Furnishings

Designers:           John Lamb Lyon, Daniel Cottier
Date:                c.1879
Original Location:   Sydney, NSW
Patron:              The Governor of New South Wales.

**Description:**
Ceiling decoration incorporating the same designs for the Four Seasons used at Glenyarrah (ref no.130), sourced from Cottier's designs for Cairndhu (ref no.136), with conventionalised flora. The state drawing room suite was recovered in crimson floral damask.

**Current position:**
Extant decoration, recently renovated by the Australian Historic Houses Trust.

**References:**
Ellsmore 1982, 5 & 7 Montana 2000, 134-6.

### 138  James Barnet's House, Interior Decoration

Designer:            John Lamb Lyon
Date:                c.1879
Original Location:   Clarens, Potts Point, Sydney, NSW
Patron:              James Barnet.

**Description:**
Wall decorations.

**Current position:**
Not known.

**References:**
Ellsmore 1982 , 5; Gould 1969, 3; Montana 2000, 134.

### 139  Mechanics School of Art, Stained Glass and Wall Decoration

Designer:            John Lamb Lyon
Date:                c.1879
Original Location:   Sydney, NSW
Patron:              Not known.

**Description:**
Decoration and glass for the School's theatre.

**Current position:**
Not known.

**References:**
Montana 2000, 132.

### 140  Woollahra House, Interior Decoration

Designer:            John Lamb Lyon
Date:                1879-86
Original Location:   Sydney, NSW
Patron:              Sir W Cooper.

**Description:**
An Adam Revival scheme in the drawing room (design in Mitchell Library Melbourne) and stencilled ceiling, painted to represent an iconographic scheme of music and musicians.

**Current position:**
Not known.

**References:**
Ellsmore 1982 , 4 & 5; Lane and Serle 1990, 206, Montana 2000, 135.

### 141  Glanworth, Interior Decoration

Designer:            John Lamb Lyon
Date:                c.1880
Original Location:   Sydney, NSW
Patron:              James Watson.

**Description:**
Interior and exterior decoration of the building.

**Current position:**
Demolished.

**References:**
Montana 2000, 147.

---

## 142  Exchange Hotel, Interior Decoration

| | |
|---|---|
| Designer: | John Lamb Lyon |
| Date: | c.1880 |
| Original Location: | Sydney, NSW |
| Patron: | Not known. |

**Description:**
Egyptianate scheme in distemper on the columns and panels of the dining room to accompany the 'largest mirror in the colony' according to the Sydney Morning Herald in 1880. The mirror was purchased from the Belgium Court at the 1879 Sydney International Exhibition.

**Current position:**
Not known.

**References:**
Montana 2000, 134.

---

## 143  Joylen, Interior Decoration, Furnishings and Stained Glass

| | |
|---|---|
| Designer: | John Lamb Lyon |
| Date: | 1883-4 |
| Original Location: | Birchgrove, Balmain, Sydney, NSW |
| Patron: | John Lamb Lyon. |

**Description:**
Lyon's own house was decorated and furnished by him with a stained glass window he designed for his own study. The upper panels of the window include the initials of John Lamb Lyon and his wife Elizabeth, and the family crest and motto. The three lower panels include portraits of the artists *Titian* and *Velasquez* and an unidentified man.

**Current position:**
The house was radically altered and approval given for demolition in 2005. The window from the study was acquired by the Powerhouse Museum, Sydney, and is extant.

**References:**
Montana 2000, 143-5;
http://www.powerhousemuseum.com/collection/database [2009].

---

## 144  South Australian English, Scottish and Australian Chartered Bank, Interior Decoration

| | |
|---|---|
| Designer: | John Lamb Lyon |
| Date: | 1881 |
| Original Location: | Not known |
| Patron: | Not known. |

**Description:**
Interior decoration.

**Current position:**
Demolished.

**References:**
Montana 2000, 147.

---

## 145  The Abbey, Interior Decoration, Furnishings and Stained Glass

| | |
|---|---|
| Designer: | John Lamb Lyon, Parnell W Johnson |
| Date: | 1883-84 |
| Original Location: | Sydney, NSW |
| Patron: | Not known. |

**Description:**
A Gothic Revival scheme in the hallway, aesthetic stained glass in the front door, a Gothic Revival sideboard, inglenook fire surround, rich stencilling, tiling and polychromy.

**Current position:**
Extant, including interior decoration.

**References:**
Forge 1981, 27 & 119; Montana 2000, 139-41.

---

## 146  The Great Synagogue Sydney, Stained and Etched Glass

| | |
|---|---|
| Designer: | John Lamb Lyon |
| Date: | c.1883 |
| Original Location: | Sydney, NSW |
| Patron: | Not known. |

**Description:**
Lyon & Cottier stained and etched glass.

**Current position:**
Extant.

**References:**
http://www.sydneyarchitecture.com [2009].

---

## 147  New South Wales Club, Interior Decoration

| | |
|---|---|
| Designer: | John Lamb Lyon |
| Date: | c.1884 |
| Original Location: | 71 Bligh Street, Sydney, NSW |
| Patron: | Not known. |

**Description:**
Classical-style decoration.

**Current position:**
Not known.

**References:**
Ellsmore 1986, 12.

---

## 148  Weemala Interior Furnishings

| | |
|---|---|
| Designer | John Lamb Lyon |
| Date: | c.1885 |
| Original Location; | Faulconbridge, NSW |
| Patron: | Andrew McCulloch. |

**Description:**
A country house furnished for a wealthy businessman.

**Current Position:**
Subsequently renamed Eurama and now ruinous following destruction in a bushfire in 1968.

**References:**
http://www.bmlocalstudies.blogspot.com [2010].

## WORKS OF KNOWN OR APPROXIMATE DATE NOT ASSOCIATED WITH PLACES

### 149 Stained Glass Exhibited at the Colonial and Indian Exhibition: *Australias*

Designer:        John Lamb Lyon
Date:            1886
Location:        South Kensington, London
Patron:          Not known.

**Description:**
An allegorical figure of Australia assumed to have been the window produced by Lyon.

**Current position:**
Not known.

**References:**
Montana 2000, 144.

## WORKS OF NO KNOWN DATE

### 150 St John's Church of England Toorak, Stained Glass

Designer:           John Lamb Lyon, possibly before Lyon, Cottier & Co
Date:               Not known
Original Location:  Toorak, Stonnington, VIC
Patron:             Not known.

**Description:**
Memorial window to WC Cornish, probably the first major work by John Lamb Lyon.

**Current position:**
Extant.

**References:**
Victorian Heritage Database website:
http://vhd.heritage.vic.gov.au/places/heritage/1170 [2009].

### 151 All Saints Anglican Church Condobolin, Stained Glass

Designer:           Lyon, Cottier & Co
Date:               Not known
Original Location:  McDonnell Street, Condobolin, NSW
Patron:             Not known.

**Description:**
A full set of geometric windows, it is estimated that the windows at All Saints were made and installed in several stages between 1880 and the 1890s. It is rare for a regional church to have a full set of Lyon & Cottier windows. The other known examples of regional churches in NSW with comparable sets of Lyon & Cottier windows are: St Patrick's Catholic Church, Boorowa; Anglican Church of the Resurrection, Jamberoo; and St Mary's Catholic Church Mudgee (Heritage Office Survey, 2006).

**Current position:**
Windows restored in 1978.

**References:**
NSW State Heritage Register:
http://www.heritage.nsw.gov.au/07_subnav_01_2.cfm?itemid=5055594 [2009].

### 152 Anglican Church of the Resurrection Jamberoo, Stained Glass

Designer:           John Lamb Lyon
Date:               Not known
Original Location:  Jamberoo NSW
Patron:             Not known.

**Description:**
A full set of Lyon & Cottier windows. The other known examples of regional churches in NSW with comparable sets of Lyon & Cottier windows are: St Patrick's Catholic Church, Boorowa; All Saints Anglican Church Condobolin; and St Mary's Catholic Church Mudgee (Heritage Office Survey, 2006).

**Current position:**
Extant.

**References:**
NSW State Heritage Register:
http://www.heritage.nsw.gov.au/07_subnav_01_2.cfm?itemid=5055594 [2009].

### 153 Christ Church Cathedral Grafton, Stained Glass

Designer:           John Lamb Lyon
Date:               Not known
Original Location:  Grafton NSW
Patron:             Not known.

**Description:**
E window, in memory of the second bishop of the diocese.

**Current position:**
Extant.

**References:**
*Church Standard* 1913, 51.

### 154 St Andrew's Cathedral Church Sydney, Stained Glass

Designer:           Lyon, Cottier & Co
Date;               Not known
Original Location:  Sydney, NSW
Patron:             Not known.

**Description:**
Chancel and clerestory windows.

**Current position:**
Extant.

**References:**
http://enwikipedia.org/wiki/St._Andresw%27s_Cathedral,_Sydney [2009].

## 155  St John's Anglican Church, Reredos of Encaustic Tiles

Designer:            John Lamb Lyon
Date:                Not known
Original Location:   Georges Plains, NSW
Patron:              Not known.

**Description:**
The church, by Edward Gell, was opened in 1868. The reredos made of encaustic tiles showed *The Apostles' Creed*, *The Lord's Prayer*, *The Ten Commandments* and *The Beatitudes*.

**Current Position:**
The church survives but the interior features have been removed.

**References:**
http://www.austcemindix.com/cemetery [2020].

## 156  St Mary's Catholic Church Mudgee, Stained Glass

Designer:            John Lamb Lyon
Date:                Not known
Original Location:   Mudgee, NSW
Patron:              Not known.

**Description:**
A full set of geometric windows, it is estimated that the windows at All Saints were made and installed in several stages between 1880 and the 1890s. It is rare for a regional church to have a full set of Lyon & Cottier windows. The only other known examples of regional churches in NSW with comparable sets of Lyon & Cottier windows are: St Patrick's Catholic Church, Boorowa; Anglican Church of the Resurrection, Jamberoo; All Saints Anglican Church, Condobolin (Heritage Office Survey, 2006).

**Current position:**
Windows restored in 1978.

**References:**
NSW State Heritage Register
http://www.heritage.nsw.gov.au/07_subnav_01_2.cfm?itemid=5055594.

## 157  St Matthew's Church Albury Australia, Stained Glass

Designer:            John Lamb Lyon
Date:                Not known
Original Location:   Albury, NSW
Patron:              Not known.

**Description:**
Subject: *The Calling of St Matthew*.

**Current position:**
Destroyed by fire, 1991.

**References:**
http://life.csu.edu.au/~dspennem/Varia/St.Matthews/SM_Blacket.html [2009].

## 158  St Patrick's Church Boorowa, Stained Glass

Designer:            John Lamb Lyon
Date:                Not known
Original Location:   Boorowa
Patron:              Not known.

**Description:**
A full set of Lyon & Cottier windows. The only other known examples of regional churches in NSW with comparable sets of Lyon & Cottier windows are: All Saints Anglican Church, Condobolin; Anglican Church of the Resurrection, Jamberoo; St Mary's Catholic Church Mudgee (Heritage Office Survey, 2006).

**Current position:**
Not known.

**References:**
NSW State Heritage Register:
http://www.heritage.nsw.gov.au/07_subnav_01_2.cfm?itemid=5055594 [2009].

# WORKS ATTRIBUTED ON STYLISTIC AND OTHER GROUNDS

## 159  St Peter's Church Cooks River Parish, Stained Glass

Designer:            John Lamb Lyon
Date:                1875-83
Original Location:   Cooks River Parish, NSW
Patron:              Not known.

**Description:**
A large series of windows thought to be manufactured by Lyon, Cottier & Co. Most of the windows are in memory of a particular person or family.

**Current position:**
Extant.

**References:**
http://stpeterscooksriverhistory.wordpress.com/articles-of-interest/ [2009].

## 160  Ayers House, Painted Decoration

Designer:            John Lamb Lyon, Charles Gow
Date:                *c.*1873
Original Location:   Adelaide, SA
Patron:              Not known.

**Description:**
Hand-painted ceilings and stencilled woodwork in the State Dining Room.

**Current position:**
Extant.

**References:**
http://www.hosking.wattle.id.au/~laurel/parahtml/conservation_plan.html.

## 161  The Acacias, Painted Decoration

| | |
|---|---|
| Designer: | John Lamb Lyon, Charles Gow |
| Date: | *c.*1873 |
| Original Location: | Adelaide, SA |
| Patron: | Not known. |

**Description:**
Interior decoration.

**Current position:**
Not known.

**References:**
http://www.hosking.wattle.id.au/~laurel/parahtml/conservation_plan.html.

## 162  Swifts, Interior Decoration

| | |
|---|---|
| Designer: | John Lamb Lyon |
| Date: | *c.*1880 |
| Original Location: | Darling Point, Sydney, NSW |
| Patron: | Not known. |

**Description:**
1880's-style decorations that may be in part attributed to Lyon, Cottier & Co and possibly in part to the Italian art decorator Signor Lorenzinin.

**Current position:**
Not known.

**References:**
Montana 2000, 134.

## 163  Glenleigh, Interior Decoration

| | |
|---|---|
| Designer: | John Lamb Lyon |
| Date: | 1882–84 |
| Original Location: | Regentville, NSW |
| Patron: | James Ewan. |

**Description:**
Elaborate decorated interior now attributed to Lyon, Cottier & Co.

**Current position:**
The decoration has been revealed by the owners with a view to preservation.

**References:**
New South Wales Heritage Council website:
http://www.visit.heritage.nsw.gov [2009].

# 5. LYON, WELLS, COTTIER & CO WORKS IN AUSTRALIA

## WORKS OF KNOWN OR APPROXIMATE DATES ASSOCIATED WITH PLACES

**164  Christ Church Old Cathedral St Arnaud, Stained Glass**

| | |
|---|---|
| Designer: | John Lamb Lyon |
| Date: | 1887 |
| Location: | St Arnaud, VIC |
| Patron: | Not known. |

**Description:**
E window, three lancets: *Crucifixion*, flanked by *David* and *Saint with Sword*. In memory of Valentine Nott Mogg.

**Current position:**
Not known.

**References:**
Zimmer 1984, 111.

**165  Alton, Interior Decoration**

| | |
|---|---|
| Designer: | Andrew Wells, John Lamb Lyon |
| Date: | c.1887 |
| Original Location: | Mount Macedon, VIC |
| Patron: | Sir George Verdon. |

**Description:**
Sir George Verdon's summer retreat contained decoration with Wells's Renaissance and Eastern patterns.

**Current position:**
Not known.

**References:**
Montana 2000, 149.

**166  English, Scottish & Australian Chartered Bank, Interior Decoration**

| | |
|---|---|
| Designer: | Andrew Wells assisted by John Ross Anderson |
| Date: | c.1887 |
| Original Location: | Collins Street, Melbourne, VIC |
| Patron: | Sir G Verdon. |

**Description:**
Medieval-style decoration incorporating heraldic ornament, diapers, emblems and crests of Britain and Australia.

**Current position:**
Extant.

**References:**
Ellsmore 1982, 6: Montana 2000, 76 & 146-9.

**167  Sir George Vernon's Residence, Interior decoration**

| | |
|---|---|
| Designer: | Andrew Wells |
| Date: | c.1887 |
| Original Location: | Collins Street, Melbourne, VIC |
| Patron: | Sir G Vernon. |

**Description:**
Situated above the bank, this scheme of decoration gave full rein to Wells's talents: 'terracottas, cinnamons and deep brick reds were enlivened with Persian blues, rich salmons, yellow, rose and gold leaf' (Montana 2000, 149). The scheme incorporated embossed Japanese leather papers within the wall fills and Tynecastle Tapestry paper, painted and lacquered, formed some of the dadoes.

**Current position:**
Extant.

**References:**
Australian Dictionary of Biography 2006; Montana 2000, 146-9.

**168  All Saints Anglican Church, Stained Glass**

| | |
|---|---|
| Designer; | John Lamb Lyon |
| Date: | 1888 |
| Original Location: | Hunters Hill, Sydney |
| Patron: | Not known. |

**Description:**
The church, completed in 1888, contained a fine E window and several chancel and nave windows by the respected local firm of Lyon, Cottier & Co. in a Gothic Revival style in warm russet colours.

**Current position:**
Not known.

**References:**
Baker.

**169  Cliveden, Interior Decoration**

| | |
|---|---|
| Designer: | Andrew Wells |
| Date: | 1888 |
| Original Location: | East Melbourne |
| Patron: | Sir W Clarke. |

**Description:**
A surviving photograph shows friezes and panels in Italianate styles.

**Current position:**
Demolished by the Hilton Hotel Group in 1968.

**References:**
Montana 2000, 151-4.

## 170 St Mary's Catholic Church, Interior Decoration

Designer:            Andrew Wells, assisted by J Ross
                     Anderson
Date:                1888
Original Location:   St Kilda, VIC
Patron:              Not known.

**Description:**
Decoration of the chancel and chapel.

**Current position:**
Not known.

**References:**
Ellsmore 1986 , 12; Montana 2000, 151.

## 171 Booloominbah, Stained Glass and Interior Decoration

Designer:            John Lamb Lyon, Andrew Wells
Date:                *c.*1889
Original Location:   Armidale, New England, NSW
Patron:              F White.

**Description:**
Adaptations of Millais paintings for the stained glass, Sir Walter
Scott and Shakespeare themes used in the library windows
and Kate Greenaway-style nursery glass.

**Current position:**
Extant as part of the University of New England, NSW.

**References:**
Montana 2000, 156-8.

## 172 Union Bank, Interior Decoration

Designer:            Andrew Wells
Date:                *c.*1889
Original Location:   Sydney, NSW
Patron:              Not known.

**Description:**
Hand-painted Renaissance-style designs on a gold ground.

**Current position:**
Not known.

**References:**
Montana 2000, 149.

## 173 All Saints' Anglican Church Hunters Hill, Stained Glass

Designer:            John Lamb Lyon
Date:                1889
Original Location:   Anglican Church, Hunters Hill,
                     Sydney, NSW
Patron:              Not known.

**Description:**
The windows were installed in stages.

The E window was dedicated to the memory of Shepherd
Smith, a past General Manager of the Bank of New South
Wales. A copy was made for Grafton Cathedral (ref no.151). It
depicts the theme of the hymn *Te Deum Laudamus*. The centre
light depicts the *Crucifixion* and *Christ's Victory over Death*. The

lower panel shows *The Last Supper*. The upper foils: *Sanctus,
Sanctus, Sanctus,* (Holy, Holy, Holy) and *Father, Son and Holy
Spirit.*

The other Chancel windows, all by Lyon Cottier & Wells are:
on N side: *Children Borne to and from Heaven*; on S side: *The
Road to Emmaus* (Luke 24:13-35) and the *Children's Window*;
on N side of Nave (from the crossing back); *Scenes from the
Life of Christ, Saints Augustine, Aiden* and the *Venerable Bede.*

**Current position:**
Extant.

**References:**
Anglican Parish of Hunters Hill website:
http://www.huntershill.anglican.asn.au [2009].

## 174 Union Bank of Australia Melbourne, Interior Decoration

Designer:            Andrew Wells
Date:                1890
Original Location:   Collins Street, Melbourne, VIC
Patron:              Not known.

**Description:**
Italian Renaissance-style decorations.

**Current position:**
Demolished.

**References:**
Montana 2000, 149.

## 175 National Mutual Life Association Sydney, Interior Decoration

Designer:            Andrew Wells
Date:                *c.*1890
Original Location:   Sydney, NSW
Patron:              J Sulman.

**Description:**
A gouache design survives, probably by Wells.

**Current position:**
Not known.

**References:**
Montana 2000, 150-1.

## 176 Vaucluse House, Interior Decoration

Designer:            Andrew Wells, John Lamb Lyon
Date:                *c.*1890
Original Location:   Vaucluse, NSW
Patron:              Not known.

**Description:**
Ceiling in Neo-Renaissance style, based on a Parisian source
in a folio belonging to John Lamb Lyon.

**Current position:**
Not known, the House is in the care of the Australian
Historic Houses Trust. [Update on condition before
publication?]

**References:**
Ellsmore 1982,  4&5; Montana 2000, 142.

## 177  Stonington, Interior Decoration

| | |
|---|---|
| Designer: | Andrew Wells |
| Date: | 1891 |
| Original Location: | Stonington, Melbourne. VIC |
| Patron: | J Wagner. |

**Description:**
Wall and ceiling decoration.

**Current position:**
Not known.

**References:**
Montana 2000, 155.

## 178  St Joseph's Church, Stained Glass

| | |
|---|---|
| Designer: | John Lamb Lyon |
| Date: | 1893 |
| Location: | Hobart, Tasmania |
| Patron: | Not known. |

**Description:**
The window over the sacristy door shows *St Joseph, the Sacred Heart* and *St Aloysius*. In memory of Fr Joseph Aloysius Sheehy.

**Current position:**
Extant.

**References:**
http://www.passionistshobart.org.au/index.php/parish-history/51-st-josephs-church [2009].

## 179  St Joseph's Church, Orange, Interior Decoration

| | |
|---|---|
| Designer: | Andrew Wells |
| Date: | 1897 |
| Original Location: | Orange, NSW |
| Patron: | Not known. |

**Description:**
Interior decoration in transepts.

**Current position:**
Not known

**References:**
http://users.netwit.net.au [1999]; http://www.cathchurch.net/nsw/parish/Orange [2010].

## WORKS OF KNOWN OR APPROXIMATE DATE NOT ASSOCIATED WITH PLACES

## 180  Stained Glass Including *Australia* Exhibited at Melbourne Centennial Exhibition

| | |
|---|---|
| Designer: | John Lamb Lyon |
| Date: | 1888 |
| Original Location: | Melbourne, VIC |
| Patron: | Not known. |

**Description:**
Stained glass exhibits including *Australia*, *Four Views of Old Scotch Towns*, heads after Holbein, figures from Tennyson, *Angel with Harp*, figure of *Music*, flower panels. Australia could be the same panel exhibited in London two years earlier.

**Current position:**
Not known.

**References:**
Montana 2000, 155.

## 181  Painted Vase with Illustration of Sir Joseph Banks

| | |
|---|---|
| Designer: | John Lamb Lyon |
| Date: | *c.fl*1880 |
| Original Location: | Not known |
| Patron: | Not known. |

**Description:**
Pottery vase of pseudo-Classical krater shape, painted by Lyon Cottier & Co, with medallion portrait of Sir Joseph Banks surrounded by waratah flowers, said to have been made from Lithgow clay, possibly at Lithgow NSW but perhaps in Sydney, NSW.

**Current position:**
Held by the Powerhouse Museum, Sydney, NSW.

**References:**
Powerhouse Museum website:
http://www.powerhousemuseum.com/ [2009].

## 182  Designs for Stained Glass Windows and Painted Ceilings

| | |
|---|---|
| Designer: | John Lamb Lyon and Andrew Wells |
| Date: | 1888–1907 |
| Original Location: | Not known |
| Patron: | Not known. |

**Description:**
Twenty-one original designs for windows and ceilings of churches, institutions and private residences.

**Current Position:**
Held in the State Library, NSW.

**References:**
http://acms.sl.nsw.gov.au.
Zielinski (www.prudhoecatholics.co.uk/history6.htm) [2009].

# SELECTED BIBLIOGRAPHY OF PUBLICATIONS
# AND DOCUMENTS

The bibliography lists the sources cited in the text, as well as the principal sources of reference and contextual works consulted in the preparation of this book. Unpublished sources are listed first, followed by published sources. Within published sources, those relating specifically to Daniel Cottier, William Leiper, and Dowanhill Church precede sources of more general relevance. Catalogues of exhibitions and sales are listed under the name of the venue or company which held them, unless the name of an author or editor is given on the title page. Unsigned articles are listed under the name of the publication. A date in square brackets after a website address indicates the date on which that website was consulted.

## UNPUBLISHED SOURCES
**Archival Sources:**

ACLA 1-16, Fifteen unpublished letters and one invoice, Daniel Cottier of Cottier & Co, London, to William Smith, Aberdeen City Architect (4 Feb 1875-22 Nov 1876), Aberdeen Central Library Archives
DCR, Dowanhill Church Records, Glasgow Archives, Mitchell Library, Glasgow
Alexander MacDonald of Kepplestone, Aberdeen City Council Archives, Town House, Aberdeen
Metropolitan Museum NY
Powell Records, Records of James Powell and Sons, Glass Manufacturers, London.
*Young's Glasgow Scraps*, Mitchell Library, Glasgow

**Dissertations and Research Papers:**

Borland, CM 1995 *The Domestic Architecture of William Leiper in Helensburgh, 1871-1909*, undergraduate dissertation, Glasgow School of Art
Correia, MF 2007 *Characterization of the Materials and Techniques of Daniel Cottier's Painted Scheme for Dowanhill Church, Glasgow, Together with the Conservation Treatment of a Portrait of the Rev William Dickie (Studio no. 1669)*, MA dissertation, Northumbria University
Donnelly, Max 1998 *Cottier And Company (1864-1915) Establishing a Context for the Second Glasgow School*, MA dissertation, Sotheby's Institute, London
Down, GM 1975 *Nineteenth Century Stained Glass in Melbourne*, MA dissertation, University of Melbourne
Ellsmore, D 1993 (1) 'Art Decorations in Australia: The Artists and the Craftsmen', paper given at Historic Interiors Conference, Adelaide (23-25 Apr 1993)
Ellsmore, D 1993 (2) *Nineteenth-Century Painted Decorations in Britain and Australia: An Approach to Conservation*, doctoral dissertation, University of York

Farina, B 1997 *The Development of Old English Painted Furniture of the English Aesthetic Movement*, MA dissertation, Sotheby's Institute, London
Fowle, F 1994 *Alexander Reid in Context: Collecting and Dealing in Scotland in the Late 19th and Early 20th Centuries*, doctoral dissertation, University of Edinburgh
Giedraityte, DI 1982 *Stained and Painted Glass in the Sydney Area, ca. 1830-ca. 1920*, MA dissertation, University of Sydney
Goodfellow, P [nd] 'William Leiper', typescript, courtesy of J Kinchin
Greig, T and Clarkson, AG 1978 *William Leiper*, undergraduate dissertation, Mackintosh School of Architecture, Glasgow
Gurney, G 1978 *Olin Levi Warner (1844-1896): A Catalogue Raisonné of his Sculpture and Graphic Works*, doctoral dissertation, University of Delaware
Herron, A 1984 *Historical Directory to Glasgow Presbytery*, typescript (copies in Glasgow Archives and Glasgow Presbytery Office)
Hobler, M 1987 *In Search of Daniel Cottier: Artistic Entrepreneur, 1838-91*, Master's dissertation, City University of New York
Komar, JA 1991 *The Importance of John Moyr Smith's Life and Work in the Context of Design Reform*, graduate dissertation, University of Glasgow
Leishman, J 1991 *A Study of Dowanhill Church, 1823-1991*, graduate dissertation, University of Glasgow
Logan, S 1998 *West United Presbyterian Church, Millport, Isle of Cumbrae: A Study of the Interior*, undergraduate dissertation, Glasgow School of Art
Melville, J 2001 *John Forbes White and George Reid: Artists and Patrons in North-East Scotland 1860-1920*, doctoral dissertation, University of Edinburgh
Nieswander, J 1988 *Liberalism, Nationalism and the Evolution of Middle-Class Values: The Literature on Interior Decoration in England, 1875-1914*, doctoral dissertation, Westfield College, University of London
Rush Bambrough, S 2001 *Glass Painting in Scotland, 1830-1870*, doctoral dissertation, University of Glasgow
Small, S 1996 'Development of Dowanhill Estate', unpublished paper (18 Sept 1996)
Urquhart, G 2002 *List of Early Residents of Villas in Dowanhill Estate*, Glasgow West Conservation Trust

**Reports:**

Allardyce, F 1998 *Dowanhill Church, Glasgow: Addendum Report*, Historic Scotland, Edinburgh

*Dowanhill Church: Structural Report* 1984 commissioned by Four Acres Charitable Trust from Walter Underwood & Partners, Glasgow, with Appraisal of Cottier and Drawings of Cottier Patterns by Michael Donnelly

## PUBLICATIONS
### Daniel Cottier:
Advertisements:
Cottier & Co 1882 'Messrs Cottier & Co., Interior Decorators', advertisement, *The Critic*, 2 (8 Apr 1882), 11
Cottier & Co 1984 'One of a Kind: Steinway and Son Grand Piano [...] Case Designed by Cottier & Company, Circa 1889, Serial Number 69376', *Antiques*, 125 (May 1984), 1033

### Catalogues of Exhibitions and Sales:
American Art Galleries 1913 *Illustrated Catalogue of the Artistic Property, Fine Antique and Modern Furniture, Important Flemish Tapestries, Stained Glass, Textiles and Other Objects of Household Utility and Embellishment of the Well-Known House of Cottier and Company of New York*, New York (19-26 Nov 1913)
Anderson Galleries 1915 *Catalogue of Paintings, Art Objects, Books, Fixtures and Artistic Furniture, Comprising the Entire Stock of [...] Cottier and Company*, New York (12 Mar 1915)
Anderson Galleries 1923 *Drawings and Paintings from the Collections of [...] the Late Daniel Cottier*, New York (7-8 Nov 1923)
Brinton, C 1912 *Walter Greaves (Pupil of Whistler), Being a Catalogue of Paintings, Drawings and Etchings [...] Exhibited at the Cottier Gallery January 11 to February 10, with Full Bibliographical and Critical Introduction*, New York
Christie's 1998 *Decorative Arts, Including British and Continental Ceramics*, Glasgow (23 Sept 1998), 56, lot 266
Christie, Manson & Woods 1914 (1) *Catalogue of Decorative Furniture and Porcelain, the Property of Alexander Allan Webbe [...] Mrs. Cottier*, London (23 Apr 1914)
Christie, Manson & Woods 1914 (2) *Catalogue of Modern Pictures and Water Colour Drawings, Chiefly of the Continental Schools, the Property of Mrs. Cottier*, London (23 Apr and 1 May 1914)
Cottier and Co 1878 *Fine Old Paintings and Water-Color Drawings [...] Imported by Cottier & Co. [...] Sold at [...] Association Hall*, New York (23-24 Apr 1878)
Durand-Ruel 1892 *Collection Cottier Catalogue: Catalogue of Ancient and Modern Pictures, Important Works of the French, English and Dutch Schools*, Paris-New York

### Books and Articles:
*American Art News* 1913 'Cottier Stained Glass', 116 (16 Apr 1913), 2
*Architect* 1891 'The Late Daniel Cottier', 47 (13 May 1891), 323-4

*Art Interchange* 1879 (2) 'Art Galleries', III:6 (17 Sept 1879), 52 [Cottier & Co gallery]
*Art Journal* 1878 (1) 'Notes: Cottier's Art Rooms', 4 (March 1878), 94 [Cottier & Co gallery]
*Art Journal* 1878 (2) 'The Cottier Sale of Pictures', 4 (June 1878), 192 [Cottier & Co]
*Art Journal* 1879 (1) 'Notes: New Pictures in New York Galleries', 5 (Jan 1879), 31-2 [Cottier & Co gallery]
*Art Journal* 1879 (2) 'Notes: Art Alcove at the Society Library', 5 (July 1879), 191 [Cottier & Co]
*Builder* 1874 'Stained Glass', 32 (1874), 424
*Century Magazine* 1882 'Some of the Union League Decorations', 23:5 (March 1882), 745-52
Coakley, F 1999 'Lezayre Window', www.isle-of-man.com/manxnotebook/people/artists [Cottier window] [2003]
Cook, C 1874 'Culture and Progress: Cottier and Company', *Scribner's Monthly*, 8 (Aug 1874), 500-1
*Decorator and Furnisher* 1882 'Trade Opinions', 30 [Cottier & Co furniture]
Dickie, W 1930 'Daniel Cottier', *Dowanhill Church Monthly Record* (May-June 1930), 3-4
Donnelly, Max 1999 'Daniel Cottier: Pioneer of Aestheticism', *Journal of the Decorative Arts Society*, 23 (1999), 32-51
Donnelly, Max 2001 'Cottier and Company, Art Furniture Makers', *Magazine Antiques* (New York), 37 (2001), 91-120
Donnelly, Michael 1998 (1) 'Daniel Cottier', *Glasgow Herald* (2 Oct 1998)
Donnelly, Michael 1998 (2) 'Daniel Cottier's Work', *Glasgow Herald* (16 Oct 1998)
Ellsmore, D 1982 'The Decorators Lyon and Cottier', *Historic Houses Journal*, 1 (Mar 1982), 2-7
Frelinghuysen, AC 2007, 'Daniel Cottier and Company, Spring', *Metropolitan Museum of Art Bulletin* (Fall 2007), 50
Gould, B 1969 *Two Van Gogh Contacts: EJ Wisselingh, Art Dealer; Daniel Cottier, Glass Painter and Decorator*, London
*Harper's Weekly* 1881 'The Union League Club House' (19 Feb 1881), 118 [Cottier & Co interior decoration]
Henley, WE 1892 'Daniel Cottier, 1838-1891', in Durand-Ruel 1892, ix-xiii
*Journal of Decorative Art and British Decorator* 1902 'The Late Daniel Cottier', 22 (May 1902), 145
Kinchin, J 1996 'Daniel Cottier', in Banham, J (ed) *Encyclopedia of Interior Design*, London
'Montezuma' 1880 [Montague Marks], 'My Note Book', *Art Amateur*, 2 (Apr 1880), 91 [paintings at Cottier & Co]
'Montezuma' 1888, 'My Note Book', *Art Amateur*, 18:5 (Apr 1888), 104 [paintings at Cottier & Co]
*The Nation* 1878 (1) 'Notes: Review of an Exhibition of Cottier & Co, 817 Broadway, New York' (18 Apr 1878) [Cottier & Co gallery]
Wells, A 1902 'The Late Daniel Cottier', *Journal of Decorative Art and the British Decorator*, XXII (May 1902), 142-5

**William Leiper:**

*Academy Architecture* 1891 'Park Circus Interior', 3 (1891), 127

*Academy Architecture* 1894 (1) 'Interior: Moredun, Paisley', 6 (1894), 82

*Academy Architecture* 1894 (2) 'Interior: Clarendon, Helensburgh', 6 (1894), 83

*Academy Architecture* 1899 'Knockderry Castle, Cove – Additions', 11 (1899) 68

*Architect* 1880 'Illustrations: The Great State Saloon, Imperial Yacht "Livadia"' (23 Oct 1880), 259-60 [Leiper interior design]

*Architect* 1889 'The Fall of Templeton's Mill, Glasgow' (27 Dec 1889), 369-71

*The Bailie* 1878 'Men You Know' (20 Feb 1878), 5

*Builder* 1900 'Staircase, Kelly House' (24 Feb 1900)

*Builder* 1916 'William Leiper', Obituary (2 Jun 1916)

*Builder's Journal* 1898 'Men Who Build: William Leiper RSA, FRIBA', vi (12 Jan 1898), 487-9

*Building News* 1885 'Kinloch Moidart, Inverness' (26 Jun 1885)

*Building News* 1887 'Building Intelligence: Hyndland Church' (6 May 1887)

*Building News* 1890 'Kelly House, Wemyss Bay' (6 Jun 1890)

Davison, TR 1882 'Rambling Sketches, no. 83: "Cairndhu"', *British Architect* (22 Sept 1882), 453-4

Davison, TR 1889 'Modern Architecture in Scotland, No. XXIII: "Ruthven"', *British Architect* (13 Sept 1889), 181-2

Dawson, T 2000 'Monument to the Victorian Fantasy Builder', *Sunday Times* (9 July 2000)

*Dictionary of Scottish Architects* 2008 'William Leiper', http://www.scottisharchitects.org.uk [2009]

*Glasgow Herald* 1916 'Death of a Glasgow Architect', Obituary of William Leiper (29 May 1916)

Green, S 1992 'William Leiper's Houses in Helensburgh', *Architectural Heritage*, III (1992), 32-42

Green, S 2001 'William Leiper's Churches', *Architectural Heritage*, XII (2001), 38-50

*Helensburgh & Gareloch Times* 1916 'William Leiper', Obituary (31 May 1916)

Hume, JR 1995 'The Scottish Houses of William Leiper', in Gow, I and Rowan, A (eds) *Scottish Country Houses 1600-1914*, Edinburgh, 285-297

McNab, WH 1916 'William Leiper, R.S.A., J.P.[F.]. Born 21st May 1839; died 27th May 1916', *Journal of the Royal Institute of British Architects*, xxiii (1916), 302-4

*Scotland in Trust* 2008 [Stained Glass Panel: Robert Burns], *Scotland in Trust*, 25:3 (2008), cover

Walker, D 2001 'William Leiper', *Grove Online Dictionary of Art*

Worsdall, F 1966 'A Victorian Architect: William Leiper RSA 1839-1916', *Scottish Field* (June1966), 30-31

**Dowanhill Church:**

*Building News* 1865 [Dowanhill UP Church] (18 Aug 1865)

*The Courier* 1996 'The Cottier Comes of Age' [Glasgow] (25 Oct 1996)

*Daily Mail* 1865 'New United Presbyterian Church at Partick' (8 Aug 1865)

Dickie, W 1916 (1) 'In Praise of the House of God', sermon in *Dowanhill United Free Church Jubilee* 1916, 5-10

Dickie, W 1916 (1) 'God, the Dwelling Place of His People in All Generations', sermon in *Dowanhill United Free Church Jubilee* 1916, 11-15

Dickie, W 1926 *History of Dowanhill Church 1823-1923*, Glasgow

Douglas, D 1989 'Concerted Effort to Save Old Kirk', *Scotland on Sunday* (12 Feb 1989)

*Dowanhill Church Centenary* 1923 *Dowanhill Church, Partick, Glasgow: Centenary Celebrations, 1823-1923* [printed leaflet], Glasgow

*Dowanhill Parish Church Monthly Record* (DCMR) [printed newsletter], formerly

*Dowanhill Church Monthly Record* (to Aug 1962), *Dowanhill United Free Church Monthly Record* (to Oct 1929), and *Dowanhill United Presbyterian Church Monthly Record* (to 1900)

*Dowanhill Parish Church* 1966 *Dowanhill Parish Church, Partick, Glasgow: Centenary Celebrations 1866-1966* [printed booklet], Glasgow

*Evening Citizen* 1962 [Induction of Rev Henry Chisholm] (8 Sept 1962).

*Glasgow Herald* 1866 (1) [Dowanhill UP Church] (10 Nov 1866)

*Glasgow Herald* 1866 (2) [Dowanhill UP Church] (12 Nov 1866)

*In Memoriam* 1935 *In Memoriam, Rev. William Dickie, M.A., D.D., 15th March, 1854-15th March, 1935*, Glasgow

Lawrie, TM 1891 *Notices of Dowanhill Church, 1825-1888*, Glasgow

Robertson, D 2007 'Dowanhill Church', *Journal of the Scottish Society for Art History*, 12 (2007), 83-5

Sotheby's 1983 (2) *Catalogue of Ceramics, Glass and Furniture*, Chester (6-7 Sept 1983) [includes Dowanhill Church furniture]

**General Sources:**

Adam, S 1877 *Stained Glass: Its History and Modern Development*, Glasgow

Adam, S 1896 *Truth in Decorative Art*, Glasgow

Adam, S 1908 'Stained Glass in Glasgow: Past and Present', paper presented at the Old Glasgow Club, 18 Jan 1904, *Old Glasgow Transactions*, 1 (1900-1908), 8-9

Agius, P 1978 *British Furniture, 1880-1915*, Woodbridge, Suffolk

*Alexander Thomson Society Newsletter* 1991 'St Vincent Street Church', 2 (Oct 1991), 4

*American Architect and Building News* 1877 'Decorative Fine-Art Work at Philadelphia: American Furniture', 2 (13 Jan 1877), 12-13

*American Architect and Building News* 1878 [Decoration of Trinity Church, Boston], 3:111 (9 Feb 1878), 46

*Appleton's Dictionary of New York* 1883-91, New York

*Art Interchange* 1879 (1) 'Three Examples of Monticelli', II:9 (30 Apr 1879), 71 [Monticelli at Cottier & Co gallery]

*Artistic Country-Seats* 1886, 5 vols, New York

*Artistic Houses* 1883-4, 2 vols, New York

Aslin, E 1969 *The Aesthetic Movement: Prelude to Art Nouveau*, London

Aslin, E 1986 *E.W. Godwin: Furniture and Interior Decoration*, London

*Australasian Decorator and Painter* 1909 'Personal: Mr. John Lyon' (1 Aug 1909), 263-4

*Australasian Decorator and Painter* 1916 'Death of Mr. John L. Lyon' (1 Jul 1916)

*Australian Dictionary of Biography* 2006, http://adbonline.anu.edu.au/adbonline.htm

*The Bailie* 1919 'Men You Know, No. 2426', XCIV (16 Apr 1919), 3-4 [on Hugh McCulloch]

Baird, MU 1935 'Tribute by the Rev. Matthew Urie Baird, M.A., East and Belmont Church, Aberdeen, Brought up under Dr. Dickie's Ministry at Dowanhill', in *In Memoriam, Rev. William Dickie, M.A., D.D., 15th March, 1854-15th March, 1935*, Glasgow

Banham, J et al. 1991 *Victorian Interior Design*, London

Baxter, W 1935 'Rev. William Dickie, D.D., 1854-1935', *DCMR* (Mar-Apr 1935), 1

Bell, AM 1863 *Sermon Reading and Memoriter Delivery*, Edinburgh

Bell, D 1997 *The Historic Scotland Guide to International Conservation Charters*, TAN 8, Edinburgh

Bicknell, S 1996 *The Making of the Victorian Organ*, Cambridge

Billings, RW 1849 *The Infinity of Geometric Design Exemplified*, Edinburgh

Billings, RW 1851 *The Power of Form Applied to Geometric Tracery*, Edinburgh

*The Biographer* 1894 'J Moyr Smith' (15 Oct 1894); reprint in *Glazed Expressions*, 9 (Spring 1985)

Bird, E 1973 'International Glasgow', *Connoisseur*, 184 (Aug 1973), 248-257

Bolger, D 1986 *In Pursuit of Beauty: Americans and the Aesthetic Movement*, New York

Bristow, IC 1996 *Interior House-Painting Colours and Technology 1615-1840,* London

British Museum 1963 *Layard and His Successors: Assyrian Explorations and Discovery in the XIXth Century*, London

Brogden, WA 1998 *Aberdeen: An Illustrated Architectural Guide*, 2nd edn, Edinburgh

Brooke, J 1989 *Discerning Tastes: Montreal Collectors 1880-1920*, Montreal

*Builder* 1874 'Stained Glass', 32 (1874), 424

Burke, DB et al. 1986 *In Pursuit of Beauty: Americans and the Aesthetic Movement*, New York

Cameron, I 1936 *Angus our Precentor*, London

Campbell, P 2001 'David Wilkie in Constantinople', *Journal of the Scottish Society for Art History*, 6 (2001), 27-36

Cannon, L 1990 'The Stained Glass Revival', *SSCK Journal* (Aug 1990), 1:3

Cannon, L 1991 *Stained Glass in the Burrell Collection*, Edinburgh

*Catalogue of the Avery Architectural Library* 1895, New York [visual record of Cottier windows]

Chadwick, O 1970 *The Victorian Church, Part II (1860-1901)*, London

Chevreul, M-E 1854 *The Principles of Harmony and Contrast of Colours, and their Applications to the Arts*, trans from French by Martel, C, London

*Church Standard* 1913 'Our Australian Cathedrals. No. X. – Christ Church Cathedral, Grafton' (3 Oct 1913), 51

Clark, TM 1878 'The Decoration of Trinity Church, Boston', *The Nation*, 657 (31 Jan 1878), 77

Clarke, BFL 1969 *Church Building in the Nineteenth Century*, 2nd edn, London

Cockerell, SC 1915 'Ford Madox Brown on Art Education', *Burlington Magazine*, 28 (Nov 1915), 66-7

Cohen, D 2006 *Household Gods: The British and their Possessions*, New Haven

Cohen, M 2005 'Restoration as Re-creation at the Sainte-Chapelle', *Res*, 48 (Autumn 2005), 135-54

Cohen, M 2007 'La Sainte-Chapelle du Moyen Age à la lumière des archives de la restauration. Problèmes et solutions', in Hédiger 2007, 211-27

Cole, C 1879 'Painted Glass in Household Decoration', *Harper's New Monthly Magazine*, 59 (Oct 1879), 655-64

Cook, C 1879 'Painted Glass in Household Decoration', *Harper's Magazine*, 59 (1879), 655-64 [Cottier & Co glass]

Cook, C 1878 *The House Beautiful*, New York

Cooper, J 1987 *Victorian and Edwardian Furniture and Interiors*, London

Cousland, J 1862 'Remarks on Modern Church Architecture', paper delivered to the Glasgow Architectural Society, 17 March 1862, *Daily Mail* (18 March 1862)

Cowen, P 1985 *A Guide to Stained Glass in Britain*, London

Crawford, WM 1985 *Pendower, Newcastle upon Tyne: Notes on a Victorian Mansion*, Newcastle

Crawford Municipal Art Gallery 1981 *'Got Cork': An Exhibition on the Centenary of William Burges, 1827-1881, Architect of St Fin Barre's Cathedral*, Cork

Crook, JM 1981 (1) *William Burges and the High Victorian Dream*, London

Crook, JM 1981 (2) *The Strange Genius of William Burges 'Art-Architect', 1827-1881*, Cardiff

Cruft, K, Dunbar, J and Fawcett, R 2006 *The Buildings of Scotland: Borders*, London

Cumming, E 2006 *Hand, Heart and Soul: The Arts and Crafts Movement in Scotland*, Edinburgh

Curl, JS 1991 *The Art and Architecture of Freemasonry*, London

Curl, JS 1995 (1) 'St Vincent Street Church as a Mnemonic of the Temple of Solomon', *Alexander Thomson Society Newsletter*, 12 (Jan 1995), 6-10

Curl, JS 1995 (2) 'Meanwhile, Back at the Temple', *Alexander Thomson Society Newsletter*, 14 (Dec1995), 5-6

Curl, JS 1996 'More Temple Talk', *Alexander Thomson Society Newsletter*, 16 (May 1996), 15-16

Curl, JS 1997 'St Vincent Street and the Temple of Solomon', *Alexander Thomson Society Newsletter*, 18 (Feb 1997), 5

Curl, JS 2001 'Thoughts on Thomson', *Alexander Thomson Society Newsletter*, 28 (Feb 2001), 16

Dalglish, C and Driscoll, ST 2009 *Historic Govan*, Scottish Burgh Survey, Oxford

Dalziel Brothers 1881 *Dalziels' Bible Gallery: Illustrations from the Old Testament from Original Drawings*, London

D'Angelo, D 1994 'The End of Queen's Park Church', *Alexander Thomson Society Newsletter*, 9 (Feb 1994), 7-12

Davis, MC 1991 *The Castles and Mansions of Ayrshire*, Ardrishaig

Davis, MC 1996 *Scots Baronial: Mansions and Castle Restorations in the West of Scotland*, Ardrishaig

Davison, R 1882 'Rambling Sketches No. 83: "Cairndhu"', *The British Architect* (22 September 1882)

Davison, R 1886 'Rambling Sketches: Two Houses by William Leiper', *The British Architect* (26 Jan 1886), 42-3

Day, L 1887 'Victorian Progress in Applied Design', *The Art Journal*, Special Number

*Decoration* 1885 'Decoration at Mr Pearce's House' (Sept 1885) [decoration by Andrew Wells]

*Decoration* 1887 'Painted Decorations by Andrew Wells' (Jan 1887)

Dey, M and Irwin, F 1985 *Alexander MacDonald: From Mason to Maecenas*, Aberdeen

Dickie, W and Dobbie, T 1895 *Sermon Preached on 21 April 1895, on the Death of Rev. Thomas Lawrie*, Glasgow

*Dictionary of Scottish Architects* 2008 http://www.scottisharchitects.org.uk [2009]

Doak, AM 1968 *The First Hundred Years of the Glasgow Institute of Architects*, Glasgow

Donnelly Max 2001 'British Furniture at the Philadelphia Centennial Exhibition', *Furniture History*, 37 (2001) 91-120

Donnelly, Michael 1981 *Glasgow Stained Glass: A Preliminary Study*, Glasgow

Donnelly, Michael 1990 'Glasgow's Glorious Glass', *History Today*, 40 (May 1990), 29-33

Donnelly, Michael 1997 *Scotland's Stained Glass: Making the Colours Sing*, Edinburgh

Drummond, A and Bulloch, J 1975 *The Church in Victorian Scotland 1843-1874*, Edinburgh

Dumas, C 1983 'Art Dealers and Collectors', in Royal Academy *The Hague School: Dutch Masters of the 19th Century*, London, 125-36

Eadie, J 1872 *Ecclesiastical Cyclopaedia*, 4th edn, London

Eastlake, CL 1868 *Hints on Household Taste in Furniture, Upholstery and Other Details*, London

*Edinburgh Review* 1867 'Modern Glass Painting', *Edinburgh Review*, 255 (Jan 1867)

Edwards, B 1984 'Challenge to a Townscape: The Future of Glasgow Churches', *Country Life* (9 Aug 1984), 404-6

Ellis, A 1996 'Homer at Holmwood', *Alexander Thomson Society Newsletter*, 16 (May 1996), 3-7

Ellsmore, D 1983, '19th-Century Decorators', in Stapleton, M (ed), *Historic Interiors*, Sydney, 34-43

Ellsmore, D 1986 'Scottish Influences in Nineteenth Century Decorative Arts in Australia', *Heritage Australia*, 5:3 (1986), 10-13

Errington, L 1983 *Master Class: Robert Scott Lauder and his Pupils* Edinburgh

Evans, D 1986 'Albert Pinkham Ryder's Use of Visual Sources', *Winterthur Portfolio*, 21:1 (Spring 1986), 21-40

*Evening Times* 1893 [Obituary of Ford Madox Brown] (19 Oct 1893)

Eyre-Todd, G (ed) 1909 *Who's Who in Glasgow in 1909*, Glasgow

Farr, D 1993 *Thomas Gambier Parry, 1816-1888, as Artist and Collector*, London

Ferry, E 2003 'Decorators May Be Compared to Doctors: An Analysis of Rhoda and Agnes Garrett's *Suggestions for House Decoration in Painting, Woodwork and Furniture 1876*', *Journal of Design History*, 16:1 (2003), 15-33

Field, G 1835 *Chromatography, or, a Treatise on Colours and Pigments, and of their Powers in Painting*, London

Field, G 1850 *Rudiments of the Painters' Art: Or a Grammar of Colouring, Applicable to Operative Painting, Decorative Architecture, and the Arts*, London

Fisher, A [nd] *Paisley Abbey: A Guide for Those Interested in the Stained Glass Windows*, Paisley

Forge, S 1981 *Victorian Splendour: Australian Interior Decoration, 1837-1901*, Melbourne

Fowle, F 1991 'The Hague School and the Scots: A Taste for Dutch Pictures', *Apollo* (Aug 1991), 108-11

Fowle, F 1997 'Alexander Reid: The Influential Dealer', *Journal of the Scottish Society for Art History*, 2 (1997) 24-35

Freylinghuysen, AC 1995 'The Aesthetic Movement in Newport', *Magazine Antiques*, 147 (Apr 1995), 570-77

Fridlander, ED 1921 *Matthew Maris*, London

The Gallery, 191 Piccadilly 1865 *Exhibition of 'Work', and Other Paintings by Ford Madox Brown at the Gallery, 191 Piccadilly […] A.D. MDCCCLXV*, London

Garrett, R and A 1876 *Suggestions on House Decoration in Painting, Woodwork and Furniture*, Art at Home Series, London

Gere, C 1989 *Nineteenth Century Decoration: The Art of the Interior*, London

Gere, C and Hoskins, L 2000 *The House Beautiful: Oscar Wilde and the Aesthetic Interior*, London

Gere, C and Whiteway, M 1993 *Nineteenth Century Design, from Pugin to Mackintosh*, London

Gettens, RJ and Stout, GL 1966 *Painting Materials: A Short Encyclopaedia*, New York

Gifford, J 1988 *The Buildings of Scotland: Fife*, London

Gifford, J 1996 *The Buildings of Scotland: Dumfries and Galloway*, London

Gifford, J and Walker, FA 2002 *The Buildings of Scotland: Stirling and Central Scotland*, London

Gifford, J, McWilliam, C and Walker, D 1984 *The Buildings of Scotland: Edinburgh*, London

Gildard, T 1888 'Greek Thomson', *Proceedings of the Royal Philosophical Society of Glasgow*, XIX (30 Jan 1888), 191-200

Girouard, M 1977 *Sweetness and Light: The 'Queen Anne' Movement, 1860-1900*, Oxford

Girouard, M 1979 *The Victorian Country House*, 2nd edn, New Haven and London

*Glasgow Herald* 1893 'Ford Madox Brown, 1821-1893', Obituary (9 Oct 1893)

Godwin, EW 1863 'The Sister Arts and their Relation to Architecture', newscutting in *Archive of Art & Design*, AAD 4/561, reprinted in Kinchin and Stirton 2005, 35-9

Godwin, EW 1865 *Handbook of Floral Decoration for Churches*, London

Godwin, EW 1866-8 'Painted Decoration', series of articles, *Building News* (20 Apr, 25 May, 22 June, 3 Aug, 10 Aug, 7 Sept, 16 Nov, 1866); (4 Jan, 20 Apr, 19 Jul, 18 Oct 1867); (3 Jan 1868)

Godwin, EW 1872 'Wall Painting', *The Architect* (24 Feb 1872), 87

Godwin, EW 1875 'The Present Aspect of Decorative Painting', *The Architect* (11 Sept 1875), 140-1

Godwin, EW 1876 'Scraps for Students. —V. Competitions and Clients', *The Architect* (20 May 1876),

Gomme, A and Walker, D 1987 *The Architecture of Glasgow*, 2nd edn, London and Glasgow

Gow, I 1992 *The Scottish Interior*, Edinburgh

Hamilton, W 1882 *The Aesthetic Movement in England*, London

Hansen, EF, Walston, S and Bishop, MH 1993 *Matte Paint: Its History and Technology, Analysis, Properties and Conservation Treatment*, Malibou

Harbron, D 1949 *The Conscious Stone: The Life of Edward William Godwin*, London

*Harper's Weekly* 1880 'Maurits Frederik Hendrik de Haas' (24 Jul 1880), 475 [Dutch art at Cottier & Co]

*Harper's Weekly* 1881 [New York Society Library], 25 (19 Feb 1881), 118

Harrison, M 1975 'Contemporary Glass One Hundred Years Ago', *Glass* (6 Jan 1975), 36-9

Harrison, M 1980 *Victorian Stained Glass*, London

Harrower, IM 1918 *John Forbes White*, Edinburgh and London

Harvey, C and Press, J 1991 *Design and Enterprise in Victorian Britain*, Manchester

Haweis, ME (Mrs HR Haweis) 1879 *The Art of Decoration*, London

Haweis, ME 1882 *Beautiful Houses*, London

Hawthorne, Nathaniel 1871-2 *Passages from the English Note-books of Nathaniel Hawthorne*, 2 vols, Boston, Mass

Hay, DR 1838 *The Laws of Harmonious Colouring Adapted to Interior Decorations with Observations on the Practice of House Painting*, Edinburgh

Hay, DR 1843 *Proportion, or the Geometric Principle of Beauty Analysed*, Edinburgh

Hay, DR 1846 *First Principles of Symmetrical Beauty*, Edinburgh

Hay, DR 1853 *The Orthographic Beauty of the Parthenon Referred to a Law of Nature. To Which are Prefixed a Few Observations on the Importance of Aesthetic Science as an Element in Architectural Education*, Edinburgh

Hay, DR 1854 *The Harmonic Law of Nature Applied to Architectural Design*, Edinburgh

Hediger, Christine (ed) 2007 *La Sainte-Chapelle de Paris. Royaume de France ou Jérusalem céleste? Actes du Colloque (Paris, Collège de France, 2001)*, Turnhout

Heuffer, FM 1896 *Ford Madox Brown: A Record of his Life and Work*, London

Hird, R 1997 'Durham Cathedral Organs', www.dur.ac.uk/r.d.hird/cathhist.htm [2003]

*History of Architecture and Building Trades in Greater New York*, 1899, New York

*A History of Colombia University, 1754-1904* 1904 New York

*Historic Wall and Floor Coverings* 1998, Conservation Manual No 10, Glasgow

Howarth, T 1993 'Queen's Park Church', *Alexander Thomson Society Newsletter*, 7 (Jun 1993), 11

Howell, P and Sutton, I (eds) 1989 *The Faber Guide to Victorian Churches*, London and Boston

Hume, JR 1987 'Hyndland Church, 1887-1987', *Hyndland News*, special centenary edition, Glasgow

Jeans, F 1963 *100 Years: 1863-1963. Lansdowne-Woodside Church Centenary*, Glasgow

Jervis, S 1983 *High Victorian Design*, Woodbridge, Suffolk

Jones, O 1856 *The Grammar of Ornament*, London

Kelly, TD 2006-7 'The Manna of Ecclesiology: Contributions by Members of the Church Service Society to the Development of Scottish Ecclesiology from 1863', *The Church Service Society Record*, 42 (Winter 2006-7), 3-32

Kermode, RD 1954 *The Annals of Kirk Christ Lezayre*, Douglas, Isle of Man

Kinchin, J 1991 'A Revolution in Paper-Hanging: Scottish Wallpapers 1850-1910', *Scottish Art Review*, XVII (1991), 16-21

Kinchin, J and Stirton, P (eds) 2005 *Is Mr Ruskin Living Too Long? Selected Writings of E.W. Godwin on Victorian Architecture, Design and Culture*, Oxford

Kirchoff, biblio details date

Lambie, B 1998 *Notes on Cornhill House*, www.cornhillhousehotel.com

Lambourne, L 1996 *The Aesthetic Movement*, London

Lane, T and Serle, J 1990 *Australians at Home: A Documentary History of Australian Domestic Interiors from 1788 to 1914*, Melbourne

Larner, G and C 1979 *The Glasgow Style*, Edinburgh

Layard, AH 1853 *Discoveries in the Ruins of Ninevah and Babylon [...] Being the Result of the Second Expedition Undertaken for the Trustees of the British Museum*, London

Leask, HG 1962 *Christ Church Rathgar: The Story of One Hundred Years*, Dublin

Leniaud, J-M 2007 'La Sainte-Chapelle. Monument du XIXe siècle , in Hediger 2007, 181-195

Leniaud, J-M and Perrot, F 2007 *La Sainte Chapelle*, Paris

Leopold, AK 1986 *Victorian Splendour: Re-Creating America's 19th-Century Interiors*, New York

Lewis, A, Turner, J and McQuillan, S (eds) 1987 *The Opulent Interiors of the Gilded Age: All 203 Photographs from 'Artistic Houses'*, New York

Livio, M 2002 *The Golden Ratio: the Story of PHI, the World's Most Astonishing Number*, New York

MacArthur, R and Morse, F 1890 *A History of Calvary Baptist Church, New York*, New York

MacDonald, Greville 1924 *George MacDonald and his Wife*, New York

Macdonald, RH 1856 *Rambles Round Glasgow*, 2nd edn, Glasgow

MacDonald, S 1987 'Gothic Forms Applied to Furniture: The Early Work of Bruce James Talbert', *Furniture History* (1987), 39-52

McEwan, P 1988 *Dictionary of Scottish Art and Architecture*, Woodbridge, Suffolk

McFadzean, R 1979 *The Life and Work of Alexander Thomson*, London

Mackinnon, L 1935 *Recollections of an Old Lawyer*, Aberdeen

McKinstry, S 1993 'Solomon's Temple in St Viucent Street', *Alexander Thomson Society Newsletter* 8 (Oct 1993), 10-12

McKinstry, S 1994 'Cherubim over St Vincent Street', *Alexander Thomson Society Newsletter*, 11 (Oct 1994), 4-5

McKinstry, S 1995 (1) 'St Vincent Street Church as Solomonic Polemic: A Case of Submasonic Polemic?', *Alexander Thomson Society Newsletter*, 13 (May 1995), 8-10

McKinstry, S 1995 (2) 'Tau, Thomson, or Trabeation', *Alexander Thomson Society Newsletter*, 14 (Dec 1995), 9, 12

McKinstry, S 1996 'St Vincent Street Church, the Tau and the "Three A's"', *Alexander Thomson Society Newsletter*, 17 (Nov 1996), 11

McWilliam, C 1978 *The Buildings of Scotland: Lothian, Except Edinburgh*, Harmondsworth

Madigan, MJ 1982 *Nineteenth-Century Furniture: Innovation, Revival and Reform*, New York

Mathews, B 1972 *The Organs and Organists of Salisbury Cathedral* Salisbury

Mavor, J 1923 *My Window on the Street of the World*, London

Mayer, R 1987 *The Artists' Handbook of Materials and Techniques*, London

Measom, G 1859 *The Official Illustrated Guide to the Lancaster and Carlisle, Edinburgh and Glasgow, and Caledonian Railways*, Murray & Son, Glasgow

Meikle, W 1883 *The Illustrated Guide to St Giles Cathedral, Edinburgh*, Edinburgh

Melville, J 1998 'Art and Patronage in Aberdeen 1860-1920', *Journal of the Scottish Society for Art History*, 3 (1998), 16-23

Merrill, L 1992 *A Pot of Paint: Aesthetics on Trial in 'Whistler v Ruskin'*, Washington

Midant, J-P 2002 *Viollet-le-Duc: The French Gothic Revival*, Paris

Miers, M 2008 *The Western Seaboard: An Illustrated Architectural Guide*, Edinburgh

Minto, CS 1970 *John Forbes White: Miller, Collector, Photographer, 1831-1904*, Edinburgh

Montana, A 2000 *The Art Movement in Australia: Design, Taste and Society 1875-1900*, Carlton South, Victoria

Mora, P, Mora, L and Philippot, P 1984 *Conservation of Wall Paintings*, London

Munro, AM 1909 *Records of Old Aberdeen*, 2 vols, Aberdeen

Muthesius, H 1904-5 *Das englische Haus*, Berlin

Muthesius, S 1992 'We Do Not Understand What is Meant by a "Company" Designing: Design Versus Commerce in Late Nineteenth-Century English Furnishing', *Journal of Design History*, 5:2 (1992), 113-119

*The Nation* 1878 (2) 'The National Academy Exhibition – Final Notice', 674 (30 May 1878) [bust of Cottier by Olin Warner]

*The Nation* 1879 'Exhibition by the Society of American Artists – II' (3 Apr 1879), 237-8 [Monticelli at Cottier & Co gallery]

Nesfield, WE 1862 *Specimens of Mediaeval Architecture*, London

*New York Times* 1892 [Cottier window, Avery Architectural Library] (5 Jun 1892)

Norton, B 1978 *Trinity Church: The Story of an Episcopal Parish in the City of Boston*, Boston

Orbach, J 1987 *Victorian Architecture in Britain*, Blue Guide, London, 1st edn

Pach, W 1910 'New York as an Art Center', *Harper's Weekly* (26 Feb 1910) [Cottier & Co gallery]

*Paris Universal Exhibition: Catalogue of the British Section 1867*, London

Parry, L (ed) 1996 *William Morris*, London

Parry, TG 1858-60 'Whitewash and Yellow Dab – Nos. I-IV', *The Ecclesiologist* (1858), 112-5, 372-6; (1859), 232-8; (1860), 36-40, 78-82

Parry, TG 1862 'Wall Painting versus English Climate', *The Ecclesiologist* (1862), 134-42

Parry, TG and Burchett, R 1864 *Catalogue of the Exhibition of Stained Glass, Mosaic, etc., Designed and Executed by British Artists, Arranged in the North and West Cloisters of the South Kensington Museum under the National Art Training Schools*, London

Pater, W 1877 'The School of Giorgione', *Fortnightly Review* (Oct 1877), reprinted in Pater, W 1948 *Selected Works*, Aldington, R (ed), London, 269-84

Paul, RM 1998 *Partick Anecdotes*, Helensburgh

Pert, G 1995 *Perspectives on Camphill*, Glasgow

Pevsner, N 1968 *Studies in Art, Architecture and Design: Victorian and After*, London

Pevsner, N and Richmond, I 1992 *Northumberland*, The Buildings of England, 2nd edn, London

Pickvance, R 1967 'A Man of Influence: Alexander Reid (1854-1928)', *Scottish Art Review*, XI:3 (1967), 5-9

Pollak, F, et al. 1998 *St Giles Cathedral: Stained Glass Windows*, 2nd edn, Bath

*The Power of the Pulpit and Good Preaching, by a Layman* 1887 Glasgow

Price, NS, Talley Jr, MK and Vaccaro, AM 1996 *Historical and Philosophical Issues in the Conservation of Cultural Heritage*, Malibou

Quincy, A 1979 *John Loughborough Pearson*, New Haven

Reed, P 1993 *Glasgow: The Forming of the City*, Edinburgh

Reid, HMB 1910 *The Supreme Importance of Preaching; and The Practical Training of Preachers: Two Addresses*, Glasgow

Reynolds, P, Muir, L and Hughes, J 2002 *John Horbury Hunt: Radical Architect 1838-1904*, Sydney

Rickards, LC (ed) 1995 *Studies in Art, Architecture and Design: Victorian and After*, London

Roberts, D 1842 *The Holy Land. Syria, Idumea, Arabia, Egypt and Nubia, from Drawings Made on the Spot by David Roberts, R.A., with Historical Descriptions by the Rev. George Croly, LL.D.*, London

Rush, SJ 1994 'Alexander Thomson, Daniel Cottier and the Interior of Queen's Park Church', in Stamp, G and McKinstry, S (eds) *'Greek' Thomson*, Edinburgh, 176-185

Rutledge, M 1986 'Lyon, John Lamb (1835-1916)', *Australian Dictionary of Biography*, Melbourne, vol 10, 182-3

Sato, T 1991 *Japan and Britain: An Aesthetic Dialogue, 1850-1930*, London

Sheahan, K 2004 'James Cook Windows at Cranbrook School, Sydney', *Cook's Log*, 27:4 (2004), 43-5

Sherry, B 1983 'Secular Stained Glass in Australia', *Australian Antique Collector*, 26 (Jun-Dec 1983), 44-9

Sherry, B 1991 *Australia's Historic Stained Glass*, Sydney

Sinclair, F 1984 *Scotstyle – 150 Years of Scottish Architecture*, Edinburgh

Skinner, J 1838 *The Scottish Endowment Question: Ecclesiastical and Educational*, Glasgow

Small, JW 1885 *Examples of Furniture Ancient and Modern*, Edinburgh

Small, R 1904 *History of the Congregations of the United Presbyterian Church, from 1733 to 1900*, 2 vols, Edinburgh

Small, S 2009 *Greater Glasgow*, Edinburgh

Smith, B 1992 *DY Cameron: The Vision of the Hills*, Edinburgh

Smith, JM 1887, *Ornamental Interiors*, London

Soros, S and Weber, S (eds) 1999 *E. W. Godwin: Aesthetic Movement Architect and Designer*, New Haven

Sotheby's 1983 (1) *A Series of Specialist Sales*, Chester (4-7 Oct 1983), lots 1278-9 [paintings by Rev William Dickie]

Spalding, B 1990 *Bygone Partick*, Ochiltree

Spalding, B 1992 *Bygone Partick, 2*, Ochiltree

Spencer, R 1972 *The Aesthetic Movement: Theory and Practice*, London

Sprott, GW 1882 *The Worship and Offices of the Church of Scotland*, Edinburgh

Stamp, G 1995 (1) 'The Victorian Kirk: Presbyterian Architecture in Nineteenth-Century Scotland', in Brooks, C and Saint, A (eds) *The Victorian Church: Architecture and Society*, Manchester, 98-104

Stamp, G 1995 (2) 'Holmwood House, Glasgow', *Country Life* (20 July 1995) 50-3

Stamp, G 1997 '"At once classic and picturesque [...]"', *Alexander Thomson Society Newsletter*, 18 (Feb 1997), 6-12

Stamp, G 1998 (1) 'Gildard on Thomson', *Alexander Thomson Society Newsletter*, 20 (Jan 1998), 1-10

Stamp, G 1998 (2) 'Viva the Villa', *Glasgow Herald* (16 Oct 1998)

Stamp, G 1998-9 'The Library of the Architectural Section', *Alexander Thomson Society Newsletter*, 22 (Oct 1998), 4-7, 10-12, 16; 23 (Feb 1999), 4-7

Stamp, G 2001 'Henry-Russell Hitchcock and the Caledonia Road Church', *Alexander Thomson Society Newsletter*, 29 (July 2001), 2-3

Stamp, G 2002 *An Architect of Promise: George Gilbert Scott Junior (1839-1897) and the Late Gothic Revival*, Donington, Lincolnshire

Stamp, G and McKinstry, S 1994 *'Greek' Thomson*, Edinburgh

Stapleton, A 1996 (1) 'Thomson's True Disciples', *The Alexander Thomson Society Newsletter*, 17 (Nov 1996), 4-5, 8-9

Stapleton, A 1996 (2) 'John Moyr Smith 1839-1912', *Journal of the Decorative Arts Society* (1996), 18-28

Stark, D 2004 *Charles Rennie Mackintosh & Co, 1854-2004*, Catrine, Ayrshire

Stevenson, JJ 1880 *House Architecture*, 2 vols, London

Stratten and Stratten 1891 *Glasgow and its Environs: A Literary, Commercial and Social Review Past and Present*, London

Street, GE 1863 'On Mediaeval Embroidery', *Ecclesiologist*, CLVIII (October *1863*), 255-80

Sumner, WL 1955 *Father Henry Willis, Organ Builder, and his Successors*, London

Surtees, V 1971 *The Paintings and Drawings of Dante Gabriel Rossetti (1828-1882): A Catalogue Raisonné*, Oxford

Talbert, B 1867 *Gothic Forms*, Birmingham

Talbert, B 1876 *Examples of Ancient and Modern Furniture*, London

Taylor, E 1999-2000 'The Sacred and Aesthetic Principles of Alexander 'Greek' Thomson's Architecture', *Alexander Thomson Society Newsletter*, 25 (Aug 1999) 5-15; 26 (Feb 2000) 4-14; 27 (Sept 2000) 19-27

Thomas, S 1997 'Approaches to the Treatment of Historic Painted and Decorated Interiors', *Journal of Architectural Conservation*, 3:1 (Mar 1997)

Thomson, A 1864 'On the Unsuitableness of Gothic Architecture to Modern Circumstances', address to the Glasgow Architectural Society, 18 April 1864, see Thomson 1999, 53-61

Thomson, A 1866 'An Inquiry as to the Appropriateness of the Gothic Style for the Proposed Buildings for the University of Glasgow', *Builder* (19 May 1866), 368-71

Thomson, A 1874 'The Development of Architecture:- The Spirit of the Egyptian Style', Haldane Lectures, No. 2, reprinted in Thomson 1999, 126-130

Thomson, A 1994-5 'Dear George [...]', letters of Alexander Thomson to his brother, *Alexander Thomson Society Newsletter*, 11 (Oct 1994), 3-4, 11-12; 12 (Jan 1995), 9-11

Thomson, A 1999 *The Light of Truth and Beauty: The Lectures of Alexander 'Greek' Thomson, Architect, 1817-1875*, Stamp, G (ed), Glasgow, 1999

Thomson, DC 1907 'The Brothers Maris', *Studio* (1907), xxiv

*Trial of the City of Glasgow Bank Directors* 1905, Glasgow

Treuherz, J 1985 'Ford Madox Brown and the Manchester Murals', in Archer, JHG (ed), *Art and Architecture in Victorian Manchester*, Manchester

*Twenty-Five Learmonth Terrace, Edinburgh* [nd], Edinburgh: No. 2 (City of Edinburgh)

Van Gogh, V 1958 *The Complete Letters of Vincent Van Gogh*, 2 vols, London

*Villa and Cottage Architecture: Select Examples of Country and Suburban Residences Recently Erected* 1868, London

Viollet-le-Duc, E-E 1854-68, *Dictionnaire raisonnée de l'architecture française du XIe au XVe siècle*, 10 vols, Paris

Viollet-le-Duc, E-E 1858-75 *Dictionnaire du mobilier français*, 6 vols, Paris

Walker, D 1967 'James Sellars, Architect, Glasgow 2nd December 1843-9th October 1888', *Scottish Art Review*, XI:1 (1967), 16-19

Walker, D 1967 'James Sellars, Architect, Glasgow II (1880-1888)', *Scottish Art Review*, XI:2 (1967), 21-24

Walker, D 1991 (1) 'The Rhind Lectures 1990-91: A Synopsis. The Revival of Medieval and Early Renaissance Architecture in Scotland, 1745-1820', *Proceedings of the Society of Antiquaries in Scotland*, 121 (455-72)

Walker, D 1991 (2) 'Scotland and Paris: 1874-1887'

Walker, D 1994 *Historic Scotland: Notes for the Guidance of the Professional Advisors*, Edinburgh

Walker, L 1995 'Women Architects', in Attfield, J and Kirkham, P (eds) *A View from the Interior: Feminism, Women and Design*, London

Watson, M 'Statement of Significance: Window by John Lamb Lyon', http://www.powerhousemuseum.com

Webster, C and Elliott J 2001 *'A Church as it Should Be': The Cambridge Camden Society and its Influence*, Donington, Lincolnshire

Wells, A 1892 'Decoration', *Building and Engineering Journal* (Australia and New Zealand) (7 May 1892), 186-8

Williams, JL 1992 *Dutch Art and Scotland: A Reflection of Taste*, Edinburgh

Williamson, E, Riches, A and Higgs, M 1990 *The Buildings of Scotland: Glasgow*, Harmondsworth

Willsdon, C 2000 *Mural Painting in Britain 1840-1940: Image and Meaning*, Oxford

Wilkinson, JG 1837 *Manners and Customs of the Ancient Egyptians*, London

Wilmot, R 2009 'Examining "Authenticity" in Two Contemporary Conservation Projects in Scotland: Charles Rennie Mackintosh's Dysart Kirk Murals and Daniel Cottier's Painted Decorative Scheme at Cottier's Theatre, Glasgow', *Conference Proceedings*, Fisk, T and co-editor (eds), publisher, place, 'Fisk, T(ed), forthcoming'

Wornum, R 1856 *Analysis of Ornament*, London

Wu, NY (ed) 2002 *Ad Quadratum: The Practical Application of Geometry in Medieval Architecture*, AVISTA Studies in the History of Medieval Technology, Science and Art, Aldershot

Zielinski, P 2005 *History of the Parish of Our Lady and St Cuthbert, Prudhoe*, www.prudhoecatholics.co.uk/history6.htm [2009]

Zimmer, J 1984 *Stained Glass in Australia*, Melbourne

Zukowski, K 2006 *Creating the Artful Home: The Aesthetic Movement*, Salt Lake City

**Websites Not Otherwise Listed in the Bibliography:**

Anglesey Abbey: http://www.nationaltrust.org.uk.

Anglican Parish of Hunters Hill: http://www.huntershill.anglican.asn.au

Ayers House, Adelaide; The Acacias, Adelaide: http://www.hosking.wattle.id.au/~laurel/parahtml/conservation_plan.html

Edmund Blacket: http://en.wikipedia.org/Edmund_Blacket

Columbia Museum of Art: http://www.columbiamuseum.org

Dundee St Mary's: http://www.dundeestmarys.co.uk

Charles de Kay: http://helenadekaygilder.org

Knockderry House Hotel: http://www.knockderryhouse.co.uk

Links Hotel, Montrose: http://www.linkshotelmusic.com

National Academy of Design New York: http://www.nationalacademy.org

National Museums of Scotland: http://www.scotlandsimages.com

National Trust for Scotland:
http://www.nts.org.uk

New South Wales Government:
http://www.planning.nsw.gov.au/mediarelplan/
fs20080318_686.html

New South Wales Heritage Council:
http://www.visit.heritage.nsw.gov

New South Wales State Heritage Register:
http://www.heritage.nsw.gov.au

Organ Historical Trust of Australia:
http://www.ohta.org.au

Pittsburgh History and Landmarks Foundation:
http://www.phlf.org

Powerhouse Museum, Sydney:
http://www.powerhousemuseum.com

Pruhhoe, Northumbria:
http://www.prudhoecatholics.co.uk/history6.htm
Rijksmuseum, Amsterdam: www.rijksmuseum.nl

Roxland Estates:
http://www.fivepoundahouse.com

Spanierman Gallery, New York:
http://www.spanierman.com
http://www.sydneyarchitecture.com

St Andrew's Cathedral, Sydney:
http://en.wikipedia.org/wiki/St._Andrew%27s_
Cathedral,_Sydney

St John's Anglican Church, Georges Plains:
http://www.austcemindix.com/cemetery

St Joseph's Church, Hobart:
http://www.passionistshobart.org.au/index.php/parish-
history/51-st-josephs-church

St Joseph's Church, Orange:
http://users.netwit.net.au;  http://www.cathchurch.
net/nsw/parish/Orange

St Matthew's Church, Albury, NSW:
http://life.csu.edu.au/~dspennem/Varia/St.Matthews/
SM_Blacket.html

St Peter's Church, Cooks River Parish, NSW:
http://stpeterscooksriverhistory.wordpress.com/articles-
of-interest State Library, New South Wales: http://acms.
sl.nsw.gov.au

Unitarian Church of Montreal:
http://www.ucmtl.ca

Victoria and Albert Museum, London:
http://www.vam.ac.uk

Victorian Heritage Database:
http://vhd.heritage.vic.gov.au/places/heritage

Visit Cumbria:
http://www.visitcumbria.com

Weemala, Faulconbridge:
http://www.bmlocalstudies.blogspot.com

# INDEX

The following index identifies the individuals, organisations, buildings and places referred to in this publication. The index does not cover the Introduction, References, Captions or Appendices.